THE SECULAR BIBLE

Today's secularists too often have very little accurate knowledge about religion, and even less desire to learn. This is problematic insofar as their sense of self is constructed in opposition to religion. Above all, the secularist is *not* a Jew, *not* a Christian, *not* a Muslim, and so on. But is it intellectually responsible to define one's identity against something that one does not understand? And what happens when these secularists weigh in on contentious political issues, blind to the religious back-story or concerns that inevitably inform these debates?

In *The Secular Bible: Why Nonbelievers Must Take Religion Seriously*, Jacques Berlinerblau suggests that atheists and agnostics must take stock of that which they so adamantly oppose. Defiantly maintaining a shallow understanding of religion, he argues, is not a politically prudent strategy in this day and age. But this book is no less critical of many believers, who – Berlinerblau contends – need to emancipate themselves from ways of thinking about their faith that are dangerously simplistic, irrational, and outdated. Exploring the Hebrew Bible, or Old Testament, from the perspective of a specialist, nonbeliever, and critic of the academic religious studies establishment, Berlinerblau begins by offering a provocative answer to the question of "who wrote the Bible?" The very peculiar way in which this text was composed provides a key to understanding its unique power (and vulnerability) in the modern public sphere. In separate chapters, he looks at how the sparse and contradictory words of Scripture are invoked in contemporary disputes about Jewish intermarriage and homosexuality in the Christian world. Finally, he examines ways in which the Qur'ān might be subject to the types of secular interpretation advocated throughout this book. Cumulatively, this book is a first attempt to reinvigorate an estimable secular, intellectual tradition, albeit one that is currently experiencing a moment of crisis.

Jacques Berlinerblau, who holds separate PhDs in ancient Near Eastern languages and Sociology, is Associate Professor of Comparative Literature and Languages at Hofstra University and Visiting Professor of Jewish Civilization at Georgetown University. He has published numerous scholarly books and articles, including *Heresy in the University: The Black Athena Controversy and the Responsibilities of American Intellectuals.*

The Secular Bible

Why Nonbelievers Must Take Religion Seriously

JACQUES BERLINERBLAU

Hofstra University

CAMBRIDGE
UNIVERSITY PRESS

CAMBRIDGE UNIVERSITY PRESS
Cambridge, New York, Melbourne, Madrid, Cape Town, Singapore,
São Paulo, Delhi, Dubai, Tokyo, Mexico City

Cambridge University Press
The Edinburgh Building, Cambridge CB2 8RU, UK

Published in the United States of America by Cambridge University Press, New York

www.cambridge.org
Information on this title: www.cambridge.org/9780521618243

First published 2005
Reprinted 2005, 2006

A catalogue record for this publication is available from the British Library

Library of Congress Cataloging in Publication Data

Berlinerblau, Jacques.
The secular Bible: why nonbelievers must take religion seriously / Jacques Berlinerblau.
p. cm.
Includes bibliographical references and index.
ISBN-13: 978-0-521-85314-9 (hardback)
ISBN-10: 0-521-85314-1 (hardback)
ISBN-13: 978-0-521-61824-3 (pbk.)
ISBN-10: 0-521-61824-X (pbk.)
I. Bible. O.T - Introductions. 2. Secularism.   I. Title.
BS1140.3.B47   2005
221.6′6 - dc22   2005012432

ISBN 978-0-521-85314-9 Hardback
ISBN 978-0-521-61824-3 Paperback

To Ippolita and Cyrus
Petite famille heureuse

The *Old* Testament – that is something else again: all honour to the Old Testament! I find in it great human beings, a heroic landscape, and something of the very rarest quality in the world, the incomparable naïveté of the *strong heart.*

Friedrich Nietzsche, On the Genealogy of Morals

Yes, our first ancestors, our Adams and our Eves, were, if not gorillas, very near relatives of gorillas, omnivorous, intelligent and ferocious beasts, endowed in a higher degree than the animals of any other species with two precious faculties – *the power to think* and *the desire to rebel.*

Michael Bakunin, God and the State

Contents

Preface and Acknowledgments

The reader is forewarned that I have employed the "we" form throughout the main body of this work. By doing so I do not mean to imply that the ideas expressed here represent the unified position of a group of scholars. Nor do I want to suggest that my ideas are so overpoweringly persuasive that my audience has been won over, absorbed submissively into the empire of the present author's fictitious "us." What follows are, ostensibly, my own ideas and I fully expect (and hope) that my readers will disagree with many of them. But a sense of modesty compelled even this secularist to avoid the constant insertion of "I" into sentences whose subject was God, the Holy Spirit, Moses, Origen, Ibn Ezra, and so on. Aside from the artlessness of it all, is there not something a tad narcissistic about constantly calling attention to the self when discussing such figures?

In today's academy it is everywhere assumed (but nowhere, to the best of my knowledge, persuasively argued) that the use of "I" in scholarly writing represents something of a rhetorical/ideological breakthrough. Viewed as an improvement upon the imperious, duplicitous "we" of yesteryear, the new usage has become the industry standard. Well, a few decades into the regime of the "I" perhaps it is time to take stock. Has recourse to the first-person singular significantly increased the ability of scholars to discover new ideas? Has the quality of our research improved now that the author speaks directly to the audience? Most importantly, is our readership better served or more appreciative of our work and – as a result – growing? In other words, are sales up? This is not a nostalgic call for a return to an old and troubled narrative voicing. Rather, I simply encourage a renewed attention and openness to questions of literary *style*, acknowledging the need to be less self-centered, less circumscribed, when conveying our ideas. The arguments we proffer should entice more than those interested in our arcane fields of inquiry. Perhaps the use of "we" – with both its inclusiveness and its ironic detachment (a paradox that all secularists might value) – will appeal to those beyond our parochial academic boundaries.

∾

The research for this book was conducted mostly in New York, but significant strides were made in France and Italy. In the summer of 2001, I finalized the blueprint for this study while sitting at the Pontifical Biblical Institute in Rome. A finer library for the study of Scripture I have never seen. A good deal of research was conducted in Paris where I was warmly received by Dr. Arnaud Serandour and Ms. Catherine Fauveaud of the Bibliothèque d'Études Sémitiques of the College de France. On Broadway, I am grateful to Dr. Philip E. Miller, Mr. James Cohn, Mr. Lou Massone, and Ms. Tina Weiss of the Klau Library of Hebrew Union College–Jewish Institute of Religion.

The students of my home institution, Hofstra University, are good natured to a fault. They actually seem to like hearing ideas that – to paraphrase Wellhausen – render them unfit for office. One of my undergraduate majors, Ms. Shira Blank, was especially helpful in resolving assorted bibliographical dilemmas. I also benefited immeasurably from graduate teaching stints at Drew Theological Seminary and Hebrew Union College. Indeed, it was by working at these institutions that I became intrigued, if not obsessed, with self-critical religious intellectuals.

This is a far better book than what I originally had in mind and this is due to the work of two young and highly gifted editors. Ms. Erin Carter, now of Oxford University Press, made immense contributions to the look, style, and feel of the text. I cannot exaggerate how central a role she has played in this project. Mr. Andrew Beck of Cambridge University Press has excelled in every aspect of the modern academic editor's job description – from identifying weak arguments, to suggesting new lines of inquiry, to talking the author down from the ledge.

I wish to thank my colleagues Drs. Daniel Boyarin, Jorunn Buckley, Philip Davies, Sondra Farganis, Herb Huffmon, Barbara Lekatsas, Sabine Loucif, Ilaria Marchesi, Richard Martin, Sara Reguer, David Sperling, Dan Varisco, Ziony Zevit, and Dr. Massoud Fazeli and his merry band of

Iranian expatriate economists. To members of my inner circle who were more or less ignored during the three years that this text was written I can only invoke the words of Virgil: "Friends and companions, have we not known hard hours before this?" I mention here with great fondness James Eisenberg, Ruby Namdar, and Camala Projansky. I did manage, however, to spend a little time in the excellent company of my parents Rubin and Laurette Berlinerblau, my in-laws Patsy and Pasquale Spadavecchia, the Goodmans, the Italian branch and the French branch. This work is dedicated to my wife Ippolita Spadavecchia and my son Cyrus Olivier Berlinerblau. Avoiding the obligatory suffering-but-loyal-partner motif, let me praise her for embodying everything that I associate with the term "grace." As for Cyrus: I hope that, twenty years on, he reads this book – if only so he will know what a spectacular little boy he was.

October 25th 2004
Battery Park City, New York

Introduction: Secularists and the Not Godless World

> Question: What is the opposite of faith?
> Not disbelief. Too final, certain, closed. Itself a kind of belief.
> Doubt.
>
> Salman Rushdie, The Satanic Verses

NONBELIEVERS, THE BIBLE, AND RELIGION

In all but exceptional cases, today's secularists are biblically illiterate. Truth be told, their repertoire of knowledge about religion in general leaves much to be desired. It might consist of prurient jokes about the clergy, the citation (or miscitation) of a few noxious verses from Scripture, and maybe a Bertrand Russell quote thrown in for good measure. Secularists are free, of course, to disregard issues pertaining to religious belief. They do not need to pay attention to the actual words of the Hebrew Bible/Old Testament or to those of the New Testament and the Qur'ān. Nor do they need to think about the countless ways in which such words have been interpreted. These interpretations, incidentally, inspire those manifestations of piety that so puzzle nonbelievers: the fasting and the frenzy; the pilgrims on bloodied knees; the athletic feats of sexual repression; the acts of utterly selfless grace, and the wearing of turbans, *Yarmulkes*, veils, and other forms of sacred headgear, to name but a few. Secularists are free to remain oblivious to all this.

But perhaps now is not the best time to exercise this freedom. Contrary to what so many nineteenth- and twentieth-century social theorists believed (and hoped for), the species has not abandoned its faith in the divine. Karl Marx's optimism about the impending abolishment of religion was unfounded. The masses have not turned away from their beliefs "with the fatal inevitability of a process of growth," as Sigmund Freud predicted. And no, the gods are not "growing old or dying" – to invoke Émile Durkheim's famous words. Presently, a situation prevails that few of those thinkers could have ever imagined possible: in most countries, the irreligious and areligious comprise a small minority, an exception to the rule of God. They live in a world abounding in ancient creedal antagonisms (and modern weapons). In Pakistan and India, and in Palestine and Israel, not to mention in regions where other segments of the Islamic world clash with the predominantly Christian United States, the old faiths seem to be engaging in an apocalyptic staring contest. One flinch and secularists everywhere may have the opportunity to experience the end of days right along with the euphoric faithful.[1]

This books starts from the premise that indifference to all things religious is no longer a viable option for secularists. The word "secular," after all, derives from the Latin term *saeculum*, which refers to "living in the world" or "being of the age." In light of a revitalized and often repolarized religious scene, it would seem prudent for nonbelievers to take stock of the not Godless world and age in which they live. They will need to understand how ancient sacred texts impact the lives of citizens in modern nation-states. They will need to make sense of those interfaith and intrafaith conflicts that will affect their lives for years to come. And although it may drive them to distraction, nonbelievers will need to confront religion's durability, its pervasiveness, and perhaps even its inescapability in the domain of thought and social action.

If nonbelievers were to actually think about such issues, perhaps they would eventually ponder something that is rarely discussed: the anomalous and, in some places, precarious status of secularism itself. Although statistically small in number, secularists in many nations exert cultural, intellectual, and political influence disproportionate to their size. Or, as T. N. Madan describes it, "Secularism is the dream of a minority that wishes to shape the majority in its own image, that wishes to impose its will upon history but lacks the power to do so under a democratically organized polity." To the Jewish, Christian, and Muslim fundamentalist, secularism is no dream. It is a globally hegemonic culture – the culture of (nondivinely authorized) Sex, Sex, Sex!, the culture of depravity that invokes the flood and the blinding light. It is the culture that has *temporarily* perverted the rightful order of things.[2]

It is no surprise, then, that in societies or groups where religious extremists govern or are demographically numerous, free thinkers do not fare particularly well. The indignities suffered by the novelist Salman Rushdie are instructive in this regard. The book burnings, the threats, the murders, the contempt for the mischievous sovereignty of the imagination – this is what the empowered and undersecularized in any religion have in store for critical thinkers. While we are on the topic, let it be noted that it was not a secular militia that liberated the author of *The Satanic Verses*. A telethon hosted by a tuxedoed atheist did not precipitate his eventual release. There was no walkathon in which 1 million nonbelievers raised funds for his security detail by traipsing down Fifth Avenue holding placards, wearing fanny packs, and drinking lots of bottled water. Rather, it was the largesse of various Western democracies, Anglican Britain in particular, that saw him through the whole nasty episode. These are not Godless states. They consist of a religiously moderate majority that has made its peace with secularism. It is because these moderates tolerate secularism (and are to varying degrees secularized themselves) that nonbelievers are able to persevere and prosper. The mainstream religions of the Occident are the pontoons of secularism. Only by virtue of their tacit consent can this minority remain buoyant in the arts, letters, mass media, and so on.[3]

"Secular versus religious" is a convenient dichotomy, but it is one that misrepresents a complex reality. As the presence of the tolerant religious mainstream should indicate, the lines of demarcation are quite blurry. This is partly because the centuries-long process of secularization has had great success in "taking the edge off" of most extreme forms of religious devotion in the West. As the theologian Harvey Cox once phrased it, secularization "has convinced the believer that he *could* be wrong, and persuaded the devotee that there are more important things than dying for the faith." It has also created a large class of believers who share considerable common ground with nonbelievers. We might refer to them as the "secularly religious." Think of the Jewish man who pops up every year at Yom Kippur services with his Zoroastrian wife; the Muslim woman who regularly goes drinking with her friends in a sleeveless blouse after a prayerless day at work; or the gay Christian who is deacon of his church.[4]

These examples are, admittedly, generic. Yet, they point to a substantial number of the faithful who demonstrate a self-conscious willingness to live in tension with more orthodox incarnations of their own religious traditions. The secularly religious do not have a major gripe with modernity. Old creedal antagonisms do not inflame their passions, and the burning of books is not their cup of tea. In fact, they are often friends, patrons, and even producers of the arts. Village atheists – who tend to associate all religion with religious extremism – need to ask themselves what it means to share so many similarities with those who are supposed to be their antithesis.

THE CURRENT CRISIS OF SECULAR INTELLECTUAL CULTURE

The secularist's lack of familiarity with the Hebrew Bible/Old Testament and religion in general, we have just suggested, constitutes a looming political liability. But not everything is politics. This disregard of religion also points to a crisis and paradox of secular identity. Members of the overlapping secular sectaries (e.g., "secularists," "secular humanists," "free thinkers," "atheists," "agnostics," "brights," "universists") define themselves in opposition to religions, albeit religions about which they know very little. Above all, the secularist is *not* a Jew, *not* a Christian, *not* a Muslim, even though certain contingencies may have once imposed such a designation on him or her. To construct one's self against something that one does not understand, or care much about, does not make for a very coherent, compelling, or durable self.

It does not make for an influential or rich culture of ideas either. Presently, one would be hard pressed to identify more than a few recognizable intellectuals in the English-speaking sector who speak knowledgeably about religion *qua* secularists. Informed perspectives about the post–September 11 world, Church and State relations, fundamentalisms, and so on are almost nonexistent. A secular viewpoint, or something approximating it, is most likely to be articulated by a liberal or lapsed Jewish or Christian theologian. What ever happened to secular intellectual culture? It is a culture not lacking in historical import or integrity, or in heroisms or good works on behalf of the species. Yet, it is currently experiencing something of an existential crisis. If it moves forward, it does so only by grace of inertia – momentum gathered in a prepostmodern golden age of science and reason. It is a trust fund baby, living off of the intellectual capital of Karl Marx, Friedrich Nietzsche, Émile Durkheim, Max Weber, Bertrand Russell, Sigmund Freud, and Jean-Paul Sartre – to name just a few members of the pantheon.[5]

Believing intellectuals, in contrast, are thriving once again. The enlightenment critique of religion that came to maturity in the nineteenth century did not strike the fatal blow, the "kill shot." Although staggered, theological modes of reasoning arose, dusted themselves off, focused, amended, and absorbed. From this experience, religious thinkers emerged craftier than ever. They now draw skillfully on the full range of sciences, social sciences, and humanities. In so doing, their proofs for the existence of God and the importance of belief, ritual, communities of the faithful, and so on have become increasingly rigorous and coherent. To the atheist or agnostic who wants to *rationally* justify his or her own nonbelief, we say, "*Come prepared. Come armed with erudition. Shuck the Bertrand Russell quotes, for the love of God! Your opponents have regrouped. Do not take them lightly.*"

The retreat of secular intellectuals from the domain of religious questions is most visible in the realm of contemporary higher education. For how often does a village atheist teach a course on Scripture, sacred languages, hermeneutics, or church history? How often does such a person actually have any accurate and detailed knowledge of such things? As a result, many of the West's most and least distinguished universities simply outsource their instruction of religious studies to the nearest seminary. Less promisingly, classes are sometimes taught by university chaplains or itinerant clergy. Often, one's religious studies instructor is (or was) qualified to preside over a marriage, perform a circumcision, or administer last rites. This comprises one of those exquisite ironies of the Occidental research university – a bastion of irreligious thought if there ever was one. The militantly secular academy does not sponsor the explicitly secular study of any religious issue, nor has it ever denied employment to legions of theist intellectuals (under the condition that they refrain from all manner of proselytizing activities). Although this may illustrate the university's enlightened tolerance of dissenting viewpoints, we suspect

that it says more about its complete lack of interest in this subject, if not
its fiscal priorities.[6]

Secular intellectual culture, we have claimed, is undergoing a crisis.
This crisis is aggravated by the absence of nonbelieving scholars who can
speak coherently about religion. The situation in Old (and New) Testament studies illustrates this perfectly. This discipline, whose roots burrow
deep into biblical antiquity, has always been dominated by *homines reli-*
giosi. Professional biblicists, even those teaching at secular institutions,
are usually trained in theological seminaries. The field is staffed almost
exclusively by those who read the *Witness* incessantly and piously during their youth (although as we will see, many have become secularized
themselves). Blasphemers, the morally incorrigible, and cultured despisers of religion – the types of characters who appear en masse in sociology, anthropology, and English departments – rarely venture into Old
Testament scholarship. We cite an observation made by M. H. Goshen-
Gottstein nearly 30 years ago, one that still rings true today: "practically
all academic students of the Bible remain heavily indebted to their own
tradition and upbringing.... However we try to ignore it – practically all
of us are in it because we are either Christians or Jews." As the exegete
David Clines lamented, "it's a bit of a scandal really that in the academic
context it is religious believers who are setting the tone for the study of
the Bible."[7]

This is not to deny that, here and there, a few isolated New Secularists
(i.e., refugees from a religious past) or Heritage Secularists (i.e., ethnic,
life-long secularists) have labored in the guild of biblical studies. Yet,
they have seldom scrutinized the Old Testament from a self-consciously
nontheist perspective. Although they may occasionally grumble – and
with good reason – about the overwhelmingly theological cast of the
discipline, they have proffered few alternatives. They have not posed
the really interesting questions, which go something like this: insofar
as the Hebrew Bible/Old Testament has been studied in near exclu-
sivity by Christians and Jews from antiquity to postmodernity, how
would and how *should* scholars who bracket the existence of God make
sense of sacred Scripture? What would their nontheist alternative look
like? In what ways, if any, would it differ from traditional modes of
scriptural analysis? The answers to be proposed here do not represent
a privileged or authoritative perspective. They represent *one* type of

perspective – albeit one that deserves far greater representation in secular universities.[8]

"SECULARISM" REDEFINED

But we are getting ahead of ourselves. A more fundamental question must be addressed, namely, what do we mean by "secularism"? Our understanding is somewhat idiosyncratic. As we see it, secularism cannot be reduced to a political platform insisting on the categorical separation of Church and State. It need not apotheosize humanity and its capacity to reason. No particular emphasis is placed on the importance of living exclusively in the "here and now." Nor are we seduced by the lure of hyperscientific rationality and its ability to power our triumphant march through history. Secularism, at its essence and at its absolute best, comprises an unrelenting commitment to judicious and self-correcting critique. Historically, it emerged in antagonistic dialectic with the most potent and intractable of human collective representations, that which is commonly referred to as religion. In confronting such a formidable adversary, secular thinkers forged a critical tradition of world historical significance, albeit one currently mired in a slump. Secularism's "job" consists of criticizing *all* collective representations. Its analytical energies should be inflicted on any type of mass belief or empowered orthodoxy, whether it is religious, political, scientific, aesthetic, and so on. Voltaire's Candide was certainly on to something when he declared, "isn't their pleasure in criticizing everything, in seeing faults where other people think they see beauties?" Secularism, as we envision it, is elitist and heretical by nature. When it aspires to become a popular movement, an orthodoxy, or the predicate of a nation-state, it betrays itself and is not likely to succeed.[9]

This means that the secular study of the Hebrew Bible (or any sacred text) is animated by a spirit of critique. The motto of our enterprise might just as well be *"criticize and be damned!"* We are bound by honor to cast aspersions on the integrity and historical reliability of holy documents. A secular exegete reads such works in heckle mode. He or she cannot accept that the Bible is the infallible word of God (as fundamentalists are wont to argue), nor the word of God as mediated by mortals (as the secularly religious and most biblical scholars often contend), nor the distortion of the word of God by prejudiced humans (as some radical theologians have charged). The objective existence of God – as opposed to the subjective perception of Him – is not a legitimate variable in scholarly analysis. The Hebrew Bible/Old Testament is a human product *tout court*.

Our next assumption marks a sharp break with existing secularism. Traditional approaches have always been predicated on a misty-eyed, person-centered humanism. The individual is seen as autonomous. Not under God. He or she is capable of comprehending and changing the world. Perfectible. "*You go girl!*" the secularist seems to exhort to all mankind. All this positive thinking is somewhat out of place. After all, nonbelievers categorically reject what most other humans believe to be true about the universe. Secularists are wont to think of religious beliefs as illusions, wish fulfillments, infantile projections, phantasmagoria, and so on. A wincing frustration with humanity, as opposed to an unqualified enthusiasm for its potential, would seem to be a more appropriate position for the secularist. The French novelist Michel Houellebecq recently eulogized the species in a manner more acceptable to the nonbeliever: "vile, unhappy race, barely different from the apes, which nevertheless carried within it such noble aspirations. Tortured, contradictory, individualistic, quarrelsome, and infinitely selfish, it was sometimes capable of extraordinary explosions of violence, but never quite abandoned its belief in love." That's better. That's the secular spirit.[10]

We want, then, to detach secularism from its incongruously philanthropic moorings. Following one of the grandest (and presently least appreciated) strands in social theory, we advance a less sanguine assessment of humans. They are seen as virtuosi of self-delusion. We concentrate on their vulnerability to causal factors beyond their comprehension and control. The assumptions that they always accurately understand why they do what they do, or the consequences of their actions, are contested. Not everything happens because of conscious deliberation, not everything results from an act of will. In the same vein, we assert that history is inherently ironic; the least expected, and least desired, outcomes are often the ones that come to pass. These are themes that will be visited repeatedly in our discussions of the Bible.

This skeptical appraisal of human agency, incidentally, has a lengthy intellectual genealogy. Disquisitions on our capacity for self-deception and mass deception appear in works as varied as Michel de Montaigne's essay "On the Power of the Imagination" and Freud's *The Future of an Illusion*. Marx, for his part, spoke of illusions that bind and blind entire epochs. In his youth, he exhorted humanity to awaken from the dream it was having about itself. Following Auguste Comte, Émile Durkheim referred to the "anthropocentric postulate" – that is, the misconception that societies progress because of conscious human planning. Max Weber made much of "the ironic relationship between human intentions and their historical consequences." In short, among some of the Church Fathers of secular intellectual culture, a deep skepticism concerning the divine has often been paired with *a corresponding skepticism concerning the human*. This is the omnicritical tradition we want to revive in the study of religious phenomena and is more in line with the curmudgeonly spirit of secularism.[11]

CONCLUSION: THE CHALLENGE FOR SECULAR INTELLECTUALS

It has been insisted that secularists should get to know the Hebrew Bible/Old Testament. Maybe we should also suggest, politely, that Christian and Jewish laypersons should get to know the Bible *differently*. Even within their own traditions, they will find alternatives to the simplistic readings and conceptions of Scripture to which they so often cling. College Bible professors – who are excellently positioned to make such observations – routinely express dismay at the immense bathetic gap that exists between the most sublime fruits of religious thought and the naive dogmas advocated by freshmen who have endured a basic religious education. Among many of our students, one notices a tangible poverty of knowledge concerning what their own storied intellectuals believed about the Hebrew Bible/Old Testament. They attribute to the Good Book a transparency and intelligibility that some of the most venerated thinkers in the Judaeo-Christian tradition did not believe was there.

In an effort to transcend the parallel caricatures of the Hebrew Bible that predominate in both religious and irreligious lay cultures, we propose a counterorientation called "secular hermeneutics." Aspiring to be unapologetic, it consciously performs an act of discursive aggression on Scripture and, by extension, those who hold it dear. It is a form of analysis performed in bad faith, invariably yielding un-Christian and un-Jewish readings. For these reasons, this study will be taken by some as a polemic. This charge is unavoidable and, to a certain extent, warranted. *The Secular Bible* does promote ways of thinking about Scripture that could, conceivably, neutralize claims made on behalf of sacred texts by extremists (or just about anyone else). It is virtually guaranteed to displease certain Jews, Christians, and Muslims.

But this book is not necessarily intended for secular activists. It does not seek to equip nonbelievers with refutations that will definitively trump self-righteous men and women of God. Such refutations do not exist; it is the astonishing complexity of the Old Testament that always trumps any self-righteous claim made on its behalf. Besides, the secularist fulminating about all that is irrational in religion is a doleful cliché – about as enlightening and spontaneous as a member of the Soviet Politburo flogging the Italian fashion industry in the year 1972. Mustiness, block-headishness, and predictability have come to characterize contemporary secular writings on religion; a book-length, antireligious screed would be redundant.

Our goal, then, is *not* to cast the spotlight of enlightenment reason on the dumb show of religious belief. In truth, we can only express appreciation for accomplishments made by religious students of Scripture. The scholarly bibliography on the Bible produced by nonbelievers is negligible, but the amount of research produced by Old Testament exegetes is so immense that it defies quantification. Under no circumstances can it be written off as uninteresting or uncritical. As a body of scholarship, it rivals in ingenuity and scruple anything produced within the comity of secular university disciplines. No dumb show there.

The problem with modern biblical research is that it has not gone far enough. Too often, it has deferred to tradition, censured itself, and refused to pursue the delectably blasphemous implications of its own discoveries. Even at its most critical, Old Testament scholarship is the theological equivalent of the Loyal Opposition. For these reasons, we feel obligated to draw out or amplify certain heretical leads that have been alluded to by otherwise pious scholars. Ideally, secular hermeneutics provides new theories and methods for the study of sacred texts. But often it simply reads established theories and methods through the optic of a new, highly critical orientation. We really like the theologian John Macquarrie's description of secularism as "an attitude, a mood, a point of view, a way of noticing and (equally) of failing to notice." It is this secular way of noticing that redirects or unleashes the energy of our discipline in more critical directions. This attitude of radical doubt frees us, or perhaps forces us, to speak the unspeakable truth, truths, and truthlessness of the Hebrew Bible.[12]

Part I of *The Secular Bible* is devoted to the issue of how the Hebrew Bible was composed. With more than a few winks and nods, we pose some of the most commonly asked questions about this document's origins. Who wrote it? Who do Jews and Christians think wrote it? To whom do modern scholars attribute its authorship? What does it mean? What is its enduring message to humanity? Why is it so difficult to understand?

The crucial distinction between the Bible's contents and *interpretations* of its contents tends be lost on many laypersons, whether they are secular or religious. For these reasons, we devote Part II to the problem of how Scripture is read. Of interest to us here are queries such as why is the Hebrew Bible/Old Testament so widely interpreted? What is the nature of the relation between religious intellectuals and their beloved Scriptures? Why does the text exert the history-altering effects that it does? Why is there so little agreement as to what it says? What role do readers play in constructing the Bible's "meaning"? Much attention is devoted to professional interpreters, otherwise known as biblical scholars. The reader is forewarned that we are positively obsessed with them. Exegetes are the central protagonists of the opera whose stage notes you are now reading. We have cast them in every imaginable role. They are our betrayed Madama Butterfly, our unconscionable Pinkerton, soothing Suzuki, ambivalent Sharpless, and crazy Uncle Bonze too.

This, then, is a book about the Hebrew Bible's composition and its interpreters. It is also a meditation on the predicament of secularism in a world where sacred texts are not the irrelevant artifacts that nonbelievers once thought they would be. Part III – the Judaism–Christianity–Islam component of our curriculum – provides concrete illustrations of the theories and methods discussed in Parts I and II. These chapters on intermarriage (in Judaism) and same-sex eroticism (in Christianity) examine how the Bible is dragooned into debates that affect citizens of contemporary democracies. The difficulty, if not the utter absurdity, of invoking this text in the sphere of politics is explored. Indeed, one of our central claims is that the peculiar way in which the Bible was composed in antiquity makes it far too contradictory and incoherent a source for public policy decisions in modernity. Chapter Eight compares the role of interpreters in Judaism and Christianity on one side, and Islam on the other. Here, we explore the obstacles that confront Muslim scholars who want to liberalize prevailing interpretations of the Qur'ān.

The Secular Bible is intended for scholars and cultivated laypersons. We remind our nonspecialist readers of a few rudimentary terms and concepts. "Hebrew Bible" refers to a collection of ancient documents written in Hebrew and, to a much lesser extent, Aramaic. Those documents were assembled into a fairly stable canon by Jews somewhere between the second century BCE and the first century AD. Christians generally refer to what is *roughly* the same body of texts as the "Old Testament" (although many official Christian Old Testaments are translations from Hebrew into languages such as Greek and Latin). More than 2,000 years ago Jews, and later Christians, began feverishly interpreting their Hebrew Bibles and Old Testaments. We use the phrases "Rabbinic/Talmudic literature" and "writings of the Church Fathers/patristic literature" to designate two of the most influential bodies of scriptural interpretation ever produced. The reader, ideally, will have a more nuanced understanding of these concepts by the end of this book.[13]

It is hoped that this inquiry will serve as a prototype for examinations of other foundational religious writings. In the monotheistic sphere, we envision works with titles such as *The Secular New Testament, The Secular Talmud, The Secular Church Fathers, The Secular Qur'ān*, and *The Secular Hadith*. The goal is not to establish a chain of academic franchises, but rather to outline a coherent nontheological, nonapologetic paradigm for the study of sacred Scriptures. To speak of the awesome complexity of religion critically, judiciously, and with clarity – this is the challenge and responsibility of secular intellectuals in a not Godless world.

SUGGESTIONS FOR FURTHER READING

Discussions of the current plight of secularism are appearing with increasing frequency. An excellent start would be the pitch perfect essay of Wilfred McClay, entitled "Two Concepts of Secularism," in *Religion Returns to the Public Square: Faith and Policy in America*. Eds. Hugh Heclo and Wilfred McClay. Baltimore: The Johns Hopkins University

Press, 2003, pp. 31–61. Many Indian scholars have explored secularism and its discontents in their own country. Their debates are wide ranging and entertaining, and raise issues of interest to polities far and wide. We would recommend Brenda Cossman and Ratna Kapur's *Secularism's Last Sigh? Hindutva and the (Mis)Rule of Law*. Delhi: Oxford University Press, 1999, pp. 81–135, as well as the balanced collection of essays edited by Rajeev Bhargava, *Secularism and Its Critics*. Delhi: Oxford, 1998. Of special interest is the critique of secularism in the previously mentioned volume advanced by T. N. Madan. Studies of the demise of "secularization hypothesis" (which, as we note in the Conclusion, is not the same thing as secularism) are too plentiful to be mentioned here. Rodney Stark's "Secularization, R.I.P.," *Sociology of Religion* 60 (1999) 249–273, provides a good, if somewhat strident, overview. The complex question of the absence of secularists in fields that study religion, most notably biblical scholarship, is explored in our own, "'Poor Bird, Not Knowing Which Way to Fly': Biblical Scholarship's Marginality, Secular Humanism, and the Laudable Occident," *Biblical Interpretation* 10 (2002) 267–304. One of the few works of biblical scholarship working from an explicitly non-confessional angle is Philip Davies' *Whose Bible Is It Anyway?* Sheffield: Sheffield Academic Press, 1995. A handy and reader-friendly reference guide for those who want to familiarize themselves with basic concepts involving the Bible as a text is Paul Wegner's *The Journey from Texts to Translations: The Origin and Development of the Bible*. Grand Rapids, MI: Baker Books, 1999. Finally, a wonderful, critical, "big picture" study of the Bible can be found in Robert Carroll's *Wolf in the Sheepfold: The Bible as a Problem for Christianity*. London: SPCK, 1991.

PART ONE

❧

THE COMPOSITION OF THE
HEBREW BIBLE

1

∾

Who Wrote the Bible? Ancient Responses

In the Israelite literary tradition ... authors' names are rarely reported and when they are reported the reports are almost always false.

Morton Smith, "Pseudepigraphy in the Israelite Literary Tradition."

Who wrote the Bible? This is a query that preoccupied the ancients, flummoxed countless generations of exegetes, and, as we argue later, played something of a small, significant, albeit unheralded, role in bringing about Occidental modernity. It is also a problem that has probably crossed the mind of every reflective Jewish and Christian person who has ever lived. But before we make any more sober proclamations, we should note that it does not seem to be a question that the Hebrew Bible is well equipped to answer. We are going to return to "Who wrote the Bible?" throughout this study and even take a crack at "Who wrote the Qu'rān?" The question itself, admittedly, is hopelessly simplistic, misleading, and only answerable in terms of the vaguest sociological generalizations. Be that as it may, to avoid the issue and assert something on the order of "*Who cares who wrote it! It's the message of Scripture that counts!*" is, as we will soon see, a fairly preposterous thing for a secular hermeneut (or a rational religious individual) to profess.

Why should nonbelievers bother to think about the authorship of the Hebrew Bible/Old Testament? For one, it can be used as something of a polemical trump card. Judaism and Christianity have never been able to answer this question convincingly, let alone consistently. The secularist who relishes a good scrum with religious folks can surely press the advantage here. Much more important, by pursuing this issue one comes to understand the frightful, albeit curiously endearing, complexity of Scripture's assemblage. The Byzantine manner in which the Hebrew Bible was fabricated, we will argue repeatedly, is *productive* – of speculation, of meaning, of very good and very bad ideas, not to mention the occasional cataclysmic disagreement.

So, "Who wrote the Bible?" it is. In this chapter, we explore the manner in which the Hebrew Scriptures confront and fail to confront this problem. We ask if its opinions about its own composition, and the writing process in general, are credible. From there, we glance at the answers of early Jewish and Christian exegetes who speak where the Bible is silent and who often shout it down when it does actually speak.

CREATIVITY VERSUS STENOGRAPHY

What is now known as the Hebrew Bible was originally a collection of scrolls. Accounts from roughly the first through third centuries CE report that twenty-four such scrolls comprised something of a stable Jewish canon (other sources from the same period suggest a slightly smaller number). More than half of these twenty-four books are not ascribed. By "not ascribed" we mean that nothing in their contents indicates who wrote the scroll under consideration, where it came from, the circumstances of its composition, and so on.[1]

We are never told, for example, who is narrating the drama that runs from Joshua through Judges through Samuel and into Kings. Not a word is said about the writer of Job. Who is lamenting in Lamentations? From where do Chronicles come from? Ruth and Esther fail to name their author. Scripture is mute as to the origins of these documents. But nowhere has the lack of attribution puzzled more exegetes than in the case of the first five scrolls, what would later be called the Pentateuch. The problems start at the very beginning: the Book of Genesis is either oblivious to, or unwilling to tell us about, its own textual genesis.[2]

This is no inconsequential oversight. Genesis implicitly claims to have direct access to the divine. Any mildly inquisitive reader will want to know who is relaying this privileged information. As the great biblical scholar Hermann Gunkel once phrased it: "How is anyone supposed to know what God said or thought alone or in the councils of heaven?"

This "narrator" knows everything: how Yahweh fabricated the world, His immodest assessment of the creative process (e.g., "and Elohim saw it was good"), His conversations with Himself, and so on. But the Bible's introductory text is silent about who is furnishing these data. One should never underestimate how much this silence has mystified, energized (and, in all likelihood, greatly irritated) Jewish and Christian interpreters.[3]

Although many biblical scrolls say nothing about their origins, others do speculate – ungenerously, absurdly – as to whom their writers were and how they were written. What little information they relay is often provided in the first verses of a given book. Biblical scholars commonly refer to this introductory section as a "superscription." Most view superscriptions as late additions, words prefixed (and sometimes suffixed) onto a text by meddlesome ancient scribes who themselves were pondering the "Who-wrote-the-Bible?" dilemma (see Chapter Two). The superscription of the Book of Ecclesiastes states: "Words of Koheleth, son of David, King in Jerusalem." Eleven verses later, the first-person singular is finally used, and our narrator exclaims: "I Koheleth was king over Israel in Jerusalem." This would seem to indicate that a certain Koheleth is the intellectual source of the text that we are about to read. It does not necessarily indicate that Koheleth *physically* wrote the Book of Ecclesiastes. The Hebrew of this passage – which makes no reference to writing – does not clearly permit for that precise inference.[4]

Here then is one drawback of asking "Who wrote the Bible?" In modern English, the infinitive "to write" can connote two interrelated acts: the creative act *and* actual writing. These functions are unified in the person of the novelist who both creates something and then writes it by hand (using a pen or keyboard). But in the Bible, conceptualization and stenography are often shown to be separate acts performed by entirely different individuals. Soon we will observe that very little is said in Scripture about the imaginative component of writing – the part that requires thought, inspiration, and monastic sacrifices. References to writing rarely have to do with "thinking it up" but with *writing it down* – often with God dictating over one's shoulder. Accordingly, these texts do not address the writer as artist, furrower of the brow, not-very-reluctant addict, and all the other romantic images that cluster about those who produce literature in contemporary times. Biblical "writing" consists of at least two steps: 1) the initial formulation of words that comprise a text, and, 2) the writing down (i.e., transcription) of these words. Steps one and two are not always executed by the same individual.

So, Ecclesiastes 1:1 and 1:12 only tell us that Koheleth's words stand in front of us. As best we can tell, Koheleth is held to be the source of these words. Whether the Bible wants to say that he performed the physical exertions that resulted in their being put to the scroll is anybody's guess. A similar ambiguity can be found in reports of Solomonic authorship. The superscription to the Song of Songs reads: "The Song of Songs, by/concerning [Hb. 'ăšer] Solomon." Solomon, the text appears to say, is the source or composer of the salacious poem that follows. We cannot tell if he wrote it down. While we are contemplating that difficulty, let us observe that the Hebrew of this verse is not entirely clear. The relative pronoun 'ăšer might mean "by" Solomon. If we follow this translation, then Solomon is the author (as in creator of the words). Because a woman's admiring voice is heard throughout the Song this would mean that King Solomon the Author was willing to create a work about the tremendous impression that King Solomon the Lover made on his partner.

But if we translate 'ăšer as "concerning," instead of "by," then we exonerate the monarch from the charge of hubris. The Song of Songs would be *about* Solomon. Hence, some anonymous author is describing the myrrh-scented escapades of the monarch. The same linguistic uncertainties can be found in the superscriptions of many Psalms. The widely encountered phrase (*mizmôr lĕdāwid*) is often rendered as "A Psalm of David." It might be more plausibly translated as "A Psalm about David," or "A Psalm to David." Many laypersons are convinced that David produced most of the words of the Psalter. But this is not necessarily what the biblical Hebrew says, nor what most scholars believe to be true.[5]

The first line of the Book of Proverbs reads: "Proverbs of Solomon, son of David, King of Israel." Things run smoothly for a while until we encounter Proverbs 24:23, which says: "These too are by the sages." What sages? Until this point, one could have sworn that Solomon formulated these lines. Things soon go from bad to worse. In the opening verse of the twenty-fifth chapter, the following statement is made: "These too are Proverbs of Solomon which the men of Hezekiah, King of Judah, copied [he 'ĕtîqû]." At the very least, we now have a clear example of the difference between conceptualization and stenography. The king, it would appear, came up with the Proverbs of chapter twenty-five. A few hundred years later in the time of Hezekiah (who lived in the late eighth century), Solomon's proverbs were, so it would seem, put to the scroll. Yet, our sense of relief is somewhat dampened by other troubling verses. The opening line of Proverbs chapter thirty tells us we are reading the words of one Agur son of Jakeh. The introductory sentence of chapter thirty-one communicates that we are hearing the admonishment of the mother of King Lemuel. So whose words are we reading in Proverbs? Solomon? The sages? Agur? Lemuel's mother? All the above? Who physically wrote the Book of Proverbs? Did the men of Hezekiah copy it all down, or did they just copy chapter twenty-five?[6]

The fifteen books (equivalent to four ancient scrolls) of prophecy running from Isaiah to Malachi are afflicted by these and other difficulties. The introductory verse of the Book of Ezekiel speaks in the first person – a state of affairs that might lead us to surmise that Ezekiel is its author (and perhaps also the stenographer). Problematically, the following verses proceed to speak about Ezekiel in the third person. Did Ezekiel compose the Book of Ezekiel? Did some unnamed person compose the Book of Ezekiel? Or, did Ezekiel – just for kicks – speak about himself every now and then in an oddly disembodied sort of way? This shift from third- to first-person narration occurs repeatedly throughout the prophets and elsewhere. Zechariah, for instance, speaks directly to us and then is spoken about. The Book of Daniel is recounted by, variously, Nebuchadnezzar, Daniel, and some anonymous narrative voice. None of these fluctuating voicings help to simplify the question of who wrote these texts.[7]

So far, we have looked at a variety of difficulties pertaining to biblical reports about authorship. These include 1) the Bible's unwillingness to ascribe authorship in more than half of the original scrolls, 2) a lack of textual clarity as to whether an ascribed book was created by its alleged author *and* physically written down by that same person, 3) Hebrew words that do not clearly indicate whether a text is "by" a named person or "about" him, 4) contradictory attributions of authorship within one book, and, 5) shifts in narrative voice from first to third person that make us doubt whether the narrating "I" is responsible for the text.

TEXTS JUST HAPPEN!: THE BIBLICAL CONCEPTION OF THE
ORIGIN OF TEXTS

A biblical scholar is a person who has devoted his or her life to reasoning
with a madman. We have just asked Scripture to tell us who wrote each
of its twenty-four scrolls. We concluded that its various texts say little
about the matter and what little they do say does not excel in clarity.
Compounding our frustration is that within biblical scrolls – out of the
blue – we encounter short passages that are either ascribed to Yahweh
or assorted mortals. For example, the Book of Deuteronomy never tells
us where it came from. It offers no superscription that attributes its
authorship to this or that person. Yet momentarily we will examine a short
text in Deuteronomy that claims to be created by God and transcribed
by Moses.

These ascriptions within scrolls reveal a curious and naive assumption
that runs throughout Scripture, namely, that texts just happen! As mentioned earlier, in the Hebrew Bible little is said about the "creative process." Written works seem strangely unbegotten. They exist fully formed,
prior to being written down. The final product is not the dividend of
writing and rewriting, nor tooth-gnashing and tortured contemplation.
There are no drafts. Revision is nonexistent. Rather, the finished document is simply present in God's being, awaiting an appropriate amanuen-
sis to relay its contents to a (generally unreceptive) audience of Israelites
and/or Judahites.[8]

God creates texts without discernible exertions. To this we may add
that humans transcribe or write down His words pretty effortlessly as
well. Aside from those occasions when the "Finger of God" performs the
required labor, in most cases a human being is enjoined with the task of
recording the deity's words. One might imagine, or even fear, that the
transmission of divine information via human conduits could lead to
minor or major distortions of the original. Yet, there is nothing in Scripture that would ever raise the possibility that Yahweh's utterances may
have been garbled by the mortals who recorded them. On the contrary,
the Hebrew Bible takes its own accuracy as something so obvious that it
scarcely requires comment. The reader's job does not consist of checking
for textual errata or fretting about possible mistakes made by prophets
who received revelations as the world was falling down. Rather, his or her
task is to ingest the flawless and transparent message of the text.

A few examples should illustrate the Hebrew Bible's "no fuss" understanding of textual conceptualization and transcription. In Deuteronomy
31:19, Yahweh instructs Moses to write down a poem that He has composed. Not a word is said about how the document came into being.
It is just there. The poem's passage from Yahweh's being to written or
engraved form is similarly unproblematic. Moses dutifully records it
(31:22), and to this day, the ha'ăzînû sits in Deuteronomy 32 for all to
enjoy. The same is observed as regards the ill-fated carved stones that
contained the original Ten Commandments. In Exodus 31:18, we learn
that Moses has been entrusted with two tablets inscribed by God's finger (here the deity fulfills both writerly functions). In a fit of pique the
mercurial lawgiver destroys them. Somehow, this occasions no loss of
vital data. God simply reinscribes an exact replica on humanly produced
tablets.[9]

In a quizzical passage (Isaiah 8:1), Isaiah follows Yahweh's order and
records a short prophecy of doom on a "large sheet" or "large tablet." The
ensuing oracle, as with so many others in Isaiah's prophecy, makes few
concessions to lucidity. This notwithstanding, it is once again obvious
that the creation and transcription of the text are not seen as worthy of
comment. Elsewhere, God instructs Jeremiah (36:2) to "take for yourself a
scroll and write on it all of the things that I have spoken to you about Israel
and about Judah...." A twist arises when Jeremiah dispatches Baruch to
rewrite the composition. Here we have a variant on the ordinary process
of transmission: the text passes from deity, to human, and then to another
human. But even this double movement of Scripture introduces no com-
plications. The original composition is born fully grown in Yahweh's
head. Its passage from the latter to Jeremiah's ear is apparently flawless,
as is the subsequent transmission from Jeremiah's mouth to Baruch's
hand.[10]

In most of the previous examples, the original words come from God
and are usually written down by humans. The two-step process is not
depicted as problematic. When mortals are the creative source, texts simply "happen" as well. Kings (and a queen) routinely spin out dispatches,
but not a word is said about the process by which such missives were
composed. We have no scene depicting David engaging in soul searching,
or fumbling for just the right homicidal words as he writes the letter that
will result in Uriah the Hittite's death (2 Sam. 11:14–15). Queen Jezebel
easily composes a conspiratorial missive to other residents of Jezreel. Its

contents are relayed in 1 Kings 21:8–9. Yet, the deliberations through which the letter was created are never discussed.[11]

Samuel is somehow able to jot down *all* the rules of the kingdom without any comment, fact-checking, retreat to the archives, and so on (1 Sam. 10:25). The wayward son of Proverbs is told to inscribe the Torah on the tablet of his heart (Prov. 3:3; 7:3). It is never imagined that he might flub a few lines. This is something of an incongruity because the youngster is wont to commit every imaginable blunder that a boy can make.

This "no fuss" conception of authorship is strikingly at odds with how modern scholars envision the writing of the Hebrew Bible. Actually, it is strikingly at odds with just about everything that can be empirically observed about the process of writing. Scripture is at best clueless and at worst deceitful when it comes to describing the way in which its component parts were created and transcribed. Why these depictions are so unrealistic is an open question. What we want to stress is that the Bible's confusions about its own authorship, the writing of its texts, and writing in general stimulated an incredible amount of speculation in the ancient world. Although we want to explore issues of interpretation in the second part of this study, it might be interesting to say a few words about early Jewish and Christian approaches to "Who Wrote the Bible?"

A FLAWED EQUATION: TORAH = THE FIRST FIVE BOOKS = THE WRITING OF MOSES

There are ideas found *in* Hebrew Scriptures and then there are ideas *about* Hebrew Scriptures. Anyone who wants to think clearly about Judaism and Christianity had better learn how to distinguish the two. In some places, ideas in Scripture and ancient ideas about Scripture are fairly similar. In others, the discrepancy is striking.

One idea that surfaces in both the Bible and the writings of the Rabbis and the Church Fathers consists of the belief that a given book of the Bible was written (as in conceptualized and transcribed) by one person, perhaps two, maximum three. The composition of sacred texts emerges as an intimate affair, a small-scale production involving a handful of people, usually living at one moment in history. We refer to this assumption as "monoauthorism." The Old Testament, as we saw previously, thinks in monoauthorist terms. Whenever it broaches the issue of authorship, an individual is cast as a text's creator (i.e., Qoheleth, Solomon, Agur, Isaiah, Jeremiah, Isaiah, God). At no point is it imagined that more than one person might have been responsible for a given document.

The great Rabbinic sages, whose interpretations of Scripture were written down between the first through sixth centuries CE, often thought this way as well. When contemplating the authorship of unattributed biblical texts, they typically conscripted various (individual) celebrated personages into authorial service. The Mishnaic tractate *Baba Bathra* ascribes the Book of Job to Moses. Joshua, according to the Rabbis, wrote the Book of Joshua. Jeremiah uttered the prophecies that bear his name, as well as the Books of Kings and Lamentations. The Holy Spirit (*rûah hakodesh*) – who for purposes of analysis we consider to be an individual – is seen by other Rabbinic commentators as responsible for the Books of Esther and Daniel.[12]

Here we have come across a discrepancy between ideas in and ideas about Scripture. Both the Bible and the Rabbis concur that one person is generally responsible for writing and transcribing a given text. *Yet, the authors of biblical books identified by the Rabbis are often not actually mentioned in the Bible.* With the exception of their claim that the Book of Jeremiah was composed by Jeremiah, not one of the attributions mentioned in the previous paragraph is found in Scripture itself. Actually, some of their ascriptions directly contradict those made in the Hebrew Bible. The Rabbis claim that "Hezekiah and his colleagues" wrote the Book of Isaiah, as well as the Song of Songs and Ecclesiastes. But the Bible seems to give some type of credit for these works to Isaiah, Solomon, and Koheleth, respectively.[13]

Sometimes the Rabbis surpass Scripture and deploy an "author-plus-one" logic. Here they speak of a storied Israelite whose project was completed posthumously by another. Thus, Nehemiah put the finishing touches on the Book of Chronicles started by Ezra. Gad and Nathan performed the same service in the scroll of Samuel, for Samuel of blessed memory. The team of Eleazar and Phineas wrapped up the work started by Joshua (i.e., the Book of Joshua). The Hebrew Bible, needless to say, knows absolutely nothing about these literary duos and trios. This brings us to what may be considered the showcase piece in the history of monoauthorism: the belief that Moses wrote the first five books and

Joshua completed the final few verses of the last book, Deuteronomy (in which Moses's death and burial is described).[14]

This is, again, an idea about Scripture. The Hebrew Bible never states that Moses wrote the Five Books. What it does do is make reference to a wide variety of ambiguous, shifting, and maddeningly imbricated terms such as "Torah," "the Book of Moses," "the Torah of Moses," "Book of the Torah," "Book of the Torah of Moses," "Book of the Torah of Elohim," and "Torah of Yahweh," among others. What each term meant to biblical scribes living in different times is by no means easy to discern. It is clear, however, that quite a few postbiblical commentators drew two overlapping equations when contemplating their sacred texts. First, the word "Torah" was equated with the stretch of five documents that runs from Genesis to Deuteronomy. Second, Moses was often posited as the author of "Torah" (i.e., the Five Books).[15]

The first surmise is, in the words of R. J. Thompson, "far from unimpeachable." One example should suffice to justify such misgivings. In Genesis 26:5, Yahweh expresses to Isaac his appreciation for Abraham who had kept "My commandments, My laws, and My Torah (plural)." One might ask "*what Torah?*" If Torah actually does refer to the first Five Books in their entirety, then how could Abraham (whose death is reported in Genesis 25:8) have faithfully observed the forthcoming "Torah" contained in the remainder of Genesis, Exodus, Leviticus, Numbers, and Deuteronomy?[16]

Then there is the other side of the equation, namely, the proposition that Moses wrote the first Five Books known as Torah. This assertion also lacks any scriptural substantiation. The biblicist Joseph Blenkinsopp comments: "Here and there in the Pentateuch Moses is said to have written certain things, including laws (Ex. 24:4) and the vow to expatriate the Amalekites (Ex. 17:14), but nowhere is it affirmed that the Pentateuch was authored by Moses, or indeed by anyone else. One would therefore think that what calls for an explanation is not why most people stopped believing in the dogma of Mosaic authorship, but rather why anyone believed it in the first place." But believe in it they did. The monoauthorist equation that reads "Moses wrote the Torah and the Torah equals the first Five Books" stands as one of the most intractable dogmas within Judaism and Christianity. It is an irrational and illogical assertion, yet its resiliency across the generations is truly remarkable. No one knows this better than professors of Scripture who, semester after semester, patiently field countless queries (and complaints) from student monoauthorists.[17]

Tracing the development of this idea about Scripture is a colossal undertaking. We only mention that prior to the Rabbinic era, Jewish commentators were toying with variants of this equation. Among Greek-Jewish sources, the doctrine of Mosaic authorship receives life in Philo's (ca. 20 BCE–50 CE) insistence that Moses wrote the "sacred books" running from Genesis to Deuteronomy (including the last eight verses in which his death is discussed). In *Against Apion*, Josephus (ca. 37/38–100 CE) also assigns the Five Books to Moses.[18]

This brings us back to the Rabbinic literature. *Baba Bathra* 14b famously declares "Moses wrote his own Book and the portion of Baalam [Num. 22–24]. . . . " The book in question is assumed to be the Pentateuch (although one wonders why the passage from Numbers is mentioned separately). In the tractate *Sotah* (V:6 III A) of the Jerusalem Talmud, it is said: "Moses wrote Five Books of the Torah, and then he went back and wrote the pericope of Balak and Balaam." Confronting the inconvenient fact that the last eight verses of Deuteronomy describe Moses's death, some Rabbis, as we saw previously, attributed these to his successor, Joshua.[19]

In patristic literature (i.e., the writings of the Church Fathers who lived from roughly the end of the first century CE to the eighth century CE) the association between Moses and the Five Books is postulated with far less ambiguity. Writing in the late fourth century, the quite quotable John Chrysostom opines: "And even when all humankind fell into evil ways, the creator of all did not abandon the human race . . . he sent them letters as you do to people far away from you, and this drew all humankind back again to him. It was God who sent them letters, Moses who delivered them. What do the letters say? 'In the beginning God made heaven and earth.'"[20]

Truth be told, the avid reader of postbiblical documents could find a welter of distinct authorship conjectures: that God wrote the Torah, that Moses wrote the Torah, that Moses recorded the Torah as dictated by God, that Moses wrote the Torah with the assistance of angels, that the Holy Spirit wrote the Torah, and, in a sort of underground countertradition, that Ezra rewrote the Torah. In the New Testament, we learn – although the translation is hotly contested – that "All Scripture is inspired

by God and useful..." (2 Timothy 3:16). If this were the case, then the
Old Testament in its entirety would have to be seen as, ultimately, derived
from God. In each conjecture, monoauthorist assumptions emerge. Yet,
these are different monoauthorist assumptions from those found in the
Hebrew Bible/Old Testament. Scripture and ideas about Scripture disagree – and this is an antagonism we encounter repeatedly.[21]

CONCLUSION: THE HEBREW BIBLE AS AN UNSELF-CONSCIOUS ARTIFACT

It is somewhat difficult for the Hebrew Bible to answer the question of
who wrote the Hebrew Bible. This is because it does not even know that
it is the Hebrew Bible. As a document, it displays an astonishing lack
of textual self-consciousness. It alleges to know what God thinks, but it
does not know itself. It is not aware that it is called the Hebrew Bible,
Old Testament, Scripture, the *Tanakh, Mikra, ta biblia, hai graphai, ta
hiera grammata,* or whatever other designations later Jews and Christians applied to their corpus of sacred writings. Never does the text
ascend into consciousness and declare with all the assuredness of fire-
works combusting and uncoiling in the sky: *"Read this Hebrew Bible very
carefully!"* or *"What a treasure trove of knowledge runs from Genesis to
Chronicles!"* or *"Give ear to the message of the Old Testament!"* It demonstrates no explicit recognition of being that unified body of books that
later generations referred to by the names mentioned previously. Jews
and Christians have venerated an unself-conscious artifact, one whose
embarrassing gaps in self-knowledge have always had to be filled in by later
interpreters.

So who does the Hebrew Bible think wrote the Hebrew Bible? No
answer is ever given as regards the work in its entirety. Some individual
books, and portions of books, are attributed to one given person. Some
books make attributions that are contradictory or completely illogical.
Others, as we saw above, remain completely unascribed. Through it all,
Scripture clings to its "no fuss" conception of how texts come into being.
It was only during the modern period, with its relentless, almost bullying,
suspicion of ancient wisdom that alternative, critical explanations of the
Bible's authorship could emerge en masse. This is the development that
we now examine.

SUGGESTIONS FOR FURTHER READING

A wonderful overview of biblical claims about authorship (and their dubious accuracy) is advanced in Morton Smith's "Pseudepigraphy in the Israelite Literary Tradition," in *Pseudepigrapha I: Pseudopythagorica-Lettres de Platon, Littérature pseudépigraphique juive.* Ed. Kurt von Fritz. Geneva: Vandoeuvres, 1972, pp. 191–227. Highly readable and informative accounts (and contestations) of theories of Mosaic authorship can be found in Joseph Blenkinsopp's *The Pentateuch: An Introduction to the First Five Books of the Bible.* New York: Doubleday, 1992, and S. David Sperling's *The Original Torah: The Political Intent of the Bible's Writers.* New York: New York University Press, 1998. Readers interested in tracking down important postbiblical discussions of authorship should consult B. *Baba Bathra* 14b–15a. Many opinions of various Church Fathers on the issue are conveniently collected in James Megivern, *Bible Interpretation.* Wilmington, NC: Consortium, 1978.

∾

2

"Who Wrote the Bible?": Modern Responses

And then, this original: it was not actually an original; not *the* original, when you come to look at it. It was itself a copy of a document out of God knows what distant time; upon which, then, though without precisely knowing where, one might rest, as upon a true original, if it were not itself provided with glosses and additions by the hand of the scribe, who thought thus to make more comprehensible an original text lying again who knows how far back in time; though what they probably did was further to transmogrify the original wisdom of his text.

Thomas Mann, *Joseph and His Brothers*

In the modern era, Moses the Author has been definitively – and rather ignominiously – shunted aside. The same fate has befallen an assortment of dubious monoauthorist surmises and irrational beliefs about the composition of Scripture inherited from Semitic, Hellenistic, and Latin antiquity. Contemporary scholars do not generally accept that Moses, bespectacled and sitting at the foot of Mount Sinai, penned the tale of Noah's ark. They do not maintain that Solomon composed the Song of Songs after toweling off. Nor do they often believe that – poof! – biblical texts were created effortlessly, sweatlessly, quickly. As for divine origins, well let's just say that it might be an act of grace to *not* ascribe various books of the Hebrew Bible to God or the Holy Spirit. For if those texts were indeed written, dictated, or inspired by a heavenly author, then His literary competence, not to mention His sanity, would frequently be questioned.

Take, for example, *the contradictions*. In Exodus 33:11 it is related that "Yahweh spoke to Moses face to face, as a man would speak to another."

So it comes as something of a surprise when just a few lines later Yahweh warns Moses that he cannot see His face "because no human being can see Yahweh and live." Joshua dismisses an assembly of Israelites in Judges 2:6 – which is disorienting because his death was reported in an earlier chapter. Nor is it entirely clear why Moses's father-in-law is referred to variously as Jeter, Jethro, and Reuel.[1]

The presence of *textual repetition* also leads us to doubt the sobriety of the so-called author. In Genesis alone, we encounter two creation stories, two flood stories, three tales of a patriarch pretending his wife is his sister, countless covenants, and so on. Words and verses are clearly missing from the Old Testament, and the problem of *ellipsis* raises concerns about the accuracy of our documents. Cain said something to Abel prior to murdering him, but those fratricidal sentiments are not recorded in the Masoretic text of Genesis 4:8. (Although one variant text from a collection known as the Aramaic Targumim has Cain saying, rather innocuously, "Come! Let the two of us go out into the open field." In another Targum, the boys engage in some fairly heady prehomicide banter.) Psalm 145 is an acrostic poem in which each new verse starts with a letter of the Hebrew alphabet. Yet, where is the line that should commence with the letter "*nûn*"?: nowhere to be found.[2]

Scads of biblical sentences, as we will see in Chapter Five, appear to be *ungrammatical or without discernible meaning*. Anyone who doubts this is invited to try their hand at translating the long poetic section of the Book of Job. So peculiar is its language that some have speculated that it was originally written in Aramaic and then translated back – poorly – into Hebrew. *Abrupt changes in literary and linguistic style* also typify the books of Scripture. The first creation story of Genesis 1–2:4a, with its rhythmic precision and orderly thematic development feels like a midtempo waltz. Steady and sober, one can almost hear the *tick-2-3, tick-2-3* of the conductor's baton striking the music stand. The second creation story of Genesis 2:4b-24, in contrast, accelerates and decelerates, careens from this theme to that, swerves, stops, lapses into poetry, and digresses. It is the scriptural equivalent of free jazz.[3]

It would be remiss not to mention *the hair-raisingly bewildering plot turns* that occur in so many biblical works. In the final chapter of the Book of Job, God praises and rewards Job. This would be the very same Job who has been excoriating Him across most of the story. For good measure, and as if to say, "*I can't figure Myself out either*," the deity proceeds to rebuke those who defended Him from Job's blasphemous charges. This should delight secularists far and wide.[4]

Contradiction, repetition, ellipsis, defective Hebrew, sudden stylistic shifts, perplexing turns of the plot – these are just some of the irregularities that have made exegetes think critically about traditional conceptions of who wrote the Bible. In this chapter, we survey a few distinctly modern theories of scriptural composition. The modern period, as we define it, stretches from approximately the mid-nineteenth century to the present. In more recent decades, a forceful postmodern challenge has virtually ripped Old Testament scholarship asunder. This intriguing development is discussed in Chapter Five.[5]

THE DOCUMENTARY HYPOTHESIS AND THE BIRTH OF MODERNIST EXEGESIS

Nearly every college undergraduate who has matriculated for an Introduction to Hebrew Bible/Old Testament class has been subjected to documentary hypothesis. Referred to also as "the newer documentary hypothesis," "the Graf-Wellhausen hypothesis," or more broadly, "higher criticism," it dominated biblical studies until the late twentieth century. As one noted student of the theory wrote a few years back: "Viewed as a whole, Old Testament scholarship still lives in the era of Wellhausen."[6]

In 1878, Julius Wellhausen famously averred that the "Pentateuch . . . is no literary unity, and no simple historical quantity." The story of the transcontinental tremors elicited by his *Prolegomena to the History of Israel* has been told elsewhere and need not be rehearsed here. For our purposes, it should be noted that Wellhausen was the beneficiary of centuries of critical (and often heretical) thinking on the question of the Bible's composition. By synthesizing earlier contributions and adding his own genius to the proceedings, he would advance a prototype of what became the single most influential paradigm in the history of modern biblical scholarship. Or, as one scholar phrased it, Wellhausen provided "the charter of Biblical criticism in general."[7]

In its generic incarnation, documentary hypothesis maintains that within the first five books one can identify (at least) four different sources or documents. These are typically designated by the sigla J, E, D, and P. As the twentieth century progressed, industrious (and contentious) higher critics would soon subdivide these sources into microslivers (e.g., J1, J2, J3, P1, P2, P3) or posit entirely new ones such as B, L, N, K, and S, to name a few. It is important to recall – because even biblical scholars sometimes forget – that *the sources posited by Wellhausen's theory are not synonymous with individuals.* There was no Mr. E or Mr. J. As Herbert Hahn observed years ago,

> it had been clear even to Wellhausen that neither J nor E could be regarded as the work of a single author. Each contained a number of obviously older elements, originally independent, which had been taken up into the body of the document; each had apparently been supplemented from time to time with later historical material; and each had undergone a certain amount of editorial revision in an effort to co-ordinate and harmonize the various elements in the style of the original. *The additional materials were so extensive that it was better to regard the documents as products of literary or religious schools than as the work of individual authors.*[8]

In fact, documentary hypothesis thinks far more about editors or redactors than it does about authors. It jettisoned the monoauthorist assumption that the texts of Scripture were written at one point in time by an individual or maybe two or three persons. Instead, biblical texts were seen as worked over, if you will, across the span of Israelite and Judahite history. The types of operations that the all-important redactors performed on received documents varied widely. We must assume they amended and aligned, embellished and erased, melded and moved the received documents according to the theological, political, and aesthetic demands of their day. Here and there they must have also engaged in a little "original" creative writing themselves.

Documentary hypothesis, let's just admit it, is not a very embraceable theory. It aspires to describe a hypercomplex reality. As generations of undergraduates have come to understand, it is exceedingly difficult to illustrate. Let us imagine that at some point in Israelite history a school of editors received a J document and set about working it over. Perhaps these redactors did the same to an E document in their possession. Perhaps they took the two newly edited documents and placed them side by side in a new collection. In so doing, maybe they inserted a few of their own comments to ensure a smooth transition between the two parts.

Or, perhaps they shuffled the new J and E documents into one another, leaving huge swaths of would-be Scripture on the cutting-room floor. Perhaps – and now the circuitry starts to overheat – centuries later a P(riestly) school of editors armed with the amalgamated JE document, plus a D document, performed similar operations. Higher critics have posited numerous redactorial waves throughout Israelite history, and it is here that the possibilities of textual distortion and creation achieve Borgesian dimensions. Under such circumstances, it becomes not only impossible, but rather futile, to think in terms of an author.

Although the Pentateuch may initially appear to be a unified composition, it is, in reality, "the result of editorial combination of originally independent extensive narrative sources." Stemming from different centuries, these sources have been stitched together – sometimes seamlessly – by subsequent waves of writers, editors, jurists, copyists, theologians, censors, party hacks, and so on. In the words of one exegete, modern Pentateuchal criticism works from the premise that "we are not here concerned with a unified book, compiled according to a deliberate plan by one single author, Moses for example. . . . The question is simply how this lack of uniformity is to be explained."[9]

MORE MODERNS: TRADITION HISTORY, INNER-BIBLICAL EXEGESIS, AND THE HAGGADIC HYPOTHESIS

Not every college student has had the opportunity to study theories that developed in the turbulent wake of documentary hypothesis's ascent. A rival approach, albeit one clearly influenced by Wellhausen, is commonly known as tradition history. Emerging in the early twentieth century, this school focused not only on the written form of biblical documents, but also on their oral prehistory. Among those in this school that accepted the premises of Wellhausen's theory, it was held that J, E, D, and P, as well as the Old Testament's non-Pentateuchal materials, were not originally written down. Rather, they crystallized into written form only *after* they lived long lives as orally transmitted legends, prayers, credos, prophecies, laws, cultic instructions, historical accounts, and so on.[10]

In his famous discussion of the legends of Genesis, Hermann Gunkel phrased it this way: "At the time when they were written down the legends were already very old and had already a long history behind them."

For Gunkel, the first book of the Bible "contains the final sublimation into writing of a body of oral traditions." Even when these legends were transferred to the scroll, the operation was executed not by individuals but by "schools of narrators." Another perhaps more central figure in tradition history, Martin Noth, would render the following observation about the J source: "we are dealing here with a compilation which was assembled and accumulated in the course of a long and complicated process initially involving oral transmission." "Old Testament literature," according to Ivan Engnell, one of Wellhausen's later detractors, "has the character of an oral literature which was written down only at a relatively late period."[11]

Let us bracket the question of whether we presently possess – or ever will possess – enough evidence to speak with confidence about this conjectured preliterary stage. What is intriguing about tradition history is the way in which it stretches the temporal parameters of the Bible's formation as conceived by documentary hypothesis. We can now imagine a "text" that lived a long, unstable, and constantly fluctuating existence in the oral realm, only to then live a long, unstable, and constantly fluctuating existence in the written realm as well. Once again, the concept of one sovereign original author has no place in this paradigm.[12]

To this point, we have imagined different types of specialists who performed operations on the ever-emerging, ever-unstable, precanonized Hebrew Bible. Tradition history invites us to think of oral artists who excelled in recounting, singing, or chanting. It envisions schools of narrators who eventually transposed these compositions to the scroll. Documentary hypothesis speaks of authorial schools and, in particular, editors who repeatedly reworked existing materials. A more recent approach known as inner-biblical exegesis permits us to imagine another type of contributor: the meddlesome scribe/copyist. This type of textual specialist emerged in the postexilic period. This would be somewhere after 539 BCE when, according to Hebrew Scriptures, the expatriated Judahites residing in Babylon were permitted to return to the province of Judah by Cyrus, King of Persia.[13]

In his *Biblical Interpretation in Ancient Israel*, Michael Fishbane envisioned the responsibilities of these postexilic scribes as "copying texts . . . maintaining, transmitting, and collating literary records." They were the recipients of preexisting documents that contained what

Fishbane referred to as a *traditum* (i.e., a given tradition enshrined in a text). These copyists, according to Fishbane, "received the texts of tradition, studied and copied them, puzzled about their contents, and preserved their meanings for new generations." In their zeal to clarify an obscure or problematic passage they routinely made minor – and less frequently, major – emendations on the documents they so revered. Throughout *Biblical Interpretation*, Fishbane identifies glosses, grammatical explanations, and pious revisions that had been slipped into the *traditum* by industrious copyists (and hence became a *traditum* for unsuspecting later generations).[14]

Fishbane's analysis of Psalm 68:9, although not without its critics, is useful in helping us conceptualize the small but significant interventions made by the scribes. What follows is a transliteration of the Masoretic text of the Hebrew Bible and then three standard translations of this verse. The fourth follows Fishbane's lead:

'eretz rā'ăšāh
'ap-šāmayim nāṭpû
mipnê 'ĕlōhîm
zeh sînay
mipnê 'ĕlōhîm
'ĕlōhê yiśrā'ēl

1. *King James Version*: "the earth shook, the heavens also dropped at the presence of God: *even* Sinai itself was moved at the Presence of God, the God of Israel." (68:8)
2. *New Oxford Annotated Bible*: "the earth quaked, the heavens poured down rain, at the presence of God; yon Sinai quaked at the presence of God, the God of Israel." (68:8)
3. *Jewish Publication Society*: "the earth trembled, the sky rained, because of God, yon Sinai, because of God, the God of Israel." (68:9)
4. In light of Fishbane's analysis: "the earth shook, and the sky rained because of Elohim (this is Sinai), because of Elohim, the God of Israel."

The major difference in translation lies in what Fishbane has identified as a parenthetical insertion lurking in the middle of the verse. In his view, the aside "this is Sinai" (*zeh sînay*) is a scribal addition intended to explain an apparent ambiguity. Some accommodating copyist took it upon himself to inform readers that the event described in the first half of the verse refers to a famous event in Israelite lore. The text worker, in this reconstruction, simply added a helpful comment. Fishbane writes: "a later glossator-scribe read the particular imagery of Ps. 68:9 within its particular historico-geographical context as an allusion to the Sinaitic revelation."[15]

The scribe meddled with the received text, presumably with noble intentions. So trivial or well disguised were these benevolent interpolations – and Fishbane identifies dozens of these – that their provenance was forgotten or overlooked by later generations of scribes and, eventually, biblical interpreters. Yet, these miniscule insertions often had the effect of adding new meanings and nuances to the document for future (and unwitting) readers. In a truly astonishing aside, Fishbane remarks that the Masoretic text (i.e., the "official" version of Hebrew Scriptures used by most Jews) "despite its authoritative character, is not a 'clean' or 'corrected' text-copy, but rather a compound of errors, corrections, and supplements."[16]

Fishbane's analysis often – but not in every case – points to small, modest intrusions performed by the scribes in question. It was his student, Bernard Levinson, who conceptualized larger, more aggressive interventions. In his study of Deuteronomy, Levinson pointed to the radically "transformative" work of those who wrote the fifth book of the Pentateuch. Their textual reworkings of earlier biblical texts were conscious, "creative, active, revisionist, and tendentious." These scribes had a specific political and theological agenda that they sought to implement by rewriting and in essence reformulating existing works such as the Covenant Code of Exodus (20:23–23:33). Here we are asked to envision biblical scribes who are writing in dialogue with – or perhaps better yet, shouting in opposition to – other parts of the Bible.[17]

In rounding out our sampling of distinctly modern approaches to the "Who wrote the Bible?" question, we turn to Samuel Sandmel's quirky article, published in the 1961 issue of the *Journal of Biblical Literature*. "The Haggada Within Scripture" never ceases to pop up in scholarly discussions about the Bible's composition. The criticisms that he directed at the once-regnant Wellhausian orthodoxy are less important for our

purposes than the alternative that he raised. Sandmel suggested that it
would be best to liken the composition of the Pentateuch to the early
Jewish literary genre of Haggada. One of the peculiarities of the latter
is that it often tells a story one way, and then tells what appears to be
the same story in a slightly altered form. Working from this analogy,
Sandmel reasoned that if we find a great deal of repeated, although not
identical, material in the Book of Genesis then this "fanciful retelling of
tales" may be attributable to the presence of a Haggadic narrative style.
The biblical editors thus evinced a "disinclination to expunge," and this
accounts for narrative repetition. For Sandmel, as for many others, the
Bible is "a literature which grew by accretion."[18]

This placing of different stories side by side creates logical contradictions for the modern. How could God create humans in two different ways
in Genesis 1 and Genesis 2? How could Abraham have passed his wife off
as a sister twice, only to have Issac later engage in the same behavior with
his spouse? Some believe these incongruities did not vex ancient com-
pilers. John Barton has recently proposed that the Israelite literati were
not unduly preoccupied by the need – *our* need – for a book to contain
unity, internal coherence, and closure. The editors of biblical books were
merely creating something along the lines of "anthologies of materials."
These collectors, suggests Barton, had "a weak sense of genre . . . material
which we should regard as too disparate to be juxtaposed in a single book
is freely intermingled." The image of the Bible as an anthology is central
to our secular hermeneutics and resurfaces in our later discussions about
the Bible's meaning system.[19]

CONCLUSION: ASSEMBLAGE, NOT AUTHORSHIP

Although distinct from one another, and sometimes even mutually antagonistic, the approaches surveyed previously provide a few sterling examples of modern biblical exegesis. For now we want to reiterate that modern
approaches to the "Who wrote the Bible?" question differ radically from
ancient ones. Although there are exceptions, contemporary researchers
do not typically fixate on the idea of one celebrated Israelite persona as
author (e.g., Moses, Solomon, David), nor do they accept that "texts just
happen." The writers, editors, and scribes that are conjectured to have
participated in the process of creating Hebrew Scriptures are nameless

abstractions living across hundreds of years. For this reason, the best of modern exegesis is more likely to examine assemblage, not authorship. These researchers concentrate on the long, hypercomplex, compositional process through which the Hebrew Scriptures were forged.

This having been said, there are still more than a few higher critics and others who insist on speaking about "the author" in the singular. Further, many perform their critical work on the Bible to understand the original intention or message of some ancient writer (an aspiration that we criticize in Chapter Five). Modern methods, they believe, furnish them with the tools necessary to access early and pristine strata of the Bible. These exegetes want to declutter Scripture – the better to arrive at the actual sentiments and motivations of the original biblical writers and editors. The literary scholar Regina Schwartz notes that these methods "did not so much pose a challenge to the Bible's authority as they presupposed that authority," "The motivation of most historical critics of the Hebrew Bible," writes Jon Levenson, "continues to be religious in character." There is then a "payoff" for the theologian who uses these new-fangled methods: they help him or her access unsullied revelations.[20]

Modern biblical scholars are not usually bent on blasphemy. Even so, their approaches have always lacked a certain popular appeal. Most laypersons will take a David "of flesh and blood" over a theoretical D school any day. The idea of one author who wrote a given biblical text is certainly more intuitive than that of a veritable civilization of anonymous textual tradents. It should also be added that higher critics have squabbled incessantly among one another. Nonscholars who read about this theory are confronted with a stunning array of often irreconcilable options. They are also confronted with numbingly dense prose and overdetailed reconstructions. But perhaps more than anything, the monoauthorist approach perseveres among the masses because it approximates what biblical books sometimes say about themselves and what Tradition (i.e., the teachings of the Rabbis and Church Fathers) insists is true. When it comes to Jewish and Christian laypersons, modern biblical criticism has always been a hard sell.

Let us, then, praise biblical exegetes. They demonstrate a truly admirable degree of intellectual autonomy. They are more than willing to promote theories that have little appeal to their unlettered coreligionists. They have no reluctance to disagree with biblical, not to mention classical Jewish and Christian, conceptions of scriptural authorship. Yet, it seems to us that many of the ideas discussed previously have theological consequences – troubling ones – that most biblicists are reluctant to confront. We think of the words of one of Wellhausen's contemporaries, Franz Delitzsch: "If his conclusions be true, the Old Testament cannot in any distinctive sense be the word of God." Franz Delitzsch was correct. Higher criticism, as well as other modern approaches, teems with heretical potential. Scratch its surface, and all sorts of destabilizing implications for Jewish and Christian dogma come swarming forth.[21]

It is ironic, then, that these methods are now taught in schools of Jewish and Christian theology around the world on a quotidian basis. Somehow, it has become possible to employ implicitly debunking theories such as documentary hypothesis, while maintaining that the Bible is, more or less, the word of God. How this happened constitutes one of the most interesting chapters in Western intellectual history (see Chapter Eight). It demonstrates the laudable openness to rational modes of inquiry that characterizes many religious groups in the modern Occident. It also demonstrates that theologians are smarter than secularists. They have expertly absorbed and, where necessary, smoothed over the sharpest edges of the enlightenment critique of religion.

A secular hermeneut, of course, has no desire to neutralize or detoxify critical possibilities. In the hopes of unleashing biblical scholarship's inner demons, we now want to follow the assumptions of modern exegesis to some of their logical conclusions.[22]

SUGGESTIONS FOR FURTHER READING

Many clear and informative treatments of the rise of higher criticism are available to the interested reader. Three noteworthy works are R. E. F. Friedman's *Who Wrote the Bible?* San Francisco: Harper Collins, 1987; Joseph Blenkinsopp's *The Pentateuch: An Introduction to the First Five Books of the Bible.* New York: Doubleday, 1992; and Emil Kraeling's *The Old Testament Since the Reformation.* New York: Schocken Books, 1969. A nice summary of the problems that afflict biblical literature (i.e., problems that lead scholars to assume the Bible was written by multiple authors working at different times) can be found in Alexander Rofé's *Introduction to the Composition of the Pentateuch.* Sheffield: Sheffield Academic

Press, 1999. In the past few decades, many researchers have tried to resurrect the old dogma that one person wrote the Pentateuch. Such studies are usually written by conservative theologians or, strangely enough, secular professors of English or comparative literature. R. N. Whybray, however, is neither, and his *The Making of the Pentateuch: A Methodological Study*. Sheffield: JSOT Press, 1987, advances a thoughtful and sophisticated (although we think unconvincing) refutation of documentary hypothesis. On the reemergence of "monoauthorism" among scholars see our article "The Bible as Literature?" *Hebrew Studies*, 45 (2004) 9–26. As for tradition history, the writings of Hermann Gunkel (1862–1932) have aged well. In addition to his great erudition, he was a gifted prose stylist. His genius is on display in the collection of essays entitled *Water for a Thirsty Land: Israelite Literature and Religion*. Ed. K. C. Hanson. Minneapolis: Fortress, 2001. Those who truly want to get to the heart of the matter regarding tradition history should consult what might be the most widely cited dissertation in more recent biblical scholarship, Douglas Knight's *Rediscovering the Traditions of Israel*, rev. ed. SBL Dissertation Series 9. Missoula, MT: Scholars Press, 1975. Studies of inner-biblical exegesis usually require specialist knowledge, but Esther Menn offers an accessible account in "Inner-Biblical Exegesis in the Tanak," in *A History of Biblical Interpretation: Volume 1, The Ancient Period*. Eds. Alan Hauser and Duane Watson. Grand Rapids, MI: William B. Eerdmans, 2003, pp. 55–79.

3

∾

A Secular Answer to "Who Wrote the Bible?"

Ben Bag Bag said: Turn it [i.e., the Torah] over, and (again) turn it over, for all is therein.

Aboth 5:22

Talking about texts as the products of authors, and authors meaning what they say. I suppose you'll say next that God sat and wrote down the Torah and all the commentaries, all seeing and all intending, of course.

Allegra Goodman, *Kaaterskill Falls*

It is not unusual for very religious Jews and Christians to report that reading the Hebrew Bible is an incomparable experience. They tingle when they encounter the tale(s) of creation in Genesis. Isaiah's prophecies reduce them to tears. They are overcome by the most intense emotions when mouthing the Psalms. These psychological manifestations may have less to do with the objective literary qualities of these texts than with the subjective perceptions of believers. The pious ascribe the authorship of biblical books to, variously, God, the Holy Spirit, angels, and Moses, among others. With writers such as these is it any wonder that faithful readers will be awed?[1]

By now, we have seen that no book of the Hebrew Bible claims to be written by God, the Holy Spirit, or angels. Nor do Hebrew Scriptures anywhere support the later Jewish and Christian insistence on the Mosaic authorship of the Pentateuch. But in all fairness to believers, it must be acknowledged that those who are mesmerized, enchanted, or afflicted by a "special" feeling when perusing Scripture are demonstrating sound literary instincts. In one sense, they are absolutely correct: reading the Hebrew Bible *is* an incomparable experience. Yet, this is not on account of divine origins, Mosaic authorship, or some such thing. What is remarkable about the Old Testament is its compositional history – the exceedingly peculiar manner in which it was built. After all, how many books were written across hundreds of years? How many have multiple, anonymous authors and editors? How many texts can one think of in which later contributors surreptitiously commented on, altered, erased, interpreted, melded, spliced, fudged, and cut and pasted the work of earlier ones, all to have the process begin afresh with even later generations of nameless participants? Written and assembled like almost no other text, it should come as no surprise that the Hebrew Bible reads like no other. One understands why the uninitiated impute to all this literary strangeness the presence of the ineffable divine.

Be that as it may, the uninitiated are simply wrong. That, at least, would be the harsh verdict of one who places their trust in modern biblical scholarship. When it comes to what pious Christians and Jews believe to be true about their Scriptures, even harsher verdicts could be rendered. Yet Old Testament researchers are usually reluctant to pass such judgments. Tethered by a certain interpretive conservatism, they rarely take the assumptions of our discipline to their logical, and brutally impious, conclusions. Secular hermeneutics, in contrast, is a relentlessly critical enterprise. It wants to surpass an already skeptical modern exegesis because it can and because it might be interesting to do so.

HOW MANY WROTE THE HEBREW BIBLE?

To unleash the critical potential of biblical research, we begin by stating four basic assumptions about the Bible's authorship. Our debts to modern biblical scholarship, in particular, the schools discussed in Chapter Two, should be obvious.

First, it is held that the ideal-typical biblical text was composed *transhistorically*. Ostensibly, a document that is assembled across centuries cannot be ascribed to one person. This leads us quite logically to a second premise: *polyauthorism*. We envision multiple literary "contributors" – a term preferable to "author/s" – scattered across first millennia Palestine (i.e., diachronic polyauthorism). It is also warranted to posit writers working in tandem at one given historical moment (i.e., synchronic polyauthorism). Although everyone wants to know who wrote the texts of the Bible, it might be just as well to ask how many? A specific number, obviously, is not ascertainable. We advise those pursuing this question think in terms of the cast of an opera (including all the back-stage specialists, lighting technicians, musicians, costume people, hangers-on, and so on) as opposed to a working jazz trio. Across the arc of its lifetime hundreds of people, maybe more, performed operations on a biblical text.

As for the operations that these sundry and dispersed contributors performed, we identify the following broad categories of textual meddling. By *superimposition*, we refer to the act by which one or more individuals placed a layer of words, ideas, dogma, corrections, clarifications, and so on, on top of an already existing text. Let us accept that any type of erasure within a received document also constitutes such an act. *Juxtaposition* signifies the setting of two or more originally discrete textual entities side by side. Whereas superimposition pertains to a variety of manipulations executed on one textual unit, juxtaposition concerns bringing two or more of these units into proximity. Later generations – clueless as ever – will fail to notice these acts of juxtaposition and will assume the text is an organic unity. These concepts are somewhat abstract, and illustrations follow later.[2]

For now, the major point is this: if by "author" we mean the exclusive and sovereign creator of an original and unified textual product, then our approach suggests that no biblical document had *an* author. Rather, the texts of Scripture passed through the hands of countless contributors across the span of Israelite and, eventually, early Jewish civilization. Some documents were worked over more than others. Some hands, it goes without saying, made larger and more significant contributions. Undoubtedly, the historical rhythm of this scriptural meddling was syncopated; in certain periods, given books sustained more intensive interventions. But in no case may we defer to Scripture and speak of texts that "just happened."

It is therefore very unlikely that the conscious intentions of an ancient writer or editor sit on the pages of the Bible, unscathed by the compositional process that we have been describing in this study. All erstwhile biblical authors were doomed to be rewritten and prewritten. They were rewritten by countless subsequent contributors who, for all we know, never regarded their superimpositions and juxtapositions as impositions. When we say that authors were prewritten, we start from the premise that most had to negotiate with previously existing received documents, or in very early times, oral accounts (see Chapter Two).[3]

So, who wrote the component texts that now comprise the Hebrew Bible? We respond with a vague sociological generalization: an aggregate of persons trained in various scribal arts living in first millennia Palestine. As far as we can tell, all or most of the members of the aggregate were men. Given the "plutocratic prerequisites" for entry into the scribal guild, it seems that the majority emanated from privileged social strata. Yet, the members of what Philip Davies has rightly called "a small and elite class" were not entirely homogeneous. They lived in an interstitial zone of Iron Age Palestine that tended to be visited, as it were. This means that their patriarchal and elitist impulses were shot through with the cultural influences of whatever visitors had achieved local hegemony. Depending on where in history the contributors stood, we can posit Egyptian, Assyrian, Persian, and Hellenistic influences on their thought, to name but a few.[4]

We must also assume persons with diverse forms of literary skills played a role in giving shape to the text in question. Some "wrote" in the more traditional sense. Some edited. Some added glosses, superscriptions, specifying comments, and so on. Some scotched things together. Some engaged in a sort of religious and moral "quality control" of the document. Some assembled the anthology. Others simply copied texts (albeit sometimes inaccurately) and still others tried their hand at a little transformative inner-biblical exegesis. That the members of the aggregate were ideologically and theologically heterogeneous should be clear to anyone that has ever read the Hebrew Bible.[5]

Composition by aggregate is rarely encountered in the literature of the modern era. But in the ancient Near East, it appears to have been standard procedure. In his aptly titled *The Evolution of the Gilgamesh Epic*, Jeffrey Tigay demonstrated that this famous Mesopotamian text was written "over a period of at least 1,500 years." Tigay proceeds to chart the countless feats of (what we have dubbed) superimposition and juxtaposition performed on the epic by anonymous contributors. Unlike contemporary writers, these ancient scribes were not legally, morally, or psychologically restrained by any notion of "intellectual property." Touching up (or tearing apart) a received text was common practice, regardless of how inviolable its contents were perceived to be.[6]

We remind the reader that an aggregate is not a committee. The word "committee" implies conscious coordination. Committee members work together and, unless the group is preternaturally dysfunctional, share a basic awareness that they are members of a committee. But because the documents of the Bible were built transhistorically, most of those who contributed could not have been familiar with one another. Their diffusion across centuries also ensures they shared no common objectives. Indeed, almost none of those who participated in the lengthy compositional process knew that the documents they were working on would appear, a long time later, in something called the "Hebrew Bible."

In order to properly understand this foundational text of Occidental civilization, one must be willing to abandon modern notions of authorial intentions and the author's ability to determine a text's meaning. Scripture came together in ways that almost none of its contributors could ever have foreseen. Contingency, accident, unintended consequences – those are more a part of the Bible's story than many want to acknowledge.[7]

THE BIBLE'S MEANINGS NEVER MEANT

Although the phrase "composition by aggregate" is of our own clunky coinage, similar alternatives have been alluded to by other researchers. Richard Elliot Friedman once referred to the Hebrew Bible as "the product of a community . . . the offspring of a continuing, developing culture." Stephen Geller has wondered aloud if "a collective ancient Israelite" wrote the Hebrew Scriptures. "Collective genius of the people" was the phrase Herbert Hahn once used in reference to Old Testament narrative. To say that many people composed the Hebrew Bible across many years is not necessarily a radical claim. It is a basic – even banal – premise of modern Old Testament research. It turns no heads, does little to imperil one's tenure prospects, and rarely gets one excommunicated. Yet, only a handful of biblical scholars have explored the literary, hermeneutical, and even theological implications of this claim. In part, this is because doing so requires speaking on a level of near-algebraic abstraction. Yet, the theory of composition by aggregate also raises a variety of disturbing questions about what the texts of the Hebrew Bible mean and how they came to mean what they mean.[8]

Let us begin our pursuit of these implications by making another unproblematic claim about Scripture: it positively teems with meaning. An enormously large set of messages, ideas, claims, and truths resides on the scriptural page. Michael Fishbane speaks of the ability of the Hebrew Bible to "sponsor awesome and almost unimaginable levels of meaning." In a nice turn of the phrase, the exegete Nahum Sarna likened the Tanak to the "very protoplasm of Jewish existence." The literary critic Northrop Frye once referred to the "polysemous" quality of the Bible.[9]

This belief that the Good Book says many different things is by no means a conceit of modern biblical scholarship. Many are familiar with William Blake's line from *The Everlasting Gospel*: "Both read the Bible day and night, but thou readst black where I read white." A similar suspicion is evident in Shakespeare's *The Merchant of Venice*. In Act One, Antonio remarks, "the devil can cite Scripture for his purpose." Later, Bassanio reiterates the suspicion that a panopoly of meanings dwell in the sacred text awaiting exploitation by less than savory individuals:

> In religion,
> what damned error but some sober brow
> Will bless it, and approve it with a text,
> Hiding the grossness with fair ornament?[10]

Ancient exegetes also recognized the multivalence of Scripture. Is this not what Ben Bag Bag was getting at in the quote from our epigraph? Or what the Rabbinic sages were implying when they famously remarked that the Torah had "seventy faces"? Contemporary fundamentalists notwithstanding, most exegetes (be they ancient or modern) would accept that there is an affluence of meanings to be found within Scripture. Nothing controversial there. Jewish and Christian thought can accept this premise.[11]

Somewhat less congenial to Jewish and Christian thought is our insistence that this multiplicity of meaning is entirely attributable to composition by aggregate. This would mean that the Bible's polysemous quality is *unintentional*. Its authors never intended to offer posterity such a munificent bounty of significations. This point needs to be articulated – preferably with a bullhorn in hand – because so many biblical scholars

who confront the Bible's meaning abundance insist that it was put there
on purpose. Witness a remark by Israel Knohl, author of *The Divine
Symphony: The Bible's Many Voices*: "The editors recognized that God's
word is not uniform, but that God speaks in many voices and people hear
God in many ways. They did not want to mar the divine revelation nor
detract from its fullness, so they created a pluralistic book, which contains
a variety of conceptions, a variety of customs, and a variety of laws, and
passed this rich variety down to us in the process. They understood that
the Torah does not have only one entrance, but rather, has many. Their
actions paved the way for the continuation of multivocality and variation
in later generations."[12]

We, conversely, assert that nobody consciously willed the meaning
jungle that is the Hebrew Bible into existence – *nobody possibly could*.
Rather, it is something that is coughed up or sneezed out by a very peculiar, lengthy, and convoluted process of textual assemblage. Composition by aggregate – not God, the Holy Spirit, Moses, Isaiah, a scribe
named Baruch, Ezra, D, or editors with an anachronistic commitment
to pluralism – has seeded the Hebrew Bible with all these possibilities of
meaning.

POSSIBILITIES OF MEANING

The sociologist Emile Durkheim was fond of reminding us that society is
something greater than the sum of its individual parts. Transposing this
idea to the key of Scripture, we would venture that hundreds of years of
literary gilding and latticing produces something bigger, stranger – an
alien text – alien to anything that any of the contributors had in mind.
A given biblical passage or book might indeed have a clear meaning to a
given community, but let us acknowledge that this might be a meaning
never meant.[13]

Because this is all very abstract, an example is necessary. In Genesis
18:16–33, Abraham implores God to grant clemency to the wicked
Sodomites (whom he does not even know). Yet, in Genesis 22, Abraham
robotically answers God's call to murder his beloved son Issac. Is there
not something inconsistent about his behavior? In one chapter, Abraham
actually challenges God on behalf of morally depraved strangers. In
the other, he seems homicidally indifferent to the fate of his own

child. For purposes of argument, let us accept the classic assumption of documentary hypothesis that Genesis 18 stems from J and most of Genesis 22 stems from E. In our parlance, an act of juxtaposition has occurred; two originally discrete documents have been set in proximity.[14]

As a result, many intriguing possibilities of meaning have been created. Few, if any, were intended. The placement of once distinct tales side by side has endowed Abraham with quirks of character, which could not be found in the individual portraits of him drawn by either source. The composite patriarch of Genesis 18 and Genesis 22 is the father of a multitude of interpretations. Has the destruction of Sodom described in chapters 19 to 21 darkened the good social consciousness of Abraham seen in chapter 18? Was it the glimpse of all that divine violence that suddenly made him capable of murdering his child? Does the Bible mean to say that the good of the social body is more important than that of the individual? Is Abraham just a cruel agent of patriarchy, oblivious to the suffering of child and mother? Should we read this pericope as a critique of Abraham? Has he regressed? Failed "the test" mentioned in Genesis 22:1? All these – and most likely hundreds more – are possible, unintentional, and dare we say legitimate messages to be gleaned from the juxtaposed documents. But few – perhaps none – of them were intentionally placed there by a biblical contributor.

The process that we labeled juxtaposition – the placing across time of different texts next to one another – generates abundances of meaning. In the previous example, we looked at two chapters from Genesis. Because of their proximity to one another, let us call this "close juxtaposition." Of course, when the anthology that we now know as the Hebrew Bible was canonized, all its texts were juxtaposed against all its other texts. What emerges from this is an immense number of new and unintended possibilities. The stray verse from, for example, Lamentations can now be read against one from Exodus. A single line from II Kings can be brought to bear on the Book of Job. The making of "far juxtapositions" such as these is nowhere prohibited in Scripture. (The Rabbis of the Talmudic era, by the way, might just be the unsurpassed masters of far juxtaposition.) There is, therefore, compositional juxtaposition and interpretive juxtaposition. The former has to do with the assemblage of the text, the latter with the connections that readers decide to draw.[15]

Prior to moving forward, we note that even a text written by one person will be mined with numerous significations. Our claim, however, is that there are quantitatively more possibilities of meaning in the Old Testament than, let's say, *The Merchant of Venice*. Even if the latter had been continuously interpreted for 2,000 years, its expositors would not have found as much there as they have in the Hebrew Bible. Blame it all on composition by aggregate. This is a process that exponentially increases the many meanings that naturally exist in the writings of any one author. More intellects and more contributors (representing the many and diverse cultural influences on first millennia Palestine) will invariably stimulate more possibilities in the text. If the solo writer evokes a multiplicity of meanings, than a multiplicity of contributors must do so seventyfold. The estimable Northrop Frye appears to have been veering in precisely this direction as he contemplated the effects of all the textual "smashing" wreaked by the Bible's working over: "We are so possessed by the modern notion that all the qualities we admire in literature come from the individuality of an author that it is hard to realize that this relentless smashing of individuality could produce greater vividness and originality rather than less. But so it seems to be."[16]

Composition by aggregate, it has just been suggested, is a very creative process; it brings into being countless possibilities of meaning. But what is more significant, and almost never discussed, is that the same process also yields countless *impossibilities of meaning*. For each new potential meaning that our far-flung contributors inadvertently created, they also engendered innumerable contradictions, ellipses, ambiguities, and senseless claims. Is not the lack of logical coherence that characterizes so many biblical texts the most likely outcome of its peculiar literary assemblage? Could we really expect a great deal of logical consistency from a document crafted in this manner? Have not the indefatigable labors of countless exegetes across millennia tacitly testified to the following truism: without interpretive intervention and rehabilitation, many parts of Scripture really do not make tremendous sense to faithful readers?

We would even go so far as to wonder if the canonized text, in and of itself, always makes grammatical sense. How could so many acts of superimposition *not* take their toll? Any honest modern interpreter will acknowledge that hundreds, if not thousands, of biblical verses are untranslatable. This is typically explained in terms of our deficiencies, our insufficient knowledge of an ancient tongue. A little more research, a few more textual finds from Ugarit, Ebla, and Qumran and, one day, we will be able to understand biblical Hebrew better. We find this stance problematic. Why is it unreasonable to claim that certain phrases in the witness are mere gibberish, that they have been edited into grammatical and syntactical senselessness?

Let us try and approach the problem from another angle. What would happen if we were to resurrect a preexilic ancient Israelite scribe and place him in front of the canonized Masoretic text? We believe he would be fairly perplexed by the document – not just by the Masoretic pointing and separation of originally unseparated words (which was performed somewhere between the fifth and tenth centuries AD, see Chapter Five), not just by chapter and verse divisions (which were probably added between late biblical times and the Middle Ages), but by the words and syntax. We raise, then, the possibility that composition by aggregate has resulted in biblical texts that quite literally have no sense.[17]

The point of our project, however, is not to decide in advance that each and every biblical claim, text, or theme is either incoherent or inadvertently coherent. Such an enterprise would have all its conclusions agreed on in advance and thus lack any sort of integrity. That some ancient author's message came to us intact across the ages, despite superimposition and juxtaposition, Medieval meddling, and so much else, is plausible. Yet, in a secular academic context, at least, *the burden of proof lies on those who believe this to be true*. One who starts from the premise that the text is meaningful, coherent, and true to the words of an ancient Israelite or Jew is practicing theology. One who rejects these assumptions is called a secular hermeneut.

CONCLUSION: SECULAR HERMENEUTICS – A PARASITIC ENTERPRISE

We have presented a mere synopsis of the implications of composition by aggregate. Despite its brevity, it is hoped that the reader can grasp the destabilizing potential of this theory. It does away with *the* author. Instead, it posits a series of texts constituted by the uneven deposits of anonymous contributors strewn about first millennia Palestine. It thus severs the organic bond between what an author meant to say and what a text means. What a text is said to "mean," it will be suggested later, is often enough an accident – one that involves a collision between a polysemous passage and a situated reader.

Secular hermeneutics views Scripture as not possessing a meaning, but many meanings. This does not differ radically from either classical religious conceptions or the perspective of mainstream biblical scholarship. What is different is our insistence on the inadvertent manner in which the Bible's convoluted process of composition generated all these meanings. That unsparing abundance of significations is not a divine gift or a stratagem of crafty editors who wanted us to contemplate the divine in all its multiform glory. Meaninglessness as well was brought into play by the same process, and in no small quantity. Our theory suggests that we will never know the answer to questions such as "Who wrote the Bible?", "What did the original author of the Bible want to say?", or "What was the message of Isaiah's prophecy?" Actually, we view these as inferior questions. Better ones are suggested later.

The propositions advocated here are not likely to go over swimmingly among most Old Testament scholars. Biblicists do not generally believe that Scripture is meaningless, inadvertently meaningful, or laden with such a surfeit of possible meanings that championing any particular one might be described as an expression of one's ideological commitments. Although by no stretch of the imagination an uncritical cohort, exegetes are not inclined to pursue or articulate conclusions of this nature. One need not be a sociologist of knowledge to understand why. Still, it bears repeating that our secular outrages are parasitic on the most fundamental premises of this religiously inflected discipline. To their immense credit, biblical exegetes – who are rarely secularists – have produced all the explosive raw materials. Secular hermeneutics differs mainly in its critical orientation – its eagerness to detonate.

SUGGESTIONS FOR FURTHER READING

The issue of composition by aggregate has not been explored by many, and this has much to with the sheer complexity (and tedium) involved in describing the process. Richard Elliot Friedman has gone further than any exegete in conceptualizing this problem. The essays he contributed to the 1981 volume he edited are of great use (*The Creation of Sacred Literature: Composition and Redaction of the Biblical Text.* Ed. Richard Elliot Friedman. Berkeley: University of California Press, 1981). To understand the degree of complexity involved in trying to identify how polyauthored texts develop, see Jeffrey Tigay, "The Evolution of the Pentateuchal Narratives in Light of the Evolution of the *Gilgamesh Epic*," in *Empirical Models for Biblical Criticism*. Ed. Jeffrey Tigay. Philadelphia: University of Pennsylvania Press, 1985, pp. 21–52, and in the same volume, "Conflation as a Redactional Technique," pp. 53–95. Tigay's *The Evolution of the Gilgamesh Epic*. Philadelphia: University of Pennsylvania Press, 1982, also offers a concrete demonstration of the processes of superimposition and juxtaposition discussed in this chapter.

PART TWO

❧

THE INTERPRETERS OF THE HEBREW BIBLE

4

∾

Why Is There So Much Biblical Interpretation?

Almost the whole of scripture is expressed in enigmas.

Clement, *Stromata*

And I said, "Wait, wait, I know this. This is the Song of Solomon."
  "Or as we call it in our tradition, the Song of Songs."
  "And it's about Christ making love to his Church," I said.
  "It is *not* about Christ and his Church," the rabbi declared.
I was taken aback. "Well, I used to do Bible study, and that's what it
  said in the Bible."
  "Not in our Bible," the rabbi said. He spoke very absolutely.
  "You mean like that's not your interpretation?"

Allegra Goodman, *Paradise Park*

In all likelihood, and for better or for worse, the Hebrew Bible/Old Testament is the most interpreted text in the history of the species. Countless generations of Jewish and Christian thinkers have exegeted every single word of scripture, probably no less than a few hundred times each. What is it about this ancient anthology, as opposed to *The Epic of Gilgamesh*, the Egyptian *Book of the Dead*, or the Hittite myth *The Wrath of Telipinu*, that has triggered more than 2,000 years of incessant, frenzied hermeneutic activity? Why are there – as we speak – tens of thousands of seminarians, Yeshiva *bokhurs*, college professors, and so on, who are devoting their lives to cracking scriptural enigmas? And in light of all the difficulties that it presents, why have so few thrown down their Bibles, thrown up their hands, exclaimed "*I can't make any sense of this!*", and bid adieu to Scripture? We have all heard of "writer's block" – writers even write about their own writer's block. But why is there no comparable cliché about "interpreter's block"? What is it about the encounter with Scripture that leaves exegetes so full of big ideas?[1]

In this chapter, we move from "Who wrote the Bible?" to "Who interprets the Bible?" We want to understand why intellectuals, particularly ancient ones, have devoted so much attention to the Hebrew Bible/Old Testament. Along the way, we suggest the relationship between interpreters and their cherished scriptures is just a bit more fraught with antagonism than they have generally supposed.

POWER AND THE BIBLE'S APPEAL

One obvious way of explaining the Bible's allure to interpreters is to think solely in terms of relations of power. In this way of seeing things, Scripture's timeless appeal would have nothing to do with its intrinsic qualities. Rather, its association with dominant political regimes would account for its popularity. Their sponsorship of the text would account for its centrality in cultures far and wide. There is some merit to this approach.

From Constantine's conversion in the fourth century onward, various Christian orthodoxies, ranging from the Eastern Byzantine and Western Churches to numerous reigning Protestant sects of the modern age, would establish the Old – and, of course, the New – Testament as their foundational document. In those territories ruled by the Cross, learned individuals typically read the Old Testament whether they liked it or not. (A few heretical exceptions notwithstanding, it may be said that most Christian intellectuals rather liked their First Testament.) The hegemonic position achieved by assorted Christian and Christianized ruling groups ensured the Bible would become required reading, so to speak, on the syllabus of nearly every Occidental high culture since the passing of the pagan era. Only in recent times can a Christian or Jew who is biblically unlettered be considered well educated.[2]

The political supremacy achieved by various Christianities certainly goes a long way in explaining the great quantity of scriptural interpretation in the West and beyond. But let us not succumb to university fads that reduce all literary phenomena to dynamics of power and politics. To begin with, there was intensive study of biblical texts well prior to the advent of the aforementioned dominant regimes. Although it may sound peculiar, the Bible was vigorously interpreted even before it became the Bible – by itself no less! As proponents of inner-biblical exegesis (discussed in Chapter Two) have shown, biblical texts frequently refer to, explain, amend, and gloss over other biblical texts. Prophets routinely invoke the words of other biblical books and explicate past events and passages. Within the span of the twenty-one verses that constitute the entire Book of Obadiah, we find no less than twenty references to phrases found in other texts of the Bible. "It would be false to assume," writes G. Vermes, "that biblical exegesis itself is essentially and necessarily a post-biblical phenomenon." Or, as Regina Schwartz puts it: "Biblical interpretation goes back to the Bible."[3]

Other texts from roughly the same period – texts that never made it into the Jewish canon – were also interpreting those texts that did eventually make it into the Bible. This is somewhat confusing and requires further explanation. The corpus of documents that we now know as the Hebrew Bible was assembled into a fairly stable collection somewhere between the second century BCE and the first century AD. In and around this period, however, biblical retellings, spin-offs, sequels, and interpretive treatises were also being composed. These never made it into the official Jewish canon (although some entered various Christian Old Testaments). Anyone who is familiar with this apocryphal and pseudepigraphic literature can only marvel at their writers' diligence in explicating, glossing, and elaborating on soon-to-be canonical biblical scrolls. These and other works from this time (sometimes called the "intertestamental period") display a tendency to "connect the dots" of Scripture. By this we mean that they try to explain problematic and ambiguous biblical passages by recourse to ideas not explicitly found in the Bible. For our purposes, the major point is that before Scripture was underwritten by institutions of this-wordly power, before one read the Bible because one *had* to, Jewish and Christian thinkers were feverishly exegeting its contents.[4]

Although it is true that states and empires have championed the Bible as a foundational document, their patronage cannot be adduced as the only explanation for interpreters' enduring fascination with Scripture. Did not intellectuals within heresies of early modernity (e.g., Lutheranism, Anabaptism) eagerly engage the First Testament? In light of their often violent confrontations with orthodoxy, one might expect that they would reject the core document of their adversaries. But this rarely came to pass; only the regnant interpretation of the Old Testament was challenged by the heretics. A figure such as Luther did not advance a refutation of Scripture itself. Instead, he challenged the Church's belief in the inerrancy of its scriptural understanding (and, ostensibly, the Church's scriptural understanding).[5]

The Bible was interpreted *before* the rise of worldly powers that endorsed it. In later times, it was often interpreted *against* these very powers. This bolsters our contention that something other than its association with dominant political and cultural parties lures hermeneuts en masse to Scripture. Could there be certain qualities intrinsic to the text that account for why it is interpreted so much?

REASON ONE: THE INTERPRETIVE INJUNCTION

It is a curiosity of the Hebrew Bible that its own contents are often being read and interpreted by its own protagonists. Those who relish intertextuality, halls of mirrors, or echo chambers certainly have something to savor here; the text that we are reading and interpreting is a text that has often been read and interpreted by the very characters and text that we are reading about and interpreting. Leading by example, various biblical verses sometimes shout and sometimes whisper an injunction to posterity: "*Read me! Listen to me! Understand me!*" Scripture, then, models and encourages interpretation; its own protagonists are pondering its words. To *not* spend a great deal of time on the text would be to flout one of its most basic demands.

A few examples will help illustrate this point. In the Book of Deuteronomy, many passages from previous books are quoted. The very name "Deuteronomy" (coming from the Greek translation, or maybe mistranslation, "*To deuteronomion*," of a Hebrew phrase, *mišnēh hatôrāh*, in Deut. 17:18) refers to the book's standing as a "second law." This is because much of the text reiterates earlier laws. In Deut. 5:7–18, for example, Moses recites a nearly identical version of the so-called Ten Commandments encountered in Exodus 20:3–14. Here, he is re-reading Scripture (out loud). The reader (who has, assumedly, read Exodus 20:3–14) is re-reading Scripture. The fictional Israelites (who, presumably, heard the Commandments before in Exodus) are listening, again. For these redundancies, we have the process of composition by aggregate to thank. In Exodus 24:7, we are told that Moses "took the Book of the Covenant and read it aloud to the people." The contents of the Book of the Covenant, we assume, consist of material that we have just encountered in Exodus 20:22–23:19. In other words, the lawgiver is depicted as now reciting to "the people" what we have previously read. "The people," for their part, respond unanimously and obediently as follows: "All that Yahweh has spoken, we will do and heed" (24:7).[6]

The depiction of reading biblical documents as being a pious act, performed by pious Bible characters, is seen again in the second Book of Kings. There it is reported that the High Priest Hilkiah has unexpectedly found "a scroll of the Teaching/Torah" (*sēper hatôrāh*). He passes the discovery on to Shaphan the scribe, who then reads it to King Josiah. The monarch immediately despairs, recognizing that this sacred document – which scholars have traditionally identified as a large section of the Book of Deuteronomy – was not meant to languish in some vulgar temple storage space. Having made its sojourn from oblivion, to priest, to scribe, to king, the text arrives at its next destination. Josiah summons the entire community and has it recited to all the people (who, needless to say, are contrite and appreciative). Once again, the beneficial aspects of reading and listening to Yahweh's word are simultaneously staged and sanctioned for the reader – the last stop on the text's never-ending journey.[7]

In other instances, individuals are simply, brusquely, ordered to read. In Deuteronomy 17:19, the monarch is instructed to engage Torah throughout the duration of his life. Later, Joshua is charged as follows: "Let not this Book of the Torah cease from your lips, but recite it day and night, so that you will be sure to do all that is written in it" (Josh. 1:8). Assuming the Torah mentioned in the previous examples comprises some part of the first five books as we now possess them, then we are once again reading about characters who are urged to read what we are reading and have read.

The Bible enjoins us not only to read, but also to interpret. This demand is made with somewhat more subtlety. In the Old Testament, it is a given that the various texts that the world tenders have significance beyond themselves. Hence, dreams are decoded, riddles are unriddled, toponyms are subject to (endearingly simple) etymological analysis, and accents are deciphered for information about the social identity of their speakers. The elect of God interpret and, according to our sources, they interpret well. The nonelect, in contrast, are clearly lacking in this regard. The Philistines (and many modern commentators) are baffled by Samson's word play. Nebuchadnezzar's conjure men fail miserably in the Book of Daniel. False prophets do an abysmal job of gauging Yahweh's will. King Saul – who has been fitted with a rather ostentatious dunce cap – is not much different, even when looking in the eyes of a prophet he is incapable of recognizing him as a man of God (1 Sam. 9:18–19).[8]

REASON TWO: INTERPRETIVE NECESSITY AND THE QUEST FOR THE BETTER MODEL

To this point, we have argued that the document in question models, and hence sanctifies, the acts of reading, listening to, and understanding its own contents. The Hebrew Bible wants to be understood. This truism must be followed – as quickly as possible – by the observation that *the Hebrew Bible is not easy to understand*. This is so because composition by aggregate has spawned a chaotic, sprawling, disjointed anthology, overflowing with meanings and meaninglessness, blinking neon light contradictions, ambiguities, ellipses, and numbing repetition. How can a pious intellectual possibly make it through the first chapters of Genesis without having his or her interpretive fires ignited? How can a religious community possibly live according to the often inconsistent, often incomprehensible, words of Scripture?

As a prescription for communal religious life, biblical texts could not be understood in and of themselves. They needed to be explicated, corrected, internally harmonized and, where necessary, muted by force. Let us use the term *"supplementation"* as a catch-all category for the process by which early Jewish and Christian exegetes made sense of Scripture by supplementing it with texts of their own devising. The learned deliberations of these ancient interpreters have been aggressively suffixed to the original. Some of these works have achieved sacred status in their own right. Early Christianity, for one, could not permit scripture to stand alone. Marcel Simon observes: "All patristic biblical exegesis . . . is from the outset guided by this fundamental conviction that the Old Testament, in order to be clearly understood, does not suffice by itself and that it needs a kind of retrospective illumination." The emergent Church tacked the New Testament on to the Greek translation of the Hebrew Bible, the Septuagint. Insisting that the two documents were an organic unity, various

Church Fathers dutifully tightened the connections between First and Second Testaments, raking the former for all signs of the preexisting Christ. As Cyril, Bishop of Jerusalem put it: "For there is One God of the two Testaments, who foretold in the Old Testament the Christ who appeared in the new, and who, through the preparatory school of the Law and the Prophets, led us to Christ."[9]

Nor could Judaism let Scripture stand alone. The Hebrew Bible has been yoked to the massive body of literature colloquially known as Talmud. As one scholar has written of the general goals of Rabbinic exegesis: "Inconsistencies in the biblical text had to be explained away; errors, redundancies, absurdities, or anything shocking, indecent or unworthy of divine inspiration had to be removed." Especially notable is the ever-audacious Mishneh, assumed to have been compiled somewhere around the third century CE. It was proclaimed by its authors to be an oral Torah, a divine revelation shadowing the written Torah, one that allegedly passed from Moses's mouth all the way to their ears. In the first chapter of the tractate *Aboth*, we read: "Moses received the Torah at Sinai and transmitted it to Joshua, Joshua to the Elders, and the elders to the prophets, and the prophets to the men of the great synagogue." In other words, the sages claimed to be in possession of *another Torah*, a revelation every bit as valid as that inscribed in the Bible. As we see in Chapter Six, the significance of the Mishneh, and the writings of the sages in general, for mainstream Judaism far outweigh that of the Tanak.[10]

From the point of view of logical coherence, supplementation is something of a quick fix. True, it furnished the dexterous interpreter/apologist with a good deal of material to vindicate the Bible's deficiencies. It helped expositors clarify scriptural ambiguities. Supplementation even permitted the exegete to cast the text in the "dummy" position for acts of ideological ventriloquy. In retrospect, however, the legacy of these textual supplements was to create even greater problems of logical consistency for later interpreters. As one scholar points out: "Whenever you postulate *two* sources of divine revelation, you have an unavoidable question about their relationships: precedence, subordination, co-ordination, superordination, etc."[11]

For now we should not lose sight of the consequences of supplementation. Scripture has been subdued, restrained, and rehabilitated. Interpreters have been unwitting accomplices in this process. As an aggregate, they have left behind a body of work that effectively silences the original they so revered. Yet, it is highly unlikely – note this – that any of the Bible's ancient interpreters ever consciously sensed the presence of deficiencies in the Scripture that they supplemented. The fault, they reasoned, lay not with the witness, but with the human models of analysis to which it was subjected. In an attempt to understand Scripture, exegetes constantly fabricated "better" models – and they continue to do so today. Prior to moving forward we will mention three of these models insofar as they speak volumes about the chaotic multivalence of the Bible which we have been emphasizing throughout this study.

One way of making sense of the Hebrew Bible is through allegory. This approach, most famously associated with Philo (and eventually adopted by numerous Church Fathers), was particularly useful for explaining the often dubious ethics of Yahweh's favored characters, if not Yahweh himself. The use of allegory comes with a pretty astonishing tacit assumption, namely, that *the words of the Hebrew Bible do not necessarily mean what they say*. Only by allegorizing its bewildering contents could the interpreter extract its true meaning. Thus, in his *Questions and Answers on Genesis*, Philo asks, "What is 'the tree of life?'" mentioned in the Garden of Eden narrative. Suffice it to say that for the father of allegory the tree it is not an actual tree, nor life giving, but "the best of virtues in man, namely piety, through which pre-eminently the mind becomes immortal."[12]

The baffled exegete could also speak of the text's hidden meaning. James Kugel writes in *The Bible as It Was*: "The first assumption that all ancient interpreters seem to share is that the Bible is a fundamentally cryptic document. That is, all interpreters are fond of maintaining that although Scripture may appear to be saying X, what it really means is Y, or that while Y is not openly said by Scripture, it is somehow implied or hinted at in X." Once again, the exegete grants him- or herself considerable wiggle room, license to tell us what the text says as he or she decodes or reveals its concealed "truth." Last – and this is a master stroke, really – the expositor could point to divine inscrutability. Accordingly, the Bible's seeming deficiencies are explained as ordained by the deity. Augustine went so far as to say that the imperfections in the text were placed there on purpose by God. Origen insisted that He places "stumbling blocks" before the reader. Incoherence in Scripture has become transvalued – it is now the surest sign of divinity.[13]

REASON THREE: THE BIBLE'S DIVINE PROXIMITY
("PRISONERS OF HOPE")

The crux of our argument to this point has been that the Hebrew Bible/ Old Testament: 1) wants to be and, 2) desperately needs to be understood. Yet, in searching for scriptural qualities that account for its eternal magnetic pull on intellectuals, we have yet to discuss what might be the most important internal factor of them all. This would be the text's unspoken, immodest (and, apparently, persuasive) claim that it represents Yahweh. That God's creation is recounted, that God's thoughts are read, that God's feelings are expressed, that God is quoted verbatim, that God is said to be speaking (when, in fact, He is being spoken for) points to either the remarkable arrogance of the biblical contributors or their unshakeable conviction that their access to the deity was total.

The fateful, and perhaps even unwitting, manipulation performed by the Hebrew Bible is to have convinced its readers that what stands in front of them is not a hodgepodge of texts worked over by countless men positioned across time and motivated by mundane political and theological interests. Instead, it presents itself as a self-evident treasury of the actual words, thoughts, actions, political opinions, and future aspirations of Yahweh. From early on, apparently, interpreters wholly swallowed this argument. As Kugel observes, even prior to canonization, ancient exegetes assumed "all of Scripture is somehow divinely sanctioned, of divine provenance, or divinely inspired." Not only has the text convinced its readers of its awesome God proximity, but it has also convinced them that they are the intended recipients of its message. Members of the Qumran sect, in the words of C. K. Barrett, were convinced "that the Old Testament was about themselves." They thus initiated the narcissistic current in Judaism and Christianity: for how often does one come across a devout Jew or Christian who doubts that Scripture comprises something of a personally addressed communication?[14]

This having been said, we may now point to the existence of a tension between the Bible and its interpreters. The Hebrew Bible/Old Testament is a complex, paradoxical, ambiguous, and at points incoherent text. The document, however, is oblivious to its own complex, paradoxical, ambiguous, and incoherent nature. Once again, the witness does not know itself. It fails to realize that what it says about the

deity (and a host of other things) is not always clear and consistent. As
with most documents composed in antiquity and beyond, the Hebrew
Bible is hermeneutically naive. It does not view its particular teachings
as equivocal or even susceptible to varying interpretations. Despite this,
our polysemous text does not only want to be read, listened to, and
understood, but it also wants to be read, listened to, and understood *the
right way*.

However, the Hebrew Bible can be and has been understood in quite
a few ways. Much as Yahweh came to regret the very creation that he
invoked, the biblical literati must regret at least some of the interpretive
energy that they have unleashed. When someone like the seventeenth-
century Puritan Roger Williams declared that every Christian could
"interpret the Scripture in accordance with his own understanding"
he may just have articulated the biblical contributors' worst nightmare.
Unless the contributors to Scripture were ardent pluralists, we must pre-
sume they could not possibly be in agreement with *all* the divergent
interpretations that exegetical history has produced. Insofar as tolerance
for dissenting viewpoints does not to seem to rank among their most
salient virtues, the ancient literati would certainly disapprove of all the
intellectual and spiritual diversity that they engendered.[15]

Be that as it may, this is precisely the Bible's ironic fate. It wanted to be
read and heard and understood, and interpreters obliged with a displaced
vengeance. The result was not consensus among its later readers, but
disagreement, confusion, schism, sectarianism, and strife. When Moses
and Josiah read versions of Torah to "the people" they *all* obediently
understood. In the Book of Nehemiah, Ezra – the same Ezra who many
readers just as well figured was long dead – makes a cameo appearance. He
administers a communal reading of Torah to a remorseful, weepy, albeit
grateful, public. The Hebrew of Nehemiah 8:8 is most likely corrupted,
but the text seems to say something about the people having understood
(*wayābînû bamiqrā'*) Ezra's reading. Yet, the Bible's fantasy of unanimity,
of an audience that listens, understands, cries, repents, and responds as
one, *the right way*, has never come to pass. Even before canonization,
this hope was dashed by a Babel of interpreters who collectively extracted
from the text numerous, and wildly contradictory, readings.[16]

As for interpreters, they consistently fail to recognize that they are
trapped in the prison house of the Bible's convoluted logic. They have

piously unscrambled Scripture in hopes of finding the very deity that is posited by Scripture. This brings to mind Clifford Geertz's remark that religion "draws its persuasiveness out of a reality it itself defines." Convinced by the witness's claim of its proximity to God, interpreters always have construed their job as one of making sense of its writings. Those who circumnavigate the hermeneutical circle are caught in a hermeneutical loop: they are commanded to understand a text that cannot be understood, and this motivates them to exert even greater efforts to understand it. Biblical interpreters, to borrow a phrase from the prophet Zecariah, are "prisoners of hope."[17]

CONCLUSION: "I LOVE YOU. YOU'RE PERFECT. NOW CHANGE!"

It has been our contention that factors both external and internal to the Hebrew Bible/Old Testament account for the immense, and most likely unequaled, body of expository literature that it has generated. We called attention to the document's insistence that it be read, heard, and understood. This recurring demand certainly inspires and steels the exegete to confront the bountiful mysteries provided by Scripture. Indeed, interpreters have typically viewed all those assorted connundra not as evidence of clumsy human handiwork, but as a sort of heavenly challenge to probe more deeply. The hermeneut's characteristic willingness to stay the course, to soldier through the complexities and absurdities of the document, testifies to the persuasiveness of the Bible's claim that it speaks on Yahweh's behalf.

So let us never underestimate the motivational force that the belief in Scripture's divine proximity has on exegetes. They open the book having already invested their faith in the proposition that it is underwritten by God. Much later, they close it having uncovered either meaningfulness or (among more rational types) proof of the deity's inscrutability. Of course, the belief that the text must be read is something that is inculcated by culture. The high premium placed on the Bible by Jewish and Christian orthodoxies is instrumental in luring cadres of intellectuals – until more recently, the finest a given social body could muster – to the work in the first place. This is the major external reason accounting for the abundance of interpretation that this assemblage has left in its wake.

The overarching goal of biblical interpretation has stayed the same
for millennia. Devout exegetes have defined their calling as one of understanding and explicating the document. Although this objective of "pious
understanding" has remained constant, the interpretations produced in
pursuit of this end have varied widely. This demonstrates not only the polysemous nature of the witness, but also the way in which readers situated
in different historical contexts read the Bible through their own cultural
filters. It also marks something of a deadlock in the little contest of inadvertent mutual aggressions that we have staged between the Good Book
and its interpreters. The Hebrew Bible's (unreasonable) demand to be
properly understood has caused exegetes to perform the most contorted
intellectual acrobatics in the name of clarification. Exegetes, in turn, have
unconsciously muttered chorus after chorus of "*I love you. You're perfect.
Now change!*" as they supplemented the text into something approximating irrelevance.

Biblical interpreters have not only extracted from the witness a bound-
less diversity of contradictory readings, but they have also collectively
subdued the Bible by the weight (and often the explicit substance) of their
work. The modern Jew or Christian does not read Hebrew Scripture, as
much as read it *through* the filters of Jewish and Christian interpretive
traditions. One almost feels sorry for the biblical documents. Shouted
down by the New Testament, by translations and paraphrases, by centuries of Rabbinic and patristic exegesis, by midrashim and homilies,
by "Tradition," by modern commentaries and monographs, one must
strain to hear its quirky chorus of dissonant voices. The ceaseless traffic
of exegesis, the millennial din of the interpreters, confirms the following
truism: when it comes to the Old Testament there is no text as interpreted.

SUGGESTIONS FOR FURTHER READING

The question of *why* the Bible has been so extensively and continuously
interpreted has, strangely enough, rarely been posed. Extremely well doc-
umented, however, is the early history of biblical interpretation. Given
how much specialized information there is to control when discussing,
let's say, the exegesis of Palestinian Jews in the second century AD who
spoke Aramaic as they tried to make sense of biblical Hebrew in an era of
Roman domination, teams of researchers are needed to make sense of the

classical period in Jewish and Christian interpretation. A few collections of essays come to mind. Although graying somewhat, *The Cambridge History of the Bible* (various editors) Cambridge: Cambridge University Press, 1970, offers many useful introductory essays. In the field of Rabbinics, we would recommend *Mikra: Text, Translation, Reading and Interpretation of the Hebrew Bible in Ancient Judaism and Early Christianity*. Ed. Martin Jan Mulder. Assen/Maastricht: Van Gorcum, 1988, and *The Literature of the Sages: First Part: Oral Tora, Halakha, Mishna, Tosfeta, Talmud, External Tractates*. Ed. Shmuel Safrai. Philadelphia: Fortress Press, 1987, as well as Jacob Neusner's *Introduction to Rabbinic Literature*. New York: Doubleday, 1994. For patristics, one might consult the handsome volume, *The Bible in Greek Christian Antiquity*. Ed. Paul Blowers. Notre Dame: University of Notre Dame Press, 1997. The series of Johannes Quasten, *Patrology*. Westminster, MD: Christian Classics, 1986, is also of great use. More recently, a multivolume work, *A History of Biblical Interpretation*. Eds. Alan Hauser and Duane Watson. Grand Rapids, MI: William B. Eerdmans, 2003, has shed new light on the question of biblical interpretation.

5

ร∾

Introducing Biblical Scholars and Secular Hermeneutics

These are people whose early lives were dominated by an intense religious commitment, in many cases fundamentalism, but whose adulthood is marked by quiet acculturation to the secularism of the academic world and often by a slow but steady dissatisfaction from all religious institutions. Among biblical scholars, even some of the most outspoken and effective debunkers of traditional views are – though you would never guess it – ex-clerics or graduates of theology departments.

Jon Levenson, "Theological Consensus or Historicist Evasion?
Jews and Christians in Biblical Studies"

Here in the ghetto of Biblical Studies, we are still working with a mental image of text as a word-search puzzle that can be ringed and solved, or as a box stacked with precious things, all co-ordinated by an author who imitates the foreplanning and prescience of (the secure and protecting kind of) God.

Yvonne Sherwood, *A Biblical Text and its Afterlives: The Survival of Jonah in Western Culture*

Professing at a college or seminary near you – in almost complete obscurity – are individuals commonly known as "biblical scholars." The reasons for their marginality in the academy and elsewhere are complex and rarely discussed. Let's just begin by saying that in the aggressively, even obnoxiously, secular milieu of American higher education, biblical scholars are *different*. Amidst legions of grinningly irreligious and areligious faculty, Old and New Testament researchers typically maintain (or once maintained) a pronounced faith commitment. These commitments are inextricably bound up with the Bible – that would be the same Bible that they study as academicians. So when it comes to their scholarly objectivity, exegetes are always under suspicion of having blurred the line between the personal and the professional. Rightly or wrongly, colleagues in other disciplines tend to view them as apologists, clergy, or epistemological vestiges of the premodern past.[1]

Perhaps these misgivings account for why biblicists are so underrepresented in the realm of high culture. In the last half-century few, if any, have achieved international or national recognition as public intellectuals. The work of Old Testament scholars is almost never discussed in *The New York Review of Books*, or *Granta*, or the learned little journals of opinion (although scholars in other disciplines who write about the Bible are often published in these places). The occasional spectacular archaeological discovery in the Holy Land notwithstanding, journalists canvassing the religion beat have little interest in heralding (and appropriating) their ideas. Experts in Scripture are rarely called on to serve as presidents of major universities – as they routinely were in a less secularized age. Wherever the stratosphere of intellectual life might be, it is unlikely that one will find an exegete fluttering about there.[2]

This is an unfair exclusion. Biblicists may well rank among the most humanistically learned persons on campus. Aside from having mastered Hebrew, or Greek, or Latin (if not all three), they are usually trained in rather daunting languages and literatures of ancient Near Eastern antiquity. These include Egyptian, Hittite, Ugaritic, Aramaic, Assyrian, Persian, among others. But that is not all. As Martin Marty once put it, in childhood they "were nurtured . . . in 'Jerusalem,' not 'Athens.'" This religious upbringing equipped them not only with knowledge about Scripture, but those ideas about Scripture that were once synonymous with the most rarified achievements of Occidental thought. Exegetes have thus tracked the Bible across its irony-laden sojourn through history – a survey that has endowed them with a healthy appreciation for its awesome power. (To understand irony and power – is that not a precondition for being wise?) Should the opportunity present itself, walk through a museum of premodern art or listen to a gospel choir in the company of a biblical scholar. Ask one to deliver an impromptu lecture on *The Brothers Karamazov*. It is at moments like these that one realizes how integral the Bible is to the world's cultural heritage – but biblical scholars knew that all along.[3]

And then there is the legacy, oh the magisterial legacy. Exegetes are the heirs and custodians of one of the oldest and most vaunted of intellectual traditions. The procession of those who have seriously pondered Scripture measures more than 2,000 years in length. It abounds in marble-chisel names such as Philo, Josephus, Akiva, Origen, Augustine, Ibn Ezra, Maimonides, Thomas Aquinas, Luther, Erasmus, and Spinoza, to name a few among the masses of elites. Those who do not have the humility to step to the back of this queue are advised to try their luck in a department of sociology or English. Those who are preoccupied with making original discoveries had better think twice before studying a document about which almost everything has already been said. For the young scholar with pretensions of achieving swift academic glory, few disciplines could be more uninviting than the broken-down palace of biblical scholarship. This having been said, it boggles the mind to think that biblicists are almost never accorded the esteem granted to Classicists or professors of comparative literature.

The marginalization of biblical scholars among religious laypersons is even more baffling. There is probably no text studied in the university with as much popular appeal as the Good Book. Exegetes, unlike specialists in the fiction of Thomas Mann or experts in Baroque music, study something that is actually of interest to the masses. In America's Bible Belt, at least, one would think that charismatic exegetes could achieve a little local renown – "cult status," if you will, among those faithful who want to think outside the box. Nothing too heretical. Just something a bit to the left or right of orthodox doctrine. Mind-blowing meditations on Christ, erotic allegorical interpretations of the Book of Chronicles – one can always count on a biblical scholar to do that sort of thing. Although generally devout, they pride themselves on their autonomy from religious dogma. "*We're pretty open around here*" – this is a refrain one often hears down at the seminary, be it a Conservative Jewish, Greek Orthodox, or Baptist institution. Biblicists spend so much time interrogating traditional views that, professionally speaking, they tend to think of themselves as secularists. Compared with the ways that religious officials and laypersons often think about Scripture, this self-assessment is not entirely inaccurate.

Perhaps we have stumbled onto an unpleasant truth. From the perspective of almost any religious orthodoxy, this penchant for free thought is troublesome. For biblicists know not only official doctrine, but also alternatives to it. This forbidden knowledge is a dividend of toiling in that ecumenical discipline called biblical scholarship. All this dialogue with "others" enables one to think critically, if not self-critically. Let us never forget that biblical scholars *are* scholars – of the most impressive order no less. Their feet are planted in two rivers, one of which is named "free and rational inquiry." None of this means that they are harassed or mistreated in their own religious communities. Better to say that they receive the less enthusiastic handshake, the guarded, tensile hug that has been perennially reserved for those afflicted by subversive knowledge. Many exegetes do, in fact, have the most unsimplistic and emotionally freighted relation with their religious traditions. The services of a supremely gifted artist would be required to depict it in all its staggering nuance and strangeness. To this point, regrettably, writers, poets, and filmmakers have rarely recognized the possibilities for fictional adaptation offered up by biblicists.

Unappreciated by their secular colleagues in the Academy, unknown to the religious lay masses, and not unconditionally affirmed by Church or Synagogue – this is the plight of the ideal-typical biblical scholar. And if our preceding caricature was not enough of an indignity, we devote this chapter to passing more judgments on them. Whereas their coreligionists often assail them for being too critical, we insist that they are not critical enough. Saving further remarks on the lives and passions of biblicists for Chapter Eight, we will now focus on the failings of modern exegesis. From there, we turn to its postmodern adversary. The points of conflict between these approaches are examined with an eye toward sharpening our conception of secular hermeneutics.

THE ETHOS OF THE EXEGETE

The late Robert Carroll, one of Old Testament scholarship's most singular voices, phrased it this way: "If reading the Bible does *not* raise profound problems for you as a modern reader, then check with your doctor and enquire about the symptoms of brain-death." Professor Carroll was pondering what we might call the psychological trauma of reading Scripture; the confusion created by a schizophregenic, double-binding text that insists it can and must be understood, even though it mines the road to such knowledge with every possible obstruction.[4]

Ancient exegetes who were entrusted with the task of confronting this scriptural chaos construed their assignment as making the Bible make sense. This might seem like a fairly obvious mission for them to undertake. What else were they supposed to do? Yet, they could have just as easily convinced themselves that Scripture made perfect sense and hence required no further explication. Or, they could have decreed that the document was utterly puzzling – but simply too sacrosanct to be defiled by the interpretive imagination of mortals. Under such circumstances, the supplementation discussed in Chapter Four would have been considered a sacrilegious activity.

None of that came to pass. Making the Bible make sense has been the norm in Old Testament interpretation for millennia. Even modernity, whose capacity to reconfigure all aspects of religious life is a never-ending source of awe, was unable to alter the inveterate habits of biblical scholars. "Not one academic biblical scholar in a hundred," the biblicist David Clines observed, "will tell you that their primary task is to *critique* the Bible." "For some reason," he continued, "we have convinced ourselves that our business is simply to *understand*, to *interpret*." Insofar as a university nowadays need not – should not – conform to the intellectual agenda of a theological seminary, we wonder if understanding, interpreting, and making sense of Scripture is a legitimate scholarly objective. To illustrate our concerns, we look at some of the assumptions that inform the way modern biblicists translate and interpret the Hebrew Bible.[5]

It is a sort of trade secret that the number of incomprehensible words and verses found in the Old Testament is exceedingly large. If laypersons are scarcely aware of this problem, then this is because translators do so little to apprise them of its existence. Translated biblical Hebrew is a sort of artificial dialect unto itself. It always flows, keeps its feet moving and thumbs snapping. As the French might say, it makes a good impression ("*il se présente bien*"). But untranslated biblical Hebrew – which some, incidentally, have also suggested might be an artificial dialect (see below) – does not make a good impression. It abounds in sentences that are broken, grammatically flawed, or inscrutable.[6]

In more recent decades, some have seen fit to apprise their readers that textual difficulties are present in the witness. The Jewish Publication Society's (JPS's) groundbreaking translation makes somewhat parsimonious use of footnotes set in a microfont that read "*meaning of*

Heb. uncertain." Genesis 6:3 is one of the many verses flagged with this disclaimer. In Hebrew, this curious line features the following proclamation from God: *lō'-yādôn rûhî bādām lĕ'ōlām bĕšagam hû' bāśār.* Confronted by this confounding locution, the JPS team does what translators have done for ages: it takes an impressively erudite stab at the verse's meaning:

The Lord said, "My breath shall not abide in man forever, since he too is flesh."

Because we do not feel compelled to clarify ambiguous Scripture, we translate:

Yahweh said: My breath (?) will not . . . in humanity for eternity . . . he/it is flesh."[7]

The scholars who worked on the JPS ranked among the titans of northwest Semitic languages and literatures. Their English version – elegant, learned, yet somehow fluid and endearingly simple to read – must be counted as one of the triumphs of modern translation. Their scholarly mastery of Hebrew and Aramaic, not to mention English, is indisputable. But is not the goal of academic inquiry to portray the words of historical documents as accurately as possible? Should scholars willfully mistranslate an unintelligible passage from Scripture in deference to an unspoken conviction that Scripture ultimately makes sense? In the words of Professor Carroll, would it not be better for translators to "admit defeat," as opposed to constantly connecting the dots of texts whose meanings have befuddled exegetes for thousands of years?[8]

Secular hermeneutics, in contrast, does not amend, touch up, or deodorize problematic Hebrew and Aramaic. Our translations are literal and minimalist. Adding to the artlessness of it all is our insistence on calling attention to irregularities in the text. In the (hypothetical) *Secular Bible Translation* (SBT), incomprehensibility would be placed in the foreground; ellipsis points, questions marks, parentheses, and slashes would occur more frequently than the name of God. Publishing houses would never commission a translation as unsightly as the SBT, and with a good degree of justification at that. Still, in spite of its lack of readability the SBT would be, ironically, truer to the Hebrew "original" (about which more anon) than nearly any translation ever attempted.

The unsecular assumptions of modern exegetes impact not only the way they translate, but also their approach to interpretation. Those who try to make sense of a biblical verse, chapter, book, and so on, assume, obviously, that it has a sense. At the same time they concede that in its present state, as is, Scripture needs to be made sense of. Notice the oscillation between fealty to revelation and fealty to reason. Tradition, faith, love of God, and so on, impel modern biblicists to view this as an ultimately meaningful text, so to speak. Rationality, canons of academic inquiry, empirical reality, force them to acknowledge its numerous deficiencies. If the secularist aspires to "criticize and be damned," the Old Testament scholar wants to "criticize and restore." For the majority of exegetes, the purpose of scholarly criticism is to recuperate the original sense of Hebrew Scriptures, its meant meaning, its intended message to humanity, and its essential truth. Even higher critics, as we observed in Chapter Two, aspire to declutter the witness, to tease out earlier textual strata, and to understand what the motivations were of the original authors and editors who they have uncovered.[9]

As far as secular hermeneutics is concerned, this quest for original authorial intentions is an irrational undertaking. This is because countless aspects of the Bible's compositional history fatally impede our ability to ascertain the messages that its authors had in mind. Foremost among these is the peculiar fact that the texts of the Bible had no author. It is undeniable that a writer will intentionally seed a literary work with meanings to be grasped by readers. But few things could scramble that meaning to oblivion more than the process of transhistorical polyauthorism discussed in Part I. Superimposition and juxtaposition are the enzymes of authorial intent: they break down any meaning that was meant by a writer or editor, scattering new possibilities (and impossibilities) in their destabilizing wake.

So what then might we say to that earnest Christian or Jew who is searching for "the prophet Isaiah's message"? We would begin by noting that the compositional techniques of the biblical era make it very difficult to find such a thing. We would not stop there. For textual tampering is also witnessed in postbiblical times. The Hebrew Bible as we know it is not an ancient document but a Medieval one. It is based on what is called the Masoretic text (or MT), whose most important variant is referred to as the Leningrad Codex. The latter stems from the eleventh century AD and is, at best, a copy of a copy of a copy (and so on) of some earlier canonized version of the Hebrew Bible.

But it is not an exact copy. The MT variants come replete with a maniacally complicated system of "pointings" that were superimposed on the text by the learned Masoretes. This was necessary because ancient Israelite scribes never developed a comprehensive system for marking the presence of vowels. Thus, a word that was pronounced as "bat," would usually be written in biblical times solely with consonants, as "bt." In the absence of a signifying vowel, a later interpreter who came across "bt" might not know if it should be read "bet," "beat," "bit," "bite," "but," "bait," and so on. Fearful that the meaning of Scripture was being lost, the Masoretes dutifully "vowelled" the text between the fifth and tenth centuries AD. They thus stood at a distance of up to 1,500 years from a conjectured "Isaiah." To read the Masorete-enhanced "biblical Hebrew" of the Middle Ages is most definitely not to read the biblical Hebrew of antiquity.

In a quest for authentic revelations, we could, of course, point our imaginary seeker in the direction of the far older, uncanonical (and unpointed) Dead Sea Scroll versions (or DSS) of Isaiah. Yet, insofar as those documents were copied somewhere after the second century BCE, the same doubts linger. How could we be certain that they accurately reflect the utterances of a prophet who allegedly lived as far away from the Qumran sectarians as we do from the Spanish Inquisition? The reader must recall, then, that we have no "original" of the Hebrew Bible. All we possess are witnesses like the MT, DSS, and the Samaritan Pentateuch. There are also translations of all, or parts, of the Hebrew Bible, such as the Septuagint, Aramaic Targumims, the Syriac Peshitta, Vulgate, and so on. The unsullied source that enshrines Isaiah's true prophecy has yet to be found.

A list of obstacles – whether ancient, Medieval, or modern – that prevent us from communing with the meaning meant by biblical authors could easily fill a separate book. For now, we simply state another principle of secular hermeneutics: we avoid any interpretive project that aims to ascertain what an original author or editor wanted to say. The exegete Adele Berlin has drawn an important distinction between meaning that is compositional and meaning that is exegetical. Compositional meaning was the meaning intended by the original biblical authors. Exegetical meaning refers to the meaning found by the cunning and intelligence of the exegete. We urge interpreters to avoid the vainglorious error of confusing the results of their exegesis with the actual designs (whatever those may have been) of an ancient author. We do not, however, begrudge scholars who engage in self-consciously subjective, artistic, or playfully Midrashic biblical readings. If a researcher is willing to concede that his or her interpretation is, in all likelihood, *not* what the ancients had in mind, then this is perfectly acceptable. If an exegete wants to speak about what a given text (as opposed to an author) seems (emphasis on seems) to say, then this is also reasonable. This exegete, of course, must acknowledge that the text's apparent message may never have been intended by anybody.[10]

At its very best, biblical interpretation is a thing of beauty, an art form every bit as exhilarating as skilled jazz improvisation. But improvisers in the American classical tradition rarely assume they have accessed the "truth" of a melody or discerned what the song's composer was "really trying to say." Their interpretations are self-conscious elaborations of, meditations on, and negotiations with an original. The departed and much missed singer Betty Carter was not trying to clarify "Stardust" or to restate what the composer Hoagy Carmichael believed it was supposed to sound like. These musicians do not labor under the exegete's characteristic misconception that they are restoring texts to some pristine state of meaningfulness. Biblical interpretation is like jazz in the sense that its practitioners selectively magnify and ignore some possibilities and problems inherent in the materials they confront. Biblical interpretation is unlike jazz in that its practitioners often do not always realize that they are actually doing this.[11]

We call then for an end to interpretation as typically practiced by biblical scholars. In light of the compositional history (and posthistory) of the Hebrew Bible, there is no compelling reason to believe that we can identify what any given editor or writer wanted to communicate to posterity. Conversely, secular hermeneutics endorses interpretation that self-consciously aspires to achieve the status of a work of art.

HERMENEUTICS AND SOCIOLOGY: THE POSTMODERN
CONTESTATION OF MODERNIST EXEGESIS

We are not the only ones to criticize modern biblical scholarship. In more recent years, its methods, theories, and assumptions have come under increasingly fierce assault by postmodern exegetes. Indeed, one of the major fault lines in contemporary Old Testament research is situated at the modern/postmodern divide. Although the two "schools" may disagree – bitterly – over many issues, the prevalence of theological assumptions in biblical scholarship is not one of them. Postmodern critics have shown little interest in "problematizing" a disciplinary status quo in which scholarly means are routinely used to achieve confessional ends. Indeed, most proponents of these theories are themselves graduates or employees of theological seminaries. For many postmodern theorists, secularism stands in as something of an arch villain (see the Conclusion of this book). This having been said, there are resemblances, both superficial and profound, between various postmodern initiatives and our own. This is what we want to explore now.[12]

There is – how do we say this? – far too much biblical interpretation. The vaults of biblical scholarship are overflowing with the ruminations of interpreters – many of which have yet to be digested. Making sense of Scripture has been the cognitive default mode for exegetes for well over 2,000 years. Interpreting the Bible is what exegetes do. In light of our call for an end to interpretation, one might ask: what exactly is a secular hermeneut supposed to do? Rather than interpreting with the goal of recovering the text's original intended meaning, it might be more fruitful to ponder why that meaning has always been so difficult to understand or agree on. One general explanation has been advanced here. Namely, that the Hebrew Bible has been composed through a complex, collective, diachronic process from which metastasized all manner of meaning possibilities. The secular exegete, then, might chart how it all went wrong, that is, how the Bible's tangled history of assemblage has created unintended meaning, meanings, and meaninglessness for its readership.

Our ideal interpreter, therefore, does not try to understand the original meaning of Scripture. Rather, his or her task is to understand how Scripture has been understood and why it is so difficult to understand. This initiative bears oblique affinities to higher criticism *and* its postmodern nemesis. With its attention to the Bible's process of assemblage, the former offers us excellent tools for conceptualizing how and where the derailments of biblical coherence occurred. In other words, a theory such as documentary hypothesis helps explain why breakdowns in meaning happened. Our emphasis on "meaninglessness" in Scripture dovetails with ideas found in the "deconstructive" wing of postmodernism. David Clines and J. Cheryl Exum write: "As against the 'common sense' assumption that texts have more or less clear meanings and manage more or less successfully to convey those meanings to readers, deconstruction is an enterprise that exposes the inadequacies of texts, and shows how inexorably they undermine themselves. A text typically has a thesis to defend or a point of view to espouse; but inevitably texts falter and let slip evidence against their own cause." Yet, secular hermeneutics differs from postmodern hermeneutics in the following respect: it does not explain the Bible's deficiencies by recourse to philosophical claims about the inherently self-subverting nature of *all* texts. Rather, we would explain the "faltering" or "slipping" of the Bible's meaning system as a logical consequence of composition by aggregate. Scripture certainly falters and slips, but not for the same reason that Joseph Conrad's *The Heart of Darkness* falters and slips.[13]

Much to their credit, many postmodernists have long abandoned the idea of original authors. In the words of A. K. M. Adam, these interpreters "operate freely without fear of ghostly authors looking over their shoulders, coercing them to obey 'original intentions.'" This contestation of "original intentions" is based on truly intriguing arguments about textuality, the nature of authorship, and the indomitable will of written words. We share their skepticism about accessing original intentions but, again, for a less sophisticated reason: the texts that comprise the Hebrew Bible, literally, did not have an original author.[14]

Many postmodernists charge that historical criticism is exclusively interested in composition. As such, it is useless for contemplating Scripture's world-altering effects. We concur. Of course, the charge could be reversed. Postmodern biblical analysis pays far more attention to issues of interpretation than it does to issues of assemblage. Secular hermeneutics, for its part, concentrates on both composition and interpretation. It investigates the nexus between a multivalent sacred text (be it the MT, Septuagint, Vulgate, the New Testament, or Qur'ān, etc.) and a given body of exegetes situated in time and space. It poses questions that stand at the intersection of exegesis, hermeneutics, sociology, and history. What led the group under scrutiny to read the text in this particular way? Why did they choose this meaning over that one? What contradictory evidence did they ignore in Scripture to come to their conclusion? To what degree did previous interpretive traditions (e.g., Rabbinic or patristic literature) color their reading of the Bible? And the question par excellence: what were the material and ideal interests that may have predisposed interpreters toward a particular reading? Sociology becomes the handmaiden of biblical scholarship.[15]

Let us refer to "sociohermeneutics" as a field of inquiry that scrutinizes the interplay that exists between a polysemous sacred text and culturally positioned interpreters. This initiative has a comparative dimension. It contrasts the manner in which the exact same unit of Scripture is interpreted by different communities. Yvonne Sherwood's study of the history of the interpretation of the Book of Jonah is exemplary in this regard. It reminds us that the question of intended meaning is, sociologically speaking, irrelevant. Even if there were an intended meaning in the Book of Jonah, Sherwood's analysis demonstrates that interpreters have rarely agreed as to what it was. "*Why is there so much diversity of interpretation?*" That is a far more scholarly question than "*which interpretation is correct?*"[16]

This raises a theoretical problem that just might be among the more challenging facing the guild of biblical scholars today. Can absolutely anything be found in Scripture? Are the possibilities limitless? Or, are there a constricted number of readings that the text yields? We are reluctant to say that Scripture says everything because that is tantamount to saying that Scripture says nothing. If every imaginable signification does reside in the anthology, then a preference for one over the other could only be explained in terms of the sociological coordinates and power interests of later interpreters. We think of a remark made by the late, great sociologist Pierre Bourdieu: "Religion is predisposed to assume an *ideological function, a practical and political function of absolutization of the relative and legitimation of the arbitrary.*" Following this logic, the Bible's contents become irrelevant, nullified by its own multivalence; all interpretations are but legitimations of arbitrary political desiderata. Sociology becomes the frightful overlord of exegesis.[17]

A fear of sociological overkill also explains why we are reluctant to embrace another component of postmodern inquiry, known as reader-response theory. In its most extreme versions, the theory argues that all meaning is created by readers. Readers are the real writers. Texts possess no stable or implicit meaning. The belief that all meanings can be read *out* of the text parallels the belief that all meanings reside *in* a text. Both approaches obviate the text. Both subsume humanistic-oriented inquiry concentrated on the writings in question to sociological analysis of the readers in question. Everything would be power and politics. Not wanting to discount a sensible theory, we opt for a more moderate form of reader-response theory in which both reader and text play a role in the production of meaning. Adele Berlin's observation strikes us as eminently reasonable: "readers bring something to their reading of a text . . . but [the text] influences how it is read."[18]

Old Testament research is currently experiencing a crisis of signification. Exegetes do not agree as to what the source of meaning is in the Hebrew Bible. Is it the original author? Is it the editor? Is it the text? Is it the reader alone? Is it the reader in dialectic with the author? The reader in dialectic with the text? And what kind of reader are we speaking about, anyhow? At present, our own understanding of biblical meaning goes something like this: composition by aggregate has seeded Scripture with a large finite set of significations. (We cannot bring ourselves to say "infinite" set of significations, and here we recall the quip of Mordecai Gafni that the Torah has "just seventy, not seventy-one" faces.) It is through the act of reading that these meanings are discovered, ignored, embellished, and distorted beyond recognition by sociologically situated agents.[19]

Our approach is, admittedly, deficient. For we have yet to find a logical way of proving that a limited number of meanings reside in the text. In other words, we cannot logically refute a claim that composition by aggregate has endowed Scripture with an infinity of possible meanings. Unless we do resolve this problem, all biblical interpreters might rightfully be asked to pursue advanced degrees in sociology.

CONCLUSION: POLITICS AND SCHOLARSHIP

The postmodern critique of modernist exegesis has defibrillated the ailing body of Old Testament research. The jolt has not come in the form of pulsating debate or arresting discussion between exponents of these views. In truth, little direct or meaningful dialogue presently takes place between them. Rather, it is the postmodern emphasis on issues of interpretation that has reinvigorated the discipline. Workers in the field have been forced to think about the ways that Sacred Scripture is read. In turn, this has generated interest in how these readings influence popular culture, politics, interreligious polemics, academic discourse, and so forth.

Not surprisingly, postmodern biblicists want to use their findings to provoke political and social transformation. The engaged secularist could share this aspiration. In terms of social activism, nonbelievers have an interest in comprehending the many ways in which the Bible has been read. By ransacking the coffers of interpretation, they will find a treasure trove of ready-made arguments that will permit them to respond "*the Bible does not necessarily say that!*" to self-righteous and self-appointed biblical spokespersons. But secular hermeneutics is not manifestly concerned with contemporary political issues. Sensing that this will not sit well with our postmodernist colleagues, we should qualify this statement: we are not interested in taking a particular side in contemporary political debates that invoke biblical authority. Let us qualify that once more: the side we take is the one that points to the ironies and impossibilities of coherently invoking this anthology in contemporary political debates. It is to examples of such debates that we now turn.

SUGGESTIONS FOR FURTHER READING

Until recently, biblical scholars were reluctant to devote sustained attention to themselves as producers of knowledge. Even today, many biblicists will steadfastly and agressively deny that their religious beliefs influence their own scholarship, or that produced by the discipline as a whole. A few more self-critical exegetes have confronted this possibility and many of their opinions are collected in Jacques Berlinerblau's "'Poor Bird, Not Knowing Which Way to Fly': Biblical Scholarship's Marginality, Secular Humanism, and the Laudable Occident," *Biblical Interpretation* 10 (2002) 267–304. One interesting analysis was forwarded in Norman Gottwald's *The Tribes of Yahweh: A Sociology of the Religion of Liberated Israel, 1250–1050 B.C.E., Maryknoll*. New York: Orbis Books, 1979, pp. 8–17. Stephen Moore offers a memorable description of modern biblical scholarship in the introduction to his *God's Beauty Parlor: And Other Queer Spaces In and Around the Bible*. Stanford, CA: Stanford University Press, 2001. In terms of the postmodern biblical criticism briefly discussed in this chapter, we would recommend Yvonne Sherwood's *A Biblical Text and Its Afterlives:*

The Survival of Jonah in Western Culture. Cambridge: Cambridge University Press, 2000. Sherwood's study is one of the best written works of biblical scholarship that one could hope to find. For those interested in theories of postmodernism, the collectively authored work *The Postmodern Bible* is a must. It is possibly the most sophisticated work of *theory* ever produced in the discipline. It is not, however, a pleasure of text. A more accessible primer is A. K. M. Adam's *What is Postmodern Biblical Criticism.* Minneapolis: Fortress Press, 1995. In terms of conceptualizing the relation between author, text, and reader, David Clines' *What Does Eve Do to Help?: And Other Readerly Questions to the Old Testament.* Sheffield: Sheffield Academic Press, 1990, is highly recommended.

PART THREE

∾

POLITICS AND SCRIPTURE

On Jewish Intermarriage: The Bible Is
Open to Interpretation

Rabbi Ishmael taught: 'He who marries a gentile woman and raises
up children from her, raises up enemies against God.'

P. Megillah, 4:10[1]

Just as oil will not mix with other liquids, so Israel does not mix with
the other nations of the world, as it is written [in Deuteronomy 7:3]:
Neither shalt thou make marriages with them.

Midrash Rabbah, The Song of Songs, I. 3, 2[2]

In mainstream Judaism, the Judaism established by the Rabbinic sages of
the first through sixth centuries AD, the following has been prohibited for
millennia: any marriage in which one partner is Jewish and one partner
is not. Aware, undoubtedly, that some Jews were not beyond flouting
decrees from on high, the Rabbis also tackled the question of children
born to Jewish/gentile parents. After much back and forth, a fateful (and
to some, utterly inscrutable) decision was rendered. The offspring of a
Jewish woman and a non-Jewish man was accorded the status of a Jew.
Conversely, the child of a Jewish male and a gentile female was deemed
a gentile. It was as a result of these deliberations that the prohibition
on intermarriage and the principal of matrilineal descent (i.e., basing a
child's identity on that of the mother) were soon to become integral and
lasting features of normative Judaism.[3]

The Hebrew Bible, whose various texts predate the aformentioned
Talmudic decrees by centuries, thinks differently, so to speak, about these
issues. By familiarizing ourselves with the Bible's discrepant views on
intermarriage, we hope to bring an emotionally charged religious debate

into secular relief. In 1990, the National Jewish Population Survey reported that 52 percent – 52 percent! – of American Jews married since 1985 were not wed to a Jewish spouse. That finding elicited great concern, if not outright panic, among community leaders, activists, and educators. Most deplored this development in no uncertain terms, often using the classic "self-inflicted genocide" argument with great rhetorical finesse. An earlier study predicting that only 10,420 "real" Jews would remain by the year 2076 was frequently cited. Among the more liberal denominations, in contrast, a handful resigned themselves to the social facts. They reasoned that intermarriage comprised something of a sociological *mitzvah*. After all, more gentiles were personally experiencing the splendors of Judaism. Could this not be seen as both a cause and effect of decreased anti-Semitism?[4]

If secular hermeneutics trawls for ironies across the Bible's transhistorical run, then there are a few hefty ones to be netted here. To begin with, contemporary American Jews are actually behaving in a wholly biblical manner. By this we mean that some marry within the group, and some do not. The many commentators who castigate the latter often willfully ignore or simply misunderstand the sheer whimsy of the Tanak's thinking on this issue. The great Rabbinic authorities mentioned previously, for their part, may have understood this whimsy all too well. To get Scripture to support their conception of proper Jewish partnering, they ingeniously, aggressively, and perhaps impiously supplemented the very text they believed to be a divine revelation.

This brings us to the Hebrew Bible, a document that we want to nominate for the award of Worst Proof Text Ever. Forged in the crucible of maybe 1,000 years of uneven textual tampering, it abounds in ambiguities, ellipses, and contradictions. The anthology spawns so many enigmas that even an atheist cannot help but wonder if some red, grinning, Martini-sipping demon (currently slumming it in New York's East Village, no doubt) placed it on earth to beguile the more thoughtful ones. The Hebrew Bible is a misreading waiting to happen. This claim will be borne out by an examination of its varied perspectives on intermarriage and the subsequent readings of the Rabbis.

In this and the following chapter, we put into play all the concepts pertaining to composition and interpretation discussed in parts one and two of *The Secular Bible*. We point to examples of textual tampering, which we parsed under the broad category of "superimposition." Attention is drawn to how the "juxtaposition" of documents into an anthology creates wracking incongruities, as well as excesses of meaning and meaninglessness. We watch as interpreters of yesteryear aggressively supplement Scripture, coming to the most confident – and seemingly arbitrary – conclusions about what the holy writings say. Our gaze is also fixed on contemporary biblical scholars and their commitment to translating the untranslatable and wrenching sense from scriptural senselessness. All this will help us illustrate one of our central themes, namely, that the strange way in which the Hebrew Bible was assembled in antiquity impacts how it is read in modernity. To know how the text was crafted in the past is to know something about how it works – all the ways it can work – in the present.

AGAINST INTERMARRIAGE: THE CANAANITE NATIONS

We do not lack for biblical texts that shake their heads disapprovingly at the practice of exogamy. In Genesis 24:3, Abraham makes his servant swear that he will not procure a Canaanite wife for Issac. The eventual non-Canaanite wife, Rebekkah, is later said to be embittered by the two Hittite spouses taken by her son Esau. Esau's brother, Jacob, is instructed by Issac to not wed a Canaanite.[5]

Exodus 34 has more than just Canaanites and Hittites on its mind. Yahweh warns the Israelites to refrain from making a covenant with "the inhabitant of the land." Although phrased in the singular, this term actually refers to six nations (i.e., Amorites, Canaanites, Hittites, Perizzites, Hivites, and Jebusites). Scholars often refer to these as "the Canaanite nations." Addressed to an adult male, the verse suggests that contact with the women of these nations will cause his son to forsake Yahweh:

And you will take from his daughters for your sons, and his daughters will whore after their gods, and will cause your sons to whore after their gods.[6]

A crucial passage from Deuteronomy mentions seven, not six, prohibited Canaanite peoples (all those mentioned previously plus the pleasantly named Girgashites). Once again, an Israelite is warned about the path that leads from intermarriage to apostasy. The Hebrew is a bit choppy here, especially the pronouns that tend to shift inexplicably:

And you will not marry yourselves with them. Your daughter you will not give to his son, and his daughter you will not take for your son. For he will turn your son away from Me, and they (?) will serve other gods and Yahweh will be incensed with you (plural; *bākem*) and obliterate you (singular: *wĕhišmidkā*) quickly.[7]

Similar themes are struck in Joshua's farewell address. Yet, his valedictory is characterized by a curious assertion. The prohibition on exogamy, he insinuates, stems from Torah. This is all quite puzzling. For as we are about to see, characters in Torah, as well as laws in Torah and the putative author of Torah, are not averse to connubium. But Joshua certainly is, and he goes on to announce that God will punish the Israelites if they cohabit with those peoples whom they have failed to dispossess from the land.[8]

In these examples, no general prohibition on intermarriage can be inferred. The so-called six or seven Canaanite nations mentioned previously are said to be unmarriageable. But this is not said of *all* non-Israelite peoples. Christine Hayes, who has written extensively about Israelite and Jewish conceptions of purity, remarks: "the very fact that certain groups are singled out for exclusion ... implies that other groups are permitted."[9]

EZRA AND NEHEMIAH

The shrillest voices against exogamy, those found in the Book of Ezra, would also ground their opposition to this practice on (seemingly unfounded) readings of Torah. The tale goes something like this. A scribe/priest by the name of Ezra, a returnee from the Babylonian Exile, has been informed that intermarriage is rife in Jerusalem. This upsets him, to put it mildly, and while he is engaged in somewhat dramatic displays of mourning, a certain Shechaniah makes an innovative proposal: in accordance with the demands of Torah (?), the men of the community should make a covenant to expel their foreign wives and children. Which, according to Scripture, they proceed to do![10]

Although one verse vaguely insinuates that a few individuals demurred, we soon learn that 113 Judahites obeyed the request. Earlier we remarked that in the reality-deficient Hebrew Bible texts "just happen." To this we might add that mass, public divorce is portrayed as little more than a problem of logistics and planning for inclement weather. The book ends not with a surly mob of father/husbands threatening Ezra and Shechaniah – Jeremiah style (Jer. 26:7–9) – with immediate death. Instead, it depicts the "entire congregation" contemplating the most efficient way to carry out the expulsion of their own families in light of anticipated rainstorms.[11]

The whole strange sequence of events is set in motion in Ezra 9:1, a verse that reads as if it has endured some superimposition in its day(s):

The officers approached me [Ezra] saying: "the people of Israel and the priests and the Levites have not separated themselves from the peoples of the land as (?) their abominations (*mē 'amê hā'ărātzôt kĕtô'ăbōtêhem*) the Canaanite, the Hittite, the Perizzite, the Jebusite, the Ammonite, the Moabite, the Egyptian, and the Amorite. For they have married themselves and their sons to their daughters and the holy semen (*zera' haqōdeš*) has become mixed in the peoples of the land."[12]

Ezra responds to this report by pulling the hair out of his head. Exegetes can sympathize with him. The passage features some enigmatic grammar, not to mention the obscure concept of "holy semen" (which most translators politely render as "holy seed"). Saving a philological analysis for our footnotes, we raise the possibility that textual tampering has occurred. The list of (now) eight prescribed nations appears to have been forcibly jammed into the verse. Indeed, its relation to the phrase "their abominations" is what causes the Hebrew to go awry. This scribal insertion has created possibilities and impossibilities of meaning for all of posterity to puzzle over.[13]

Throughout the Hebrew Bible it is insisted that a good Judahite or Israelite observes Torah. The Book of Ezra adds something original to the mix. A pious subject not only obeys Torah (as explicated by Ezra) but possesses and responsibly bequeaths holy semen to the appropriate persons. The phrase "holy semen" appears in only one other book of the Hebrew Bible and that usage does little to shed light on a variety of problems. First and foremost, what exactly is it? Initially, this substance would seem to exist solely in Judahite men because the passage refers to sons mixing it into the peoples of the land. But if foreign women do damage to holy semen does this mean that Judahite women actualize or activate its inherent purity? In other words, is the sanctity of holy semen preserved only on contact with the uterus of a Judahite woman? And if so, should we translate with the less gender-specific "holy essence"? Trying to make sense of texts written by an anonymous collectivity over hundreds of years is not something secular hermeneuts like to do. We simply mention that Ezra never informs us who those foreign women were. We have seen that when gaps like this arise, modern biblical scholars feel strangely compelled to fill them in. Suggestions concerning the women's identity range from surviving members of some of the eight nations, to local Judahites with whom the authors did not see eye to eye.[14]

If we were to assume the books of the Hebrew Bible sit in chronological order – which is a really bad assumption to make – then we must judge Ezra's reform a failure. For the subsequent text, the Book of Nehemiah, reports that intermarriage is rampant. In its tenth chapter, yet another reform is initiated as the members of the community take an oath: "we will not give our daughters to the peoples of the land, and their daughters we will not take for our sons." But let us never underestimate the inveterate infidelity of holy semen bearers. A little later, an exasperated and cagey Nehemiah reveals that he has found (and harassed and beaten) Judahite men married to women from Ashdod, Ammon, and Moab.

But even these passages from Ezra and Nehemiah do not unequivocally support the Rabbinic decrees of a much later time. Once again, only specific foreigners are said to be unmarriageable, not all foreigners. A comprehensive ban on intermarriage is not present in Hebrew Scripture.[15]

PREFERRING VOLUPTUOUSNESS TO GOD: INTERMARRIAGE IN HEBREW SCRIPTURES

Inconsistent to a fault, the Hebrew Bible contains passages that blatantly contradict the ones examined in the previous section. For reasons that we cannot begin to fathom, the most incongruous views on exogamous union have been juxtaposed in this anthology. Quite a few characters in Scripture married outside the group. To borrow a phrase from Josephus, they preferred "voluptuousness to God, and to a God-fearing life." Not only do some documents seem to endorse the activities of these individuals, but many rank among the most revered figures in the Bible.

Judah, whose descendants evince quite a fondness for foreigners married a Canaanite woman. Simeon, the son of Jacob, reared a son with a Canaanite wife. Joseph wed Asenath whose father is said to be an Egyptian priest. The sons of that union, Manasseh and Ephraim, went on to become ancestors of two Israelite tribes.[16]

No less a celebrated figure than Moses may have practiced exogamy, *twice*. His marriage to Zipporah, the daughter of a Midianite priest, is briefly mentioned in Exodus. Later, in the Book of Numbers, Miriam and Aaron upbraid Moses on account of his "Cushite wife." Is she one and the same as Zipporah, his Midianite wife? Another textual enigma. In any case, Yahweh does not appear to appreciate their critical input. He afflicts Miriam (but not Aaron) with leprosy. Moses's siblings may have been outraged by the Lawgiver's taste for non-Israelite women, but the same cannot be said of God as depicted in Numbers 12.[17]

Samson's fondness for Philistine women is the stuff of (very confusing) legends. Esther is "made queen" or literally "kinged" by King Ahasuerus. True, the story never explicitly says that she is his wife. Yet, it shows little concern about a Jewish virgin's intimacies with a carousing, polytheist Persian emperor. King Solomon – himself the son of a woman who was once wed to a Hittite – is notorious for his exogamous predilection. Although Solomon is reprimanded for his behavior, David's marriage to Maacah, daughter of the Aramaen King of Geshur, is noted without comment. The Book of Chronicles mentions a variety of obscure Israelites who engaged in connubium. One scholar, Sara Japhet, has suggested that this was done purposefully as a means of celebrating "the non-Israelite elements in the people of Israel."[18]

This brings us to David's great grandfather, Boaz the Judahite, who wed Ruth the Moabitess. That coupling is remarkable in the following bipartite respect. First, a law in Deuteronomy states that no Moabite, under any circumstances whatsoever, will be admitted into the "congregation of Yahweh." Second, the union of Ruth and Boaz would seem to be impermissible according to the standards of Ezra and Nehemiah. Could it be possible that King David and his line are tainted by non-holy semen/essence? Many have wondered if Ruth's tale of threshing floor Judahite/Moabite love is actually a veiled critique of, or response to, intolerant attitudes that had seized some parties (e.g., Ezra's party) in postexilic Israel.[19]

In addition to these references, we find a passage that indirectly points to the *legality* of exogamy. Deuteronomy 21:10–14 speaks of a "beautiful woman" captured in battle. According to the law, she is to be brought into her captor's house. The latter can make her his wife after he permits the woman a month of mourning for her parents. Here, marriage with a foreigner does not appear to be a threat to one's religious devotion or the community's ethnic purity.[20]

What we have then is a document that makes many incongruous claims about the rules of proper partnering. Undaunted by the contradictions, ancient exegetes typically attempted to extract a coherent "rule to live by" from the witness. Modern scholars are far more cautious and skeptical. But among them, many still try to discern what the authors of these passages truly felt about intermarriage. Secular hermeneutics, of course, is far more interested in understanding how the Bible's assemblage spawned such completely discrepant views. It is also interested in how the contradictions were productive of fresh ideas for later interpretive communities. It is to this issue that we next turn.

THE BIBLE BETRAYED?

Judaism, the scholarly axiom goes, is Rabbinic not biblical. The claim that Jews live more by the rules and ruminations of the Talmud than by the ramblings of the Tanak is exceedingly true. Rabbinic discourse, needless to say, is not monolithic; spanning centuries it includes the opinions of more than 1,500 named commentators. (Unlike the Hebrew Bible, the Talmud never tries to mask its collective composition.) It is thus not surprising that dissenting views on the question of intermarriage and matrilineality are strewn throughout this massive corpus of writings.

A few of the sages' opinions are quite tolerant and humane, especially when compared with what earlier Jewish sects had in store for their exogamous brethren. The pseudepigraphic *Book of Jubilees* (ca. 200 BCE), for example, recommends burning an Israelite woman who strays (and stoning her male relations who permitted the marriage). Nor were the Rabbinic authorities always oblivious to the real historical sources of their decrees. Shaye Cohen has convincingly argued that some Rabbis were aware that the ban on exogamy with all gentiles (with which they generally agreed) had no discernible biblical foundation. They recognized, therefore, that this broader sanction came not from Moses, but postbiblical Jewish thinkers.[21]

Yet, in the main, the tenor of Talmudic discussions leads us to believe that they would never permit Jews to engage in the types of shenanigans practiced by the biblical characters discussed in the preceding section. "To the Rabbis," writes Lawrence Schiffman, "there was no question that mixed marriages were forbidden." Their decrees are certainly in line with some words of Scripture. But they exist in tension with others. Taken as a whole, the biblical evidence simply does not warrant the categorical restriction on exogamy seen in Rabbinic supplementation.[22]

Should we conclude, finger raised in the air, "*the sages of Palestine and Babylonia have betrayed the Bible!*"? No, too melodramatic and not entirely accurate. In truth, it is simply impossible for any interpreter or interpretive tradition *not* to betray some part of Scripture. It would be more accurate to affirm that betrayal is unavoidable whenever interpreters try to extract a meaning, a truth, a law, and so on, out of a work composed in this manner. For as we saw in Part I, the very nature of the Bible's staggered collective composition freighted it with an abundance of meanings. Let's put it this way: the quest for *a* meaning is the betrayal. To a certain degree, Scripture has been complicit in its own betrayal. Aside from its cheery inconsistency, it did an exceedingly poor job of defending itself against interpretation. It never claimed to be written by God. It never insisted that its contents were inviolable. It never placed any restrictions on the alteration, adaptation, translation, erasure, embellishment, copying, and recopying of its texts. (The biblical scholar S. David Sperling has quite humorously suggested that never "in the Torah, nor in the rest of the Hebrew Bible, is there a claim that the events related actually happened.") A famous Mishnaic axiom informs us that the Rabbis set out to "make a fence round the Torah." No such defensive measures were taken up by the carefree Torah itself. This is what we meant when we dubbed the text an "unself-conscious artifact." It does not know itself, and this left it susceptible to all manner of interpretive high jinks.[23]

Unable, unwilling, to protect itself from exegetes, the Hebrew Bible remained vulnerable to the interpretive brilliance of ancient Jewish thinkers. When confronted with passages that seemed to favor exogamy, the sages generally proceeded to connect the dots of Scripture. They cleverly supplemented the Bible's elliptical testimony with evidence nowhere to be found in the Bible. When the hermeneutic dust had settled a thoroughgoing ban on intermarriage was set in place. Awed by this cavalier attitude toward God's words, a secularist, at least, should be permitted to wonder aloud: *what exactly did the Rabbis think they were doing?* Did they believe that they were merely interpreting sacred Scripture, and by this we mean, uncovering the message contained in those complex divine revelations? Did they believe that they were freely innovating; by this, we mean consciously extemporizing completely novel additions to the text that had nothing to do with the original divine revelations? Or – and this is our preferred option– did they delude themselves into thinking that their innovations were nothing but accurate interpretations? Whatever the case, this willingness to "enhance" Scripture is one of the signal characteristics of Midrashic and Haggadic biblical exegesis. It testifies to an assumption, be it conscious or not, that the Bible is pliable, emendable, and open to interpretation, as it were. It also raises the possibility discussed in Chapter Four of a psychologically vexed, tacitly hostile, relation between the Rabbis and the text.[24]

In many cases, Rabbinic supplementation demonstrates that foreign women married to Israelites were actually pious converts. Do we even need to point out that the Hebrew Bible says nothing about conversion? Thus, in *Midrash Rabbah Ecclesiastes*, Joseph's Asenath is said to be a proselyte. Unbeknownst to Scripture, Ruth too had converted. *Midrash Rabbah Ruth* quotes the biblical text of Ruth 1:16 verbatim, although it adds a few words to her famous speech. It has the Moabitess proclaim: "I will destroy all idolatry within me." As for Zipporah, Moses's (first?) wife, her father Jethro was, apparently, already on the straight path. "The fact is," according to the *Midrash Rabbah Exodus*, "that Jethro was at first a priest to idolatrous worship, but when he saw that there was no truth in it, he despised it and thought of repenting even before Moses came." His daughter Zipporah, we are told elsewhere, was a woman of great virtue who cleansed the house that she shared with Moses of every vestige of idolatry.[25]

In the case of exogamous Israelites, the Rabbis usually come to their defense as well. Esther is repeatedly lauded for her beauty, intelligence, sacrifice, and a general commitment to her (Rabbinic) Jewish ideals. David's marriage to Maacah is understood as lawful. This is accomplished by insisting that she is an example of the "beautiful captive woman" mentioned in Deuteronomy. Solomon's actions, in contrast, created difficulties. One source has God contemplating the destruction of Jerusalem in anger over his marriage to Pharaoh's daughter. Another wonders whether Solomon converted his Egyptian bride or even married her at all. Whatever the Rabbinic attitude toward a biblical character, most of the preceding enhancements are bound by a common supposition: intermarriage is a very bad thing.[26]

Let us imagine that, for whatever sociological reasons, the Rabbis wanted, or needed, to argue in favor of exogamy. Is there any doubt that they could have easily supplied the required scriptural "proof"? They would have lauded the lifestyle choices of Moses, David, Ruth, and Esther. A premium would have been placed on capturing beautiful women in battle. The Book of Nehemiah would have been ignored. Names would have been provided for each of Solomon's foreign wives with accompanying hagiographic portraiture. Legends would have been told of poems a love-struck Ezra composed for a Girgashite maiden. And another betrayal would have taken place.

We are not claiming that Scripture says everything about everything. Rather, we propose that the manner in which the text was assembled could only provide many contradictory and often incoherent answers to questions asked by later generations. As noted earlier, the study of sociohermeneutics seeks to understand why and how a given community of exegetes found the specific answers that they did. In this regard, a more comprehensive study of the sociological context of these Rabbinic discussions needs to be undertaken in a work entitled *The Secular Talmud*.

CONCLUSION: SCRIPTURE AS SIMULACRUM

In this chapter, we pointed to the discrepancies that exist between the words of the Hebrew Bible and Rabbinic readings of these words that have provided the basis for mainstream Judaism. It is not our goal to conclude that that "the Rabbis are wrong." In a way, they are "right." Of course, they could have come to exactly the opposite conclusions about intermarriage and also been "right."

What remains to be explored is the contemporary discourse about intermarriage in the public sphere. Even though it concerns an issue mostly of interest to Jewish-Americans, it typifies some problematic trends that characterize much religious/political discussion in the United States. To begin with, the debate is inexplicably bereft of secular participants. This is puzzling when we consider the following. There are as many as 1 million Jews in the United States who do not practice Judaism. Many of these nonobservant Jews, however, view themselves as "cultural" or "secular" Jews. One might suppose that a high-profile dispute about their identity and their children's identity would elicit some interest. But this has not occurred. Nor is anything heard from a cohort so large as to constitute something of a stereotype: intermarried secular Jewish intellectuals. They cannot be described as marginalized, camera shy, inarticulate, or unmedia savvy. Their silence is emblematic of how nonreligious opinion makers eschew discussions about religion – even when they are the subject under discussion.

Free of secular input, the dialogue on intermarriage is comprised of contributions made by representatives of major Jewish denominations. (Christians, perhaps out of a sense of ecumenical discretion, generally refrain from chiming in.) Of interest to us is the manner in which the Hebrew Bible figures in these intra-Jewish conversations. With the exception of the work of a few scrupulous scholars, Scripture is typically cited tendentiously or inaccurately. David Bleich opines, "from the early dawn of history the people of Israel sought to preserve their ethnic purity and legislated against intermarriage." Writing in *Commentary* magazine, the Provost of the Jewish Theological Seminary, Jack Wertheimer, remarks: "Beginning with the biblical text itself, Jewish religious writings warn of the potentially subversive link between exogamy and religious assimilation." Although such statements might grant a little biblical authority to positions held by orthodox and conservative Judaism, they are highly misleading. As we saw earlier, most biblical passages do not posit the "subversive link" mentioned by Wertheimer. Prior to Ezra, the "ethnic purity" alluded to by Bleich did not garner much attention in the Bible. Neither writer grapples with a possibility that clearly preoccupied the ancient Rabbis, namely, that only the so-called Canaanite nations, not all foreigners, are off limits to Israelites.[27]

In a roundtable staged by *Tikkun Magazine*, Blu Greenberg affirms: "Intermarriage is a violation of Jewish law. It's an abrogation of the covenantal concept of how one enters the Jewish community and peoplehood." Yet, as the case of Ruth illustrates, intermarriage is often a perfectly legitimate way to enter the community, if not the genealogy of various Messiahs. Examples of dubious assertions such as these could be multiplied at will. As a final reminder that one should do a little fact-checking before accepting any public claim made about the Bible, even when made by a scholar, we cite the following: "Since, in the realm of Jewish ideology, God's will is primary, the rule of God's Law (Torah) determines the standards and parameters of appropriate behavior. It is within this framework that intermarriage is seen as unequivocally pro-hibited. Marrying a Gentile has for thousands of years been equated with death itself, as those who intermarried were seen as severing the chain of Jewish continuity."[28]

These writers make some attempt, however misguided, to refer to bib-lical texts and concepts. Reading through the countless contributions on intermarriage one is astonished by how little sustained reflection there is on Scripture. If it is mentioned, in a newspaper article or editorial/opinion piece in a Jewish-affiliated magazine, it is mentioned in passing. The Bible, we suggest, is losing its salience in public disputation about religion even when the disputants are religious. The lessened understanding of doc-trine seems to be consonant with broader shifts in American religious discourse. The sociologist Alan Wolfe recently observed how religious groups in the United States have increasingly diminished the importance of doctrine, in favor of emotive and self-helping forms of belief. As Wolfe observes about Christian fundamentalists: "Doctrinaire they may be but interested in doctrine they are not."[29]

Most Jews and Christians who fulminate on religion's behalf do not have a complex and contradictory Scripture in mind, but a simulacrum of Scripture: a handy set of simple creedal statements about what the text does and does not mandate. This does not mean that the Bible is irrele-vant. Rather, its many dimensions have been flattened by some religious leaders who obscenely simplify the complexity of the text. Of course, all readings of Scripture are, to some degree or another, simulacra. The Rabbinic sages certainly produced selective and tendentious readings. Yet, they could never be accused of not wrestling with the tensions and diffi-culties of the Bible, nor with simplifying its contents. Among present-day commentators, in contrast, the mysteries of Scripture have, apparently, been unriddled. The Bible, it has been concluded, is clear and simple. This is an ironic and just fate for the Worst Proof Text Ever.

SUGGESTIONS FOR FURTHER READING

The amount of literature on Jewish intermarriage is large, and because it concerns an issue with "practical" applications, it is often accessible to laypersons. Of great interest is the special issue of *Judaism* 34 (1985) exclusively devoted to this topic. It features a large variety of short, punchy articles from writers representing nearly the entire spectrum of Jewish thought on mixed marriages (although there are only a few articles by women and none by secular Jews). In terms of early Judaism, the studies of Shaye Cohen are highly recommended. It is significant that Cohen reaches scholarly conclusions that he admits contradict his own personal beliefs. If more scholars in religious studies followed Cohen's lead, there would be far less need for secular hermeneutics. See his writings, "From the Bible to the Talmud: The Prohibition of Intermarriage," *Hebrew Annual Review* 7 (1983) 27 (23–39); "The Matrilineal Principle in Historical Perspective," *Judaism* 34 (1985) 5–13; "The Matrilineal Principle," in *The Beginnings of Jewishness: Boundaries, Varieties, Uncertainties.* Berkeley: University of California Press, 1999 pp. 263–307 and "Solomon and the Daughter of Pharaoh: Intermarriage, Conversion, and the Impurity of Women," *Journal of the Ancient Near Eastern Society* 16–17 (1984–1985) 23–37. A detailed and tightly argued study of the development of ideas on intermarriage in emergent Judaism can be found in Christine Hayes, *Gentile Impurities and Jewish Identities: Intermarriage and Conversion from the Bible to the Talmud.* New York: Oxford University Press, 2002.

7

∾

Same-Sex Eroticism and Jerry Falwell

The fact is that Paul treats *all* homosexual activity as prima facie
evidence of humanity's tragic confusion and alienation from God
the Creator.... Though only a few biblical texts speak of homoerotic
activity, all of them express unqualified disapproval.

> Richard Hays, "Awaiting the Redemption of Our Bodies:
> The Witness of Scripture Concerning Homosexuality"

The New Testament takes no demonstrable position on homosexuality.... The source of antigay feelings among Christians must be sought
elsewhere.

> John Boswell, *Christianity, Social Tolerance, and Homosexuality:*
> *Gay People in Western Europe from the Beginning of the Christian*
> *Era to the Fourteenth Century*

Intolerance, lust for political power masquerading as love of God, thump-
a-Bible self-righteousness – these are the qualities that American secularists ascribe to Christian fundamentalists. Perhaps no single fundamentalist conforms to their stereotype as much as the Reverend Jerry Falwell.
His stewardship of the Moral Majority, his prominent role in the rise of
the religious Right, as well as his periodic assaults on the liberal media,
have made him the object of secular fear and loathing. Then there is his
enduring and often strange obsession with gay people. Falwell has accused
the founder of the PTL television ministry, Jim Bakker, of being a homosexual. He has accused the Teletubby Tinky Winky of being a homosexual role model. He has blamed the terrorist attacks of September 11,
2001, on rampant American homosexuality (among other national vices).

But Falwell is by no means the most extreme or hateful of antigay Christian conservatives. He has, after all, invited his former speechwriter Mel White and White's gay congregants to an evening of prayer and dialogue at his Lynchburg, Virginia, church. He has also publicly and unambiguously denounced homophobic violence.[1]

The Christian Right's recent fixation with homosexuality has been attributed to a variety of factors. Some have pointed to its need for a new enemy in a postcommunist era. Institutional fund-raising, according to others, always necessitates a convenient scapegoat. Whatever the merits of these explanations, it is clear that the Christian world is devoting unprecedented attention to the question of same-sex relations. "Many of the major Christian traditions in the west," writes one scholar, "are in turmoil about homosexuality." "The gay issue," comments another, "has hung over the church like an ominous cloud during the last fifty years." We concentrate on this debate because it features many story lines that are of interest to us: convoluted sacred texts, cocksure interpreters, blurry Church-State borders, high-profile religious demagogues, pious biblical scholars, and, naturally, the conspicuous absence of secular participants. But most importantly, this analysis lets us look at how professional interpreters go about contesting or refuting dominant readings of the Bible. We refer to this as the art of "counterexegesis" and we will wonder aloud if nonbelievers have an interest in acquiring this skill. Let us begin by reviewing those scriptural passages that would appear to address the issue of what moderns, but not ancients, refer to as "homosexuality."[2]

"LYING DOWNS OF A WOMAN": HEBREW SCRIPTURE'S AMBIGUOUS TESTIMONY ON HOMOEROTICISM

The tendency, noted in our epigraph, for scholars to reach completely contradictory conclusions about what the Bible says is by no means unusual. In his 1978 book, *Jonathan Loved David: Homosexuality in Biblical Times*, Tom Horner commented that the Israelites lived within "a culture that accepted homosexuality." Robert Gagnon, in his 2001 study, *The Bible and Homosexual Practice: Texts and Hermeneutics*, remarked that "there is clear, strong and credible evidence that the Bible unequivocally defines same-sex intercourse as sin." We find neither view compelling.[3]

In the entire Old Testament there are only two verses that appear to explicitly address the legality of sexual relations between persons of the same gender. The first passage, Leviticus 18:22, is typically translated in this vein: "Do not lie with a male as one lies with a woman; it is an abhorrence." For millennia, this type of reading has caused no small amount of misery for persons in Jewish and Christian societies who have engaged in, or been accused of engaging in, homoerotic acts. It is at once ironic and disturbing that this reading is not entirely faithful to the actual Hebrew. The biblical scholar Saul Olyan (whose writings on the subject are admirably free of theological cant) has rightly observed that renderings of this kind are "interpretive, not literal." A literal, secular translation of Leviticus 18:22 might read something like this[4]:

And with a male you will not lie *lying downs of a woman* (*miškěbê 'iša*)
It is an abomination.[5]

The cryptic phrase, "lying downs of a woman" (*miškěbê 'iša*), surfaces one other time. Its appearance in a similar verse (Leviticus 20:13) does little to clarify matters:

And a man that will lie with a male *lying downs of a woman* (*miškěbê 'iša*), the two of them have committed an abomination. They will die. Their blood is upon them.[6]

It seems fairly plausible to assume some type of sexual encounter between two males is considered abhorrent and worthy of capital punishment. A Jewish or Christian man might gather from this that he had better not engage in "lying downs of a woman" with another male. But what precisely does that entail? Undeterred by the silences, and convinced that Scripture always has something coherent to say, scholars have made suggestions ranging from all homoerotic acts to solely anal sex. The absence in these passages of any reference to the age and social status of the participants has also intrigued interpreters. Age and social standing were crucial variables in Greek and Roman thinking pertaining to homosexuality, about which we do possess a decent quantity of data. With these cross-cultural parallels in mind, industrious exegetes have asked whether the person addressed in these verses was the active (i.e., insertive, higher-status) partner or passive (i.e., receptive, lower-status) partner. Further, these laws fail to mention same-sex relations between women – a silence that has spawned the most varied surmises as to what the Bible thinks about lesbianism.[7]

Earlier we called for an end to interpretation geared at discovering "original intentions." This request is aimed, in part, at making exegetes think about the usefulness, if not the sobriety, of making conjectures such as those noted in the previous paragraph. We reiterate Professor Carroll's plea for interpreters to "admit defeat." The Old Testament does not, after all, brim with information about same-sex eroticism. Petronius' *Satyricon* it is not. Nor can it be confused with Plato's *Symposium*, where many juicy details about homosexuality can be found. A secular hermeneut would begin by acknowledging the incomprehensibility of the phrase "lying downs of a woman." This would permit him or her to move on to questions that fall under the purview of what we labeled "sociohermeneutics." In particular, we would want to know how and why so many interpreters, past and present, have come to the identical conclusion. Namely, that two scant and elliptical sentences in the Old Testament comprised an unequivocal, blanket condemnation of same-sex eroticism.[8]

A partial answer to this question centers around the way interpreters have juxtaposed other Old Testament passages against those found in Leviticus. In a groundbreaking, although somewhat uneven 1955 study, the Anglican cleric Derrick Sherwin Bailey observed that "the Christian attitude to homosexual practices inevitably begins with the story of the destruction of Sodom and Gomorrah." This episode in Genesis 19, and a similar tale in Judges 19, have often been adduced as evidence of the Bible's antigay stance. Both feature an unruly mob of locals who demand "to know" male guests who are lodging in the house of a nonindigenous inhabitant of their town. In each story, the host offers to hand over to the crowd women who are sheltered in his home. This is done, apparently, in the hope that the mob will rape the women instead of the male visitors.[9]

The sins of Sodom are cited elsewhere in the Bible. It was Bailey who called attention to the curiosity that none of those references ever associate Sodom with "sodomy." In Ezekiel, for example, the crime of the infamous city is described as arrogance (*gā'ôn*, Ezek. 16:49). The prophet Jeremiah charges Sodom with adultery and lying (*nā'ôp wĕhālōk bašeqer*, Jer. 23:14). For these reasons, Bailey suggested, rather convincingly, that the prohibition on same-sex relations is not biblical. Instead, it emerged in pseudepigraphic, Apocryphal and Hellenistic Jewish writings. In our parlance, it is an idea about Scripture, not an idea in Scripture. Others have observed that a depiction of homosexual rape is not necessarily the same thing as a condemnation of homosexuality. If this were the case, then the rapes of Dinah (Gen. 34) or Tamar (2 Sam. 13) would have to be interpreted as denunciations of heterosexuality.[10]

Another passage that is brought to bear on the subject in question is Genesis 9:22. It reports an incident in which Ham saw "his father's [Noah's] nakedness." For some unspecified reason, this leads to the punishment of Ham's son, Canaan. That conundrum should not distract us from the enigmatic phrase "his father's nakedness." This is another of those irritatingly ambiguous locutions that has always inspired pious exegetes to strain for sense. Discussants in the Babylonian Talmud, for example, puzzle over whether these words refer to Ham's castration or sexual abuse of his father. In our view, the verse is too sparse and mangled to warrant such conclusions. Be that as it may, this passage has figured in traditional religious contestations of homosexuality.[11]

Some, conversely, have discerned a certain acceptance of homoeroticism or at least "homosociability" in Scripture. In 1 Sam. 18:1, we read "and the soul of Jonathan became bound with the soul of David, and Jonathan loved him as his own soul." After the death of the latter in 2 Sam. 1:26, David famously cries "wonderful was your love for me, more than the love of women!" A little earlier King Saul rebukes his son Jonathan by saying, "You son of a . . . (?), I certainly know that you have chosen the son of Jesse, to your shame and to the shame of your mother's nakedness." (1 Sam. 20:30). Tom Horner, reviewing these proclamations, as well as a rather dramatic kiss between the lads, concludes: "we have every reason to believe that a homosexual relationship existed."[12]

Perhaps. But since it is our contention that almost *any* given interpretation can be neutralized by a motivated exegete, we offer the following counterreading. King David comes in for his share of abuse in Hebrew Scripture. His acts of adultery (with Bathsheeba), murder (of Uriah), treason (as a Philistine mercenary), and even a bout of seeming impotence (with Abishag the Shunammite) are chronicled in merciless detail. We have wondered elsewhere if an anti-David current runs subversively through these stories. Looked at in this way – and we are just playing devil's advocate here – the report of David's love for Jonathan may have been derisively inserted by *homophobic* authors/editors. Reference to his affection for a man may have served as yet another form of tacit character assassination and not an endorsement of sexual love between men. This is *one* meaning we could draw from Scripture. We could draw this inference after selectively juxtaposing a few heavily superimposed verses and letting our exegetical energies run their course. Was it the meaning meant? Who knows? Who could possibly know? What kind of person thinks that he or she could know such things?[13]

THE NEW TESTAMENT EVIDENCE

In the entire New Testament only three passages bear directly on same-sex eroticism. How Christian polities far and wide could freight such pithy verses with so much humanly devastating social legislation provides yet another illustration of Scripture's vulnerability to the ideological leanings of its readers.

The former Jesuit John McNeill has referred to Romans 1:26–27 as "the strongest New Testament argument against homosexual activity as intrinsically immoral. . . . " There, Paul (or somebody claiming to be Paul) writes:

Their women exchanged natural intercourse for that against nature; and their men likewise abandoned natural relations with women and burned with lust for one another – males committing shameless acts with males and being paid in turn in their own persons the wage suited to their deviation.[14]

In continuing to look at how prevailing interpretations can be neutralized by exegetes, we quickly review a few analyses that challenge anti-homosexual readings of this and two other passages. We do so not to champion these alternative readings; secular hermeneutics is reluctant to champion *any* reading. Instead, our goal is to demonstrate the arts of counterexegesis: strategies that biblicists (and one day secularists?) use to destabilize dominant conceptions of "what the Bible says." Some counterexegesis merely flips or reverses a dominant conception of Scripture. Thus, the exegete works out proofs for the claim that homophobia is nonexistent in the Bible. A more sophisticated form of counterexegesis is one that points to the difficulty of extracting any clear lesson from the Good Book. As such, it is concluded that biblical verses are too ambiguous or contradictory to tell us much about homosexuality.

This approach (which can be applied to almost any subject in Scripture) implicitly undermines reigning interpretations.

One effective way of disarming a prevailing reading might be referred to as "deduction." Here the exegete simply draws logical inferences from the "plain" words of the Bible. On first glance, one might not conclude that Paul is referring to what we call "bisexuals" in Romans 1:26–27. A closer look, however, makes such an argument logically plausible. The passage cited previously seems to say that the men in question have "abandoned" their natural heterosexual urges for women. Only *then* did they proceed to engage in same-sex intercourse. Paul, in the words of John Boswell, derogates "homosexual acts committed by apparently heterosexual persons." If this were indeed the case, then the apostle would have nothing to say about those whom we might call "naturally" or "biologically" gay. He is therefore silent on the question of homosexual acts committed by homosexual persons. Some might protest that this reading is based on a "loophole," an unintended implication in the text. Others could charge that this rendering is anachronistic insofar as the concepts of "biological" gayness (or "gayness") never existed in antiquity. The obvious response is that religious orthodoxies have made abundant use of such loopholes and anachronisms for millennia. And this is because without recourse to such strategies no community under the sun would be able to live by the sparse and elliptical words of Scripture.[15]

Familiarity with the languages of biblical antiquity is an exceedingly useful skill for those who want to undercut orthodox interpretations. The two remaining New Testament passages addressing homosexuality feature a rather strange Greek word, *arsenokoitês*. Let us never underestimate how much havoc a skilled exegete can wreak on a dominant reading when blessed by a peculiar and poorly attested word. What follows is the New Jerusalem Bible's translation of 1 Timothy 1:8–10 – a translation that many of the commentators mentioned in this section vehemently contest[16]:

We are all well aware that the Law is good, but only provided it is used legitimately, on the understanding that laws are not framed for people who are upright. On the contrary, they are for criminals and the insubordinate, for the irreligious and the wicked, for the sacrilegious and the godless; they are for people who kill their fathers or mothers and for murderers, for the promiscuous, homosexuals [*arsenokoitês*], kidnappers, for liars and for perjurers – and for everything else that is contrary to the sound teaching that accords with the gospel of the glory of the blessed God.

Other English Bibles offer "sodomites," "homosexual perverts," or "deviants" as a reading for *arsenokoitês*. Not convinced by this rendering, the New Testament scholar Dale Martin examined appearances of this word in contemporaneous Greek documents. The contexts in which it appears suggest to him that sins of an economic nature are being discussed. He wonders if *arsenokoitein* "refers to some kind of economic exploitation, probably by sexual means: rape or sex by economic coercion, prostitution, pimping, or something of the sort." Refreshingly, Martin admits: "I am not claiming to know what *arsenokoitês* meant, I am claiming that *no one* knows what it meant."[17]

Arsenokoitês appears in another list of vices. In 1 Corinthians 6:9, we learn that *malakoi* and *arsenokoitai*, among others, will not inherit the kingdom of God. The literal meaning of *malakos* is "soft" or "soft ones." In English New Testaments *malakoi* and *arsenokoitai* have typically been viewed as having something to do with sexual activities between those of the same gender. Some translations go so far as to render both Greek words, by *one* English word: "homosexuals." McNeill, however, insisted that "there is no justification for applying *malakos* specifically to homosexuality." Following this lead, and doing the philological heavy lifting, Martin concludes that *malakos* should be translated as "effeminate." Yet, he adds the proviso that in documents of the period effeminate men were not necessarily homosexuals. "A man," he observes "could be branded as effeminate whether he had sex with men or with women." Such an interpretation makes it hard to lend sanction to a biblically based condemnation of homosexuality.[18]

Aside from simple deduction, or the introduction of philological doubt, a biblical scholar can also look to surrounding cultures as a means of filling in scriptural gaps. In his 1983 book, *The New Testament and Homosexuality: Contextual Background for Contemporary Debate*, Robin Scroggs reasoned that Paul did indeed have some sort of homosexual activity in mind, but only one specific type – pederasty of the most exploitative and abusive sort. Surveying grim reports of this practice from the Graeco-Roman world, Scroggs concludes that an outraged Paul had nothing to say about consensual relations between peers of the same gender. Finally, one can contest prevailing views by the appeal to silence. Jesus does not say a word about same-sex relations. Many interpret this as indicative of his tolerance for homosexuality or his lack of concern for this issue. Others, needless to say, come to the exact opposite conclusion.[19]

SCHOLARS, DEMAGOGUES, SECULARISTS, AND PUBLIC DISCUSSIONS OF HOMOSEXUALITY

Even though they work on the same text, mediagenic religious demagogues and biblical scholars ply their trades in very different ways. The demagogues' "methods" for understanding a passage from Scripture do not resemble any of those employed by the researchers discussed previously. They rarely go plowing through lexicons of long-dead languages. They do not concern themselves with ancient cultural context. They are not afflicted with those debilitating doubts about the Bible's meaning that crouch at the door of every conscientious exegete's psyche.

Reverend Falwell's approach illustrates these points well. For him, the Bible is "God-breathed" and possesses "the quality of being free from error in all of its statements and affirmations." It is this assumption that animates some rather confident scriptural readings. In a 1981 contribution, he declares: "God considers the sin of homosexuality as abominable.... The Old Testament law is clear concerning this issue." More recently, he opined: "I believe homosexuality is wrong, that it's moral perversion. I believe the Bible teaches that." For Falwell, the Bible has *one* clear and indisputable message. The problem lies not in figuring out what the text says – that is self-evident – but in applying that timeless, transparent communication to society writ large. Politics is the task at hand, not hermeneutics.[20]

Celebrity preachers, such as Falwell, are accomplished rhetoricians. They convey their ideas (which they construe as identical with the Bible's ideas) with finesse and technical skill. The accessibility of their presentation stands in stark contrast to that of often anticharismatic biblical scholars. The latter's writings are not generally considered to be masterpieces of nonfictional prose. Nor do biblicists excel in the domain of public speaking. Yet, for all their intellectual and stylistic differences, famous fundamentalists and obscure exegetes share one quality in common. Most biblical scholars who write about homosexuality – whether they are conservatives imploring gays to repent or radicals who are "queering" Nehemiah – *write explicitly as believers*, usually of the Christian variety.

The potential for conflicts of interest is enormous. We regret to say that this potential is often achieved. Reading through the immense scholarly bibliography on the Bible and same-sex eroticism one is struck – and dismayed – by the formulaic quality of such inquiries. The conservative Christian professor routinely affirms that the Torah, Paul, and every jot and tittle of Scripture deplore all forms of homosexuality. The liberal or radical usually engages in counterexegesis of the flip variety. It is insisted that the Bible, God, Christ, and so on, love gay men and women. As Pim Pronk put it: "The function of an appeal to Scripture is to reinforce the position one finds convincing before making that appeal."[21]

There is nothing unethical about a given scholar having religious beliefs. Things become potentially objectionable when the scholar in question studies these very same religious beliefs in his or her capacity as a scholar. The tendency of so many exegetes to come to conclusions that perfectly conform to their preexisting creedal convictions is something that members of our discipline will need to think about. Confronting this problem might do much to rehabilitate the image of the biblicist in the Academy (see Chapter Five). Of course, many in today's university might celebrate unself-critical research as a desirable change from the old chimera of objective scholarship. We, however, still cling to the belief that the virtuous thing about scholars – this might actually be our only real virtue – is a certain unpredictable independence of mind, a freedom from dogma. This is where the mission of the university intersects with the most integral ideal of secularism. Ideally, both are committed to the preservation and promulgation of critical and self-critical discourse. Celebrity clergy cannot be faulted for refraining from such discourse; their job is not to foster critical thinking skills, but to save souls. Professional academicians must be held to a higher standard. One day exegetes will routinely publish conclusions that directly contradict their personal beliefs about homosexuality. When this day comes Old Testament research will have become fully secularized.

Having chided religious demagogues and biblicists, let us now turn to secularists. Where exactly are they in public discussions of homosexuality and religion in the United States? The dialogue about this issue is mostly carried out by religious leaders and religious academicians. In response, a nonbeliever might conceivably respond: "*So? What's wrong with that?*" What's wrong, in our opinion, is that this dialogue tends to profoundly impact the lives of nonreligious people. In a predominantly Christian country such as our own, beliefs about the mandates of Scripture clearly shape public perceptions. The manner in which many Americans and their political representatives think about topics such as gay marriage, adoption, military suitability, and so on, is greatly influenced by the official positions of their respective churches. Judith Plaskow is quite correct when she claims that "the religious and public policy dimensions of sexual orientation are so thoroughly intertwined that it is almost impossible to disentangle them."[22]

Even here, our skeptical secularist might demur: "*Granted, these biblically based discussions about homosexuality have some effect on the lives of non-believers. But fortuitously all of those 'secularly religious' folks that you (plural) have spoken about routinely clash with religious conservatives. It's a bit ironic but in the process they inadvertently defend our secular values – or some reasonable facsimile of whatever those might be. Ergo, they provide the (hell)fire wall that permits us to go about our lives in peace.*" There is, admittedly, much merit to the riposte of our imaginary interlocutor. For when a fundamentalist leader makes yet another aneuerism-inducing statement about "ho-mo-sexuals," his or her most credible and vehement opposition comes not from secularists, *but from other Christians.* These would be the very same Christians who know Scripture inside out, appreciate the subtleties and complexities of its language, and understand the polysemous nature of its contents. In other words, these Christians know how to counterexegete. In terms of convincing others of the truth of his/God's message, who should Jerry Falwell fear more? Dissenting coreligionists who speak to the Christian mainstream and can persuasively challenge his readings, or biblically illiterate secularists making snarky asides about religious hypocrisy?

There is, then, an intriguing triangulation to be considered between fundamentalists, the secularly religious, and secularists. As our fictional respondent clearly sensed, the latter two constituencies often share political interests. In the sphere of social action, a pragmatic alliance could conceivably be forged between the secularly religious and secularists. It is difficult, however, to think of many cases in which this has actually happened. The rhetorical brawn in such an alliance, of course, lies with the moderate believer, not with the godless who have no scriptural grounds by which to effectively take on religious conservatives.

There are, of course, potential fault lines in our hypothetical coalition. When progressive Christian interpreters counterexegete New Testament verses on homosexuality, they tend to drive the following point home: Paul is not excoriating egalitarian, loving, committed, long-term relationships between two persons of the same gender. On the contrary, such a gay couple is affirmed in Christ. This is a humane and tolerant reading. But for some gay (and straight) people this affirmation is meaningless and suffocating. This is because many secularists reject the Judaeo-Christian emphasis on monogamous union. What is to be done with those who unrepentantly enjoy the anonymous, consensual pleasures of a good weekly trip to the bathhouse? Are they also affirmed in Christ? Their sexual behavior, obviously, cannot be easily accommodated within any system of monotheistic sexual ethics. Nor do they usually seek the Church's benediction in such matters.[23]

As this example makes clear, political partnerships between religious moderates and secularists are fraught with fissures. Truth be told, gay secularists could quite reasonably conclude that *any* alliance with religious groups is not in their best interests. The case could be made that homophobia itself has a religious geneaology. In one of the few contributions that addresses the subject of secularism and same-sex eroticism, Thomas Clark observes that "there are no good secular grounds for claiming homosexuality is either morally defective or socially harmful." Such arguments, he continues, emerge almost exclusively from religious modes of thought (although we should never rule out the existence of secular homophobes). The dilemma that confronts gay secularists is one that confronts all secularists: should they form strategic coalitions with the large and politically influential body of secularly religious? Or, are the values and objectives of nonbelievers so opposed to those of even the latter that it makes more sense to go it alone? We raise the possibility that in either scenario familiarity with the basic principles of counterexegesis may be helpful. In a society where interpretations of the Bible routinely affect the lives of all citizens, learning how to criticize claims made on behalf of the Bible is a useful civic virtue.[24]

CONCLUSION: "NOW IT CAN BE EXEGETED!"

The endeavor to extract *the* originally intended message of some putative biblical author concerning homosexuality is a hopeless task. It is an aspiration soaked in theological preconceptions about Scripture's under-lying meaningfulness. It has no place in secular inquiry. Besides, even if one person, or deity, did deposit a clear and coherent opinion about same-sex relations in the Bible, one that remained unmolested by scribes of later ages, this would not change the fact that modern exegetes are having the most difficult time agreeing on what that opinion might be.

How can this absence of interpretive consensus be explained? As always, we start by blaming the Bible. It contains few verses devoted to homo-sexuality. The verses that it does relinquish are unclear and difficult to translate. They include key terms (e.g., *miškĕbê 'iššâ, arsenokoitês*) that are ambiguous in the extreme. The passages are so slight and vague that the most basic questions, the "am I allowed to do this?" questions, about same-sex activities cannot be answered. These lines sit in the midst of a massive collection of ancient writings crammed with all sorts of verses that, if called upon, can lend this or that inflection to their murky contents. The strange, historically staggered composition of the Hebrew Bible/Old Testament seeded the canonized text with countless possible (and impos-sible) readings. The suffixing of the New Testament onto the Old expo-nentially multiplied these interpretive possibilities. To understand why there is so much disagreement, one must start by recognizing that the Bible furnishes its readers with unlimited resources for dispute.

But composition is only half the equation. Readers also play a role in discovering and generating these diverse meanings. It is they, for exam-ple, who decide to let Genesis 1:27–28 "shed light" on Leviticus 18:22 and Romans 1:26–27. The passage from Genesis seems to posit a God who creates male and female, and then urges the pair to produce large quan-tities of offspring. Does this not demonstrate, unequivocally, the Lord's preference for heterosexuality? Does this not tip the scales in favor of the antihomosexual tone that can be inferred from the cryptic Leviticus 18:22? It is a reader who juxtaposes the verse from Genesis against those from Leviticus and Romans. A different reader could line verses up in such a way that would lead to the opposite understanding of God's views on same-sex love.

Once we accept that readers extract only certain meanings from the many (albeit finite) meaning possibilities present in the text, then we are prepared to pose the sociohermeneutic question: "*why did this particular interpreter or community of readers conclude that the Bible said this (but not that)?*" How different this is from the traditional query, "*What does the Bible say?*" The latter question impels and constrains us to make the Bible make sense. The former requires us to think about the role that culture, class, social race, gender, sexual orientation, and so on, play in conditioning biblical interpretation.[25]

In this sociological vein, we suggest that particular understandings of the Bible are more likely to emerge under particular social conditions. The issue of homosexuality illustrates this well. For hundreds of years, the passages examined previously have been generally understood as scriptural condemnations of same-sex relations. Prior to the mid-twentieth century not much attention was paid to this subject. When the issue was broached, it rarely elicited the ructions that have shaken the Christian world in more recent decades. Christopher Seitz observes: "For all the issues that divided the Church in the past – over which Anabaptists, Lutherans, the Reformed, Anglicans, Methodists, Roman Catholics, Pentecostals, and others might have disagreed – tolerance or blessing of homosexual acts was never one of them." What is novel in contemporary times is the emergence of *many* explicitly and transparently progay interpretations. In an era that has witnessed the advent of gay civil rights, gay consciousness, and the rise of Queer Studies as an academic discipline, it is not a coincidence that the counterexegesis sampled in this chapter has surfaced en masse. Social conditions certainly do make possible, or at least facilitate, given readings of the Bible and their dissemination.[26]

Exegetically and sociologically speaking, ours is an age like no other in the history of biblical interpretation. Its motto might be described as "*now it can be exegeted!*" Or maybe, "*now it can be counterexegeted!*" The Index and the lashes no longer await those who blaspheme Scripture. The old orthodoxies have lost their power to suppress and brutalize heretics (although not necessarily their willingness). Today, a Christian or Jew can say pretty much anything about Scripture and live to tell about it. A sacred text whose unique assembly loaded it with a plurality of messages has finally interlocked with a secularized civilization that self-consciously aspires to be politically and culturally pluralistic. The Bible is now free to become the polysemous text that it never desired to be.

SUGGESTIONS FOR FURTHER READING

As with intermarriage, the scholarly discourse on homosexuality and the Church is immense and often quite accessible. For purposes of comparison, one might want to look at a study such as John Boswell's *Christianity, Social Tolerance, and Homosexuality: Gay People in Western Europe from the Beginning of the Christian Era to the Fourteenth Century*. Chicago: University of Chicago Press, 1981, and contrast it with, let's say, Robert Gagnon's *The Bible and Homosexual Practice: Texts and Hermeneutics*. Nashville, TN: Abingdon, 2001. A very readable and balanced introduction to the ancient data is Martti Nissinen's *Homoeroticism in the Biblical World: A Historical Perspective*. Trans. Kirsi Stjerna. Minneapolis: Fortress Press, 1998. A novel and original analysis of Rabbinic attitudes toward homosexuality can be found in Daniel Boyarin, "Are There any Jews in 'The History of Sexuality'?" *Journal of the History of Sexuality* 5 (1995) 333–355. The edited volume of Saul Olyan and Martha Nussbaum, *Sexual Orientation and Human Rights in American Religious Discourse*. New York: Oxford, 1998, offers many important statements of contemporary positions. Touching on the question of scholarly ethics in dealing with this issue is P. Deryn Guest's article, "Battling for the Bible: Academy, Church and the Gay Agenda," *Theology and Sexuality* 15 (2001) 90 (66–93).

8

໑

The Secular Qur'ān?

> Whoever loves and admires the Qur'ān loves God and his Messenger;
> whoever abhors the Qur'ān abhors God and his Messenger.
>
> Ghazzālī, *ihyā 'ulūm ad-din*

Today's secularists have an adversary and that adversary is not religion
per se. Rather, it is religious extremism and, in this regard, we hasten
to add that the secularly religious share precisely the same nemesis.
Of all the monotheistic extremisms, it is currently the Islamic variety
that nonbelievers (and others) should monitor most carefully. This is
not to downplay the dangers presented by Jews erecting trailer parks on
Palestinian lands or assassinating their own democratically elected leaders. Nor is it to disregard Christians who stalk abortion clinics and gay
bars. If properly empowered, these groups are as capable of making the
world an insufferable place (or a nonexistent place) as their Muslim coun-
terparts. Of late, however, radical Islamists have distinguished themselves
in terms of their growing numbers, the international scope of their activities, and their unbridled enthusiasm for mass homicide. The possibility
that their ancient ideology of martyrdom might one day "shake hands"
with modernity's arsenal of apocalypse is enough to make all civilized
persons edgy, especially that majority of nonextremist Muslims residing
in their immediate vicinity.

At this point, it is obligatory to declare that these militants are not
true practitioners of their faith. The real Islam has been hijacked. The
authentic message of the Qur'ān has been distorted. That revelation
enjoins us to be loving, tolerant, and peaceful – *not* to hurl civilian air-
craft down Greenwich Street in New York City. Platitudes such as this are
common in university religious studies departments where some evince a

bouncer-like commitment to shielding whatever religious tradition they study from undesirable critique. To a certain degree these platitudes are true. Yet they collide thunderously with one of the major theses of this book. We insist that there is no one, authentic message or lesson to be found in, or extracted from, Sacred Scripture. The murderous xenophobia of the Book of Joshua and the embrace of the foreigner found in the Books of Leviticus and Ruth are *both* "real" biblical messages that have been identified by exegetes. The ultranationalist Israeli right-winger who demands the expulsion of all Arabs from "Judah" and "Samaria," as well as the peacenik strumming Bob Dylan tunes on a Tel Aviv beach, can both legitimately cite the Tanak in their defense. The Hebrew Bible puts what we have referred to as "a large finite set" of messages into historical play. Interpreters, in diverse social contexts, amplify and ignore, embellish and strip down, isolate and creatively consolidate those sundry messages. And so it is with the Qur'ān and its interpreters. Al-Qaeda's reading of the divine recitation is not necessarily a false reading; better to describe it as a reading that has had little truck among Muslims across nearly 1,400 years of Islamic civilization.

There are many credible explanations for why religious militancy – a phenomenon that is, at present, relatively marginal among Jews and Christians – has established a small but significant foothold in various Muslim societies. One could point to the often disastrous effects of Western imperialism. Nor should we forget that secular regimes in Islamic lands have often served up the worst that political nonbelief has to offer. Although not denying the relevance of these and other factors, we approach this question from a somewhat less frequented avenue. We want to concentrate on intellectuals, specifically self-critical religious intellectuals. Their current absence in public institutions of Islamic theological speculation provides *one* explanation for the differing status of religious extremism among the monotheistic faiths. Ours is an argument not often heard: in history, exegesis *matters*, as do exegetes.

THE HEBREW BIBLE AND THE QUR'ĀN: A COMPARISON OF TEXTUAL CONSCIOUSNESS

We begin by comparing the ways in which the Qur'ān and the Hebrew Bible account for their own authorship. This might seem like an awfully circuitous route to take when addressing issues of contemporary religious militancy. But as we are about to see, the pursuit of the nagging, insoluble, age-old question of "Who wrote the Bible?" eventually yielded a set of responses that resulted in a dramatically new orientation toward Scripture. It also gave rise to a new class of religious critics. The orientation they espoused is theologically and politically inimical to the health of extremist movements. Nothing, but nothing, is more difficult for fundamentalists to combat than a cadre of learned opponents *within* their own religious tradition. No laser-guided missile, no economic embargo, no manifesto-toting secular movement, could do as much damage to extremist causes.[1]

We have already had occasion to note that the Hebrew Bible is not a particularly self-conscious work. It does not know its name. It shows absolutely no awareness that it is a "Bible," or even a corpus of collected documents. It equivocates as to its origins; some texts are casually attributed to certain mortals, others are said to be divinely dictated, and still others are left unsigned. Hebrew Scripture, moreover, does not seem to seriously consider that its message is anything but transparent. The possibility that readers might be utterly baffled by its peculiar contents has not, apparently, crossed the mind of those who produced the Hebrew Bible.[2]

Contrast this with the Qur'ān, a work that Stefan Wild described as the "most self-referential holy text known in the history of world religions." Wild has certainly identified a signal oddity of Islam's foundational document. The work in question knows that it is a "book." The name of this book, we are told again and again, is "the Qur'ān." Not only is it conscious of itself, but of its merits as well. It describes itself as "glorious," "wise," "clear," "the Book with the truth," and so on. So flush is this document with a sense of its incomparability that it challenges others to come up with something better. "If you doubt what We have revealed to Our servant," it affirms, "produce one chapter comparable to it." When the Hebrew Bible wants to prove the greatness of God it depicts God's greatness. The Qur'ān does that and more, it also points to the greatness of the Qur'ān. As Daniel Madigan recently put it: "The Qur'ān is both itself and *about* itself."[3]

The work in question also displays far less naivete about its interpretive afterlife than its Hebrew counterpart. Cognizant of the fact that it will be read and heard, it draws the logical conclusion that some will not read and hear it the right way. Haunted by the specter of misinterpretation, the Qur'ān launches a preemptive hermeneutical strike *by rehearsing potential criticisms of the Qur'ān*. Commenting on the curiosity that the divine transmission was sent in stages, one sura reads: "The unbelievers ask: 'Why was the Koran not revealed to him entire in a single revelation?'" The response: "We have revealed it thus so that We may sustain your heart. We have imparted it to you by gradual revelation." One well-known passage asserts that the Holy Book contains clear and ambiguous elements. The unclear sections seem to attract the scrutiny of those "whose hearts are infected with disbelief." These types of people try to explain these ambiguities, oblivious to the fact that "no one knows its meaning except God." Elsewhere it is declared that the deity actually *prevents* certain individuals from understanding His message. One thus misunderstands or criticizes the Qur'ān because one is either an unbeliever, or afflicted by God, or both.[4]

The Qur'ān's conception of its own genesis is also strikingly distinct. Readers are repeatedly reminded that it comes from, or better yet, comes down from, Allah. One would be hard pressed to think of any verses in the Old or New Testaments as explicit as the following: "This Koran could not have been devised by any but God. It confirms what was revealed before it and fully explains the Scriptures. It is beyond doubt from the Lord of the Universe." In the sura entitled "The Cave," the Prophet Muhammad is instructed to "Proclaim what has been revealed to you from the Book of your Lord." "You have received the Koran," it is reported, "from Him who is wise and all-knowing." The thirty-second sura opens, "This Book is beyond all doubt revealed by the Lord of the Universe."[5]

INTERPRETIVE QUIET ZONES AND HOTSPOTS

When looking at the history of interpretation one finds that during given periods certain issues fail to generate noise, conflict, ructions, and vitriol. Exegetes might say very little about a given scriptural problem for centuries, and what they do say indicates that the question has been answered to just about everybody's satisfaction. Discussions of same-sex eroticism among Christians, for example, were never particularly contentious prior to the mid-twentieth century. Most intellectuals seemed to agree that it was expressly forbidden by Scripture and Tradition; no need to get all worked up over proof texts when no one is demanding proof. These "interpretive quiet zones," which can prevail for long stretches of time, are the opposite of what we will call "interpretive hotspots."[6]

The concept of the quiet zone aptly describes the manner in which Muslim thinkers have engaged the question of the Qur'ān's authorship. With few exceptions, the overwhelming majority of Islamic orthodoxies, from past to present, have championed the message discussed previously. Hava Lazarus-Yafeh notes that, "The final consensus which evolved before the tenth century, and still binds Muslims to this very day, though in a slightly mitigated form, speaks about the uncreated, inimitable miracle of the Qur'ān, the transmission of which is faultless and totally reliable." Shabbir Akhtar points to a widespread belief that the text is "the literal and immutable word of Allah."[7]

That the Qur'ān comes from God is a theme that the Qur'ān certainly "puts out there." In this regard, the trajectory of Islamic theological speculation was, from the outset, angled differently from that of Judaism and Christianity. Muslim interpretive traditions have championed this idea and disseminated it across the earth. But let us not foster the illusion that the dominant understanding is "correct" or has "gotten it right." Ambiguities and contradictions *can* be found. As one famed Medieval Qur'ānic commentator acknowledged, "According to the opinion of some scholars, every verse can be understood sixty thousand ways." A dexterous secular hermeneut – preferably one trained in classical Arabic – could easily find evidence to counterexegete claims of divine authorship. Finding irregularities in the Qur'ān, incidentally, was a pastime that occupied many Jewish and Christian polemicists in the Middle Ages. Within the Islamic fold, there has also been occasional dissent. The Mu'tazila school of roughly the ninth through thirteenth centuries comes to mind. Richard Martin and Mark Woodward describe them as "theological rationalists" whose first principle was that "God can and must be known rationally." They famously argued that the Qur'ān was created, and hence was not an attribute of God. After a short period of rule (and, apparently, tyranny), their views became equated with heresy.[8]

Far less unanimity is seen in Jewish and Christian interpretive traditions. There, the question of who wrote the Bible clearly qualifies to be called a hotspot. From the Rabbis in *Baba Bathra* 14a bluntly asking, "Who wrote the Scriptures?" to the numerous contestations of early Christian heresies, the matter of scriptural authorship has always been a source of dissensus. This has much to do with silences and inconsistencies that riddle the sacred text. To give the most obvious example: on purely internal grounds, it is quite impossible to discern who wrote the first five books. How early Judaism and Christianity came to ascribe the entire composition to Moses is anybody's guess. It is not surprising, however, that voices in nearly every postbiblical generation have questioned either the Bible's account of its authorship and/or that of its canonical interpreters. Of course, in premodern times, a Jewish or Christian critic was well advised to issue such challenges quietly or cryptically or, better yet, not at all. "Let him who understands the secret be silent" – those are the memorable words of the twelfth-century Jewish polymath Ibn Ezra as he realizes that Moses could not have written various verses ascribed to him.[9]

This is not to say that the Qur'ān and the Bible are identical objects for secular analysis. They differ markedly in terms of their textual history. The most critical studies of Qur'ānic composition suggest that the text was assembled over the span of a few centuries, as opposed to the near millennium in which the Bible was probably put together. If secular hermeneutics posits a nexus between composition and interpretation, then it logically follows that the distinct composition of the Qur'ān results in distinct interpretive possibilities. These issues are best left for the specialist who writes *The Secular Qur'ān*.[10]

MODERN BIBLICAL SCHOLARSHIP: HEROISM AND LATENT SECULARIZING THRUST

In the modern Occident, circumstances eventually prevailed in which criticisms of Scripture and Tradition could be openly expressed. In the universities and seminaries of the Western world, the once infallible Hebrew Bible has been laid low, made mortal. Scholars identify cheerfully its grammatical and linguistic irregularities. They routinely list clumsy interpolations performed by ham-fisted editors. No pangs of conscience are evident when archaeologists demonstrate that the facts excavated from the soil of the Holy Land do not corroborate the depictions found in the Holy Book. More than a few modern exegetes extract (and often excoriate) what they perceive to be the ideological prejudices of various biblical authors. Discussions of their patriarchal, racist, classist, or heterosexist biases have proliferated in recent years. The sacred text is now fallible like us. Guilty, too! Verdicts of this nature are, more often than not, reached by scholars employed in Jewish and Christian institutions of higher learning.[11]

How did it ever come to this? The turbulent rise and reign (and more recent retreat in the face of postmodernism) of critical approaches to the Bible have been abundantly chronicled. We need make only a few general remarks here. Suffice it to say that the period from roughly 1500 to the present witnessed the slow, uneven, and perhaps inadvertent development of a rational and skeptical way of thinking about the composition of Scripture. The process accelerated dramatically in the second half of the nineteenth century. It was then that scholars in Europe, and soon after in North America, began to consolidate centuries of blasphemous hunches about the authorship of the Old Testament. Never slow to respond to blasphemous hunches, ecclesiastical and academic institutions immediately ascertained the heretical implications of this enterprise.[12]

The two figures most associated with these outrages, Julius Wellhausen and his Scottish colleague William Robertson Smith, are known mostly to biblicists and intellectual historians. This is unfortunate because their accomplishments are every bit as world altering as those of Darwin, Marx, Nietzsche, and Freud. Robertson Smith outraged his church for, among other things, questioning the dogma that Moses composed Deuteronomy. Wellhausen argued that the Hebrew Bible is out of chronological order. Its Prophetic sections, he famously concluded, were written prior to the laws found in the Torah. This would be a shock to an orthodox reader. For in the canonized Bible the Torah is positioned before the Prophets. The Pentateuch, he continued, was not a unified composition. Rather it was the amalgam of different documents written at different times (see Chapter Two). Of course, there were numerous other components to their arguments. But for our purposes let it be noted that questions of authorship, of "Where on earth did this text come from?", figured prominently in their research and the outcry that it elicited.[13]

These initiatives initially encountered staunch resistance. Yet, the speed by which the controversial tenets of "higher criticism" became standard, even orthodox, assumptions of modern biblical scholarship is astounding. After a few tumultuous decades in the late nineteenth century, the new orientation settled in quickly among the more liberal Protestant denominations. Catholic and Jewish scholars were somewhat slower to get with the program. But among them as well, the conversion occurred with remarkable rapidity. One might compare the Church's *Lamentabili* of 1907 and its hostility toward the newfangled approach with the *Divino Afflante Spiritu* of 1943 or the 1993 *The Interpretation of the Bible in the Church*. The latter two documents illustrate a new openness to various forms of critical inquiry. As for Jews, S. David Sperling notes that by the later decades of the twentieth century, "the Jewish quasi-taboo against higher critical study of the Pentateuch had been shattered." No longer could someone equate higher criticism with "higher anti-Semitism," as Solomon Schechter famously did in 1903.[14]

Let us linger on the most curious fact. The patriarchs, architects, and martyrs of higher criticism over a century ago were, almost exclusively, religious men. Although deeply pious, they practiced what Richard Riesen has called "believing criticism." This is defined as "an attempt to advance faith, not in spite of, but by means of, the critical method." To read about the heresy trials, excommunications, and faculty expulsions of this period is to read about religious scholars who – to their great surprise – ran afoul of their respective orthodoxies. Permit us to suggest that their inquisitors may have had a better understanding of their work than the heretics did. Modern biblical scholarship, although birthed by religious intellectuals, has a latent secularizing thrust. At best, it insinuates that the Bible does not know itself. At worst, it implies that the text is willfully deceitful in its presentation of self.[15]

We must not underestimate the world-historical significance of this development. For where else have the most learned scholars of a given religious tradition participated in a collective intellectual endeavor that is skeptical of that very tradition? The emergence of a critical and self-critical framework for the study of the Bible must be reckoned not only as an effect, but also as a cause (and stabilizer) of Occidental modernity and its attendant secularizing impulses. If some of us no longer live under the hegemony of the Book, if we are free to interpret it as we want, completely ignore it, or even heckle it, then we must see the believing critics as partly responsible for these novel privileges and pleasures.

SECULARIZING THE QUR'ĀN: THE TRIPLE OBSTACLES

Nowadays, this rational and skeptical orientation to the Hebrew Bible has become commonplace. Its carriers are mostly religious (or once religious) men and women. These believing critics perform their research within institutions of knowledge-production deemed as legitimate within the Occident (i.e., universities, seminaries). Self-censorship is fairly rare. There is no need to veil or encode one's findings about the Old Testament. The practice of critical biblical scholarship is not very dangerous. On the contrary, it is so marginalized within the Academy, the Church/Synagogue, and society at large (see Chapter Five) that one wonders if the occasional exegete doesn't relish a little joust with the religious powers that be and the scandalized masses.

A rational and skeptical framework for analysis of the Qur'ān, one carried by religious intellectuals, has never achieved legitimacy in the Islamic world. There are, in all likelihood, numerous believing critics among Muslim exegetes. Few, however, are willing or able to share their skeptical insights with the public at large. Jousting with the 'ulamā (i.e., "guardians, transmitters, and interpreters of religious knowledge, of Islamic doctrine, and law") and scandalizing the masses is something that very few intellectuals would want to do. This is one fairly obvious lesson to be learned from the Rushdie affair or the plight of a persecuted believing critic such as the Egyptian scholar Nasr Abū Zaid.[16]

A critical Qur'ānic scholarship on par with biblical studies has not developed in Muslim societies. A. P. Welch writes: "The doctrines of the eternity and perfection or inimitability of the Kur'ān contributed to its extensive influence throughout Islamic life and culture.... At the same time, these two doctrines have been the strongest factor working against the acceptance of critical studies of the Kur'ān within the modern Muslim community ... modern Muslims [are] loathe to accept methods of historical and literary criticism that have proved so fruitful in the study of other scriptures." John Wansbrough, famed for his highly skeptical assessment of Qur'ānic text and tradition, comments: "As a document susceptible of analysis by the instruments and techniques of Biblical criticism it is virtually unknown."[17]

It might be imagined that the accomplishments of modern biblical scholarship would have nudged Qur'ānic studies in a more skeptical direction. In fact, the very opposite seems to have occurred. Surveying contemporary thought, Daniel Brown observes that the modern period has witnessed an even less critical approach than seen in previous centuries. In outlining this "triumph of scripturalism," Brown concludes,

"Rather than being 'humanized' as we might expect by analogies with modern trends in Christian or Jewish thought scripture has become even more distant and untouchable." The Algerian French scholar, Mohammed Arkoun, summarizes the situation in the following manner: "As for Muslim scholarship it continues to inflict upon itself limitations, mutilations and prohibitions that only accentuate the dependency and backwardness of qur'anic studies."[18]

The question arises as to why an orientation that has become commonplace among Jewish and Christian intellectuals has failed to gain adherents among Muslim thinkers. Issues of textual origins are relevant to our answer. The Qur'ān's insistence on its divine origins constitutes one very formidable barrier. Shabbir Akhtar is certainly correct when he comments, "The idea of a critical Qur'anic scholarship is blasphemous." For how can a mortal criticize the word of God? As Akhtar phrases it, "Revelation judges men, men do not judge revelation." Could a pious Muslim easily explore the possibility that some of the text's contents were not revealed by the deity? Or that its human authors retained a patriarchal bias? Or that scribal errors have garbled its message? Or that its recollection of biblical episodes is not terrifically accurate? Any of this would be tantamount to heresy. Compounding the difficulties is the Qur'ān's own foreclosing of criticism by attributing dissent to unbelief.[19]

Mainstream interpretive traditions provide another hindrance. These have almost always amplified those sections of the Qur'ān that speak of its godly origins. Under such circumstances any attempt to apply critical methods risks confronting not only God's word, but that of the (interpretive) community at large. This brings us to the final obstruction: social structure. It would be hard to think of many arenas in the Islamic world where one can publicly engage in rational and skeptical textual criticism. There exist few institutions akin to the liberal seminaries and university religious studies departments of the West. Even if one overcame the psychological and intellectual impediments of Scripture and Tradition, fora in which heretical ideas may be expressed are extremely rare.[20]

A class of critical Muslim Qur'ānists is presently nonexistent or very marginal. In terms of our brief analysis, at least three major hurdles stand in their way. These would be 1) a text that is adamant about its divine origins although not always unimpeachably so, 2) normative interpretive traditions that have concurred for nearly the entire breadth of Islamic history (though not without exceptions), and 3) sociological factors that make the public contestation of either text or Tradition difficult, if not sometimes dangerous. In light of these triple obstacles, it will take an abundance of heroism on the part of Muslim intellectuals to secularize – that is, render amenable to criticism – the Qur'ān.

CONCLUSION: THE NEW MU'TAZILA

It is not, of course, our contention that the recent explosion of Islamic extremism is *nothing but* a consequence of the absence of skeptical Qur'ānic inquiry among Muslim theologians. The relation between the two is far more complex and mediated. We prefer to say that institutionalized believing criticism may function as a solvent of religious fanaticism, one that undermines its political potency and popularity. This means that modern biblical scholars are – however inadvertently – central and even heroic players in the saga of secular modernity. No attempt to trigger the much sought-after "Islamic Reformation" will succeed without the emergence of a comparable class in the Muslim world.

Why do we attribute such importance to believing critics? The subversive power of self-critical religious intellectuals stems from their belongingness, expertise, and creedal autonomy. By belongingness, we mean to say that these critics are members of the religious groups whose texts they are criticizing. They are "one of us" and hence immune from the predictable charge of being prejudiced or ill-disposed toward the "us" in question. Expertise refers to their possession of specialized religious knowledge. They read the sacred languages, master interpretive traditions, are fluent in doctrine, ritual, and so on. Their biographical credentials are quite similar to those of traditional religious intellectuals. Yet unlike the latter they do not spend their time articulating, transmitting, and defending orthodox dogma. Their primary fealty as scholars is to rational inquiry, not Tradition.

But one cannot very well serve two lords, and it is little wonder that these conflicting loyalties tend to get believing critics into trouble. The history of religious thought is strewn with cases (and bodies) of thinkers who – *now how'd that happen?* – accidentally wandered into the most sacrilegious territory. Their heretical findings were not usually born of animus toward religion, but of the inevitable trespass that occurs whenever reasoned inquiry is asked to visit religious belief. In earlier times, such thinkers in the Western world were often rewarded for their integrity with quite inventive forms of physical punishment. As recompense today, they are left to languish in almost total obscurity. Self-critical religious intellectuals have never been much appreciated. They should be because Judaism, Christianity, and Islam need them, as does secularism.[21]

Religious extremists, on the other hand, could clearly do without them. This is because believing critics cast doubts on the highly simplistic and tendentious readings of sacred documents that typify fundamentalist projects. In response to the fanatic's self-confident assertion that "*The Bible says this!*" the intellectual responds, "*Well, maybe not.*" In Chapter Seven, we noted that Christian conservatives and various official Christian creeds – few of whom could be described as militant – insist that homosexuality is categorically condemned in the Bible. Affirmations of this type are routinely assailed by exegetes who, for good measure, also disagree with one another. Sacred Scripture is never simple, transparent, and unequivocal. Biblical scholars are those people who bring this inconvenient fact to our attention. In so doing, they infect the social body with doubt. The fundamentalist craves immediate social action, if not social upheaval, on the basis of Scripture's alleged mandates. Believing critics, in contrast, provide the faithful with cognitive braking mechanisms, countless reasons to hesitate before acting on the Bible's behalf.

The existence of this self-critical cohort is also of great symbolic import. If Sacred Scripture and Tradition can be criticized, then why not contemporary orthodoxies, or anything else for that matter? Higher criticism, whatever its flaws may be, represents the apotheosis of the human faculty of critique. It has sanctified the once impermissible act of questioning God's Book and the venerable traditions that had protectively clustered around its imperfect body. The mere presence of a class of believing critics confers legitimacy on the most sacred of secular values. Moreover, it serves as a resource and refuge for those who are not religious. The political philosopher Tariq Ali has observed that, "In reality millions of skeptics, agnostics, and atheists currently live in the Islamic world. They dare not speak in public for fear of the response, but they will not keep silent forever." The presence of Muslim Qur'ānic scholars who publicly express their own skepticism, we submit, might embolden them to break their silence.[22]

In light of the triple obstacles discussed earlier, it would seem highly unlikely that believing criticism will achieve institutional stature in most Islamic societies. A more likely seedbed for this development would be among the diasporic Muslim intelligentsia. Wherever it comes from, it is essential that rational Qur'ānic criticism emerge from within Muslim theological circles and be predicated on ideas indigenous to its rich exegetical traditions. Omid Safi has rightly insisted that a progressive Islamic agenda must derive "its inspiration from the heart of the Islamic tradition. It cannot survive as a graft of Secular Humanism onto the tree of Islam, but must emerge from within that very entity." So we await the new (and more tolerant) Mu'tazila. One of their many tasks will consist of making the question of authorship a hotspot again.[23]

We close with a caveat. A critical orientation to Sacred Scripture is not a panacea for all of humanity's ills. Even with "higher criticism," the Occident of the twentieth century has shown itself to be vulnerable to recurring paroxysms of the most appalling violence. True, these were not typically committed in the name of religion, but this would be little consolation to the millions of victims of internal and external Western aggression. So, in good secular faith, let us not deify or reify believing criticism. It does not bring about the salvation of the species. It does, however, go a long way in dampening those irrational passions that occasionally overcome all religious groups.

SUGGESTIONS FOR FURTHER READING

A few works that we found helpful in putting together this chapter will be mentioned here. An extremely useful resource is Jane Dammen McAuliffe's *Encyclopaedia of the Qur'ān. A–D.* Leiden: Brill, 2001. Its many articles are clear, up-to-date, and balanced. Shabbir Akhtar's "Critical Qur'anic Scholarship and Theological Puzzles" and "The Limits of Internal Hermeneutics: The Status of the Qur'an as Literary Miracle," both in *Holy Scriptures in Judaism, Christianity and Islam: Hermeneutics, Values and Society.* Eds. Hendrik Vroom and Jerald Gort. Amsterdam: Rodopi, 1997, are of great interest. An honorary secular hermeneut would be the critical and learned Mohammed Arkoun. His *Rethinking Islam: Common Questions, Uncommon Answers.* Boulder: Westview Press, 1994, is an excellent primer in humanistic analysis. We must also mention the apostate

Ibn Warraq who has edited collections of studies that are highly critical of Muslim pieties. These volumes are invaluable, although the author adopts the highly confrontational attitude to religion that we view as something of a dead end for secular criticism (see the Conclusion). That having been said, Ibn Warraq is to be lauded and admired for his critical heroism. On contemporary issues, one might consult the collection *Progressive Muslims: On Justice, Gender and Pluralism*. Ed. Omid Safi. Oxford: Oneworld, 2003. In terms of today's politics, the short, readable book, *The Place of Tolerance in Islam*. Eds. Joshua Cohen and Ian Lague. Boston: Beacon Press, 2002, is also recommended.

Conclusion: Beyond Church and State: New Directions for Secularism

> The fact of the matter is that secularism in our day can claim no energizing vision and no revolutionary élan, not as in the past. Instead, it sits passive and inert, heavily dependent upon the missteps and excesses of the Religious Right or some similar foe to make its case, stir up its fading enthusiasm, and rally its remaining troops. Secularism sits uneasy upon its throne, a monarch that dares not speak in its proper name, and dares not openly propound its agenda, if indeed it still has one. For all its gains, it seems peculiarly on the defensive, old and quaint, a tenured radical who has ascended to the endowed chair of culture only to spend its days shoring up the principle of *stare decisis.*
>
> Wilfred McClay, "Two Concepts of Secularism"

As far as most secularists are concerned, sacred texts are inconsequential relics, repositories of antiquated theopolitical mumbo jumbo. But if there is as much as one tangible "policy implication" to be gleaned from the present work, then it might be stated as follows: in the post–September 11 world, nonbelievers can no longer afford to remain oblivious to the combustive interplay of Scripture and ideas about Scripture. Even the most dim-witted secularist could not fail to construe recent current events as an invitation to think through the whole religion "thing" a bit more carefully. One might think, for instance, about how Americans returned in droves to their houses of worship in the aftermath of an atrocity that illustrated (yet again) the absolute worst that religion has to offer. True, most of those newfound, autumnal congregants quickly reverted to their delinquent patterns of attendance. Yet, in no way does this demonstrate a predilection for Godlessness or nonbelief in the United States. It merely points to secularization's extraordinary success in preventing the faithful in this country from getting too overwrought.[1]

Secularists have much more to think about because, to be perfectly frank, secularism is in a state of intellectual emergency. Its worldview has matured little and remains moored in the mid-twentieth century. Its magazines of opinion have grown stale. Its leading lights are old or long dead. Lacking a cadre of public intellectuals, it is incapable of defending, or articulating, its own depassé ideals. In the West, where anything goes, secularists have even lost their ability to shock the pious. Once the pleasure of sacrilege has been democratized, what fun is there in blasphemy? This all occurs against the backdrop of a worldwide revitalization of religion. Some groups have revitalized themselves just a bit too much. Informed, critical assessments of mass religious movements are now needed more than ever. If secularism is to persevere as the minority position that it has always been (and should always be), it will need to rethink itself. In this chapter, we identify some dilemmas and desiderata that confront nonbelievers as they enter the most challenging era in their brief history.

THE SECULAR TYRANNY MYTH

We have alluded to the tendency of secularists to think of religion, *all* religion, in terms of religious extremism. Now it is undeniable that the threat posed by extremists is real. Never again will we doubt their commitment to delivering misery and suffering to as many people as possible. It must be recalled, however, that these groups are still relatively rare. A more concrete and pervasive challenge comes from a rather different cohort: religious fundamentalists who pursue their agenda by working within the parameters of the law. There is an enormous difference between, let's say, Al-Qaeda and an Islamist political party such as Turkey's defunct Welfare (Refah) Party. Similarly, the splinter group that produced the assassin of the prime minister of Israel is not the same as the religious Shas Party. This does not rule out the existence of occasional sympathies or even alliances between unlawful and lawful fundamentalists. Still, secularists need to contemplate the distinction between those who want to transform society through violence and those who want to do so by operating within existing political structures. Then again, if law-abiding fundamentalists were ever to achieve their desired transformation nothing assures us they would not obliterate the existing political structures with dispatch. We are reminded of V. S. Naipul's observation that as far as believers are concerned, "faith was full of rules," but "in politics there were none."[2]

The discerning secularist, we have repeatedly argued, must also take into account another constituency, those whom we have referred to as the secularly religious. They are true moderns, epistemologically fractured souls, grandchildren of the "believing critics" discussed in the previous chapter. Among the secularly religious in the Occident, there exists a significant contingent of political progressives. In a country like the United States, it would seem plausible for these left-leaning religious moderates to join secularists in an antifundamentalist coalition. The possibilities are intriguing. The religious Left would bring to the table its sizable numbers, its far-reaching network of civic organizations, and decades of experience in grassroots activism. Secularists, for their part, would bring to the table... *what is it again that secularists bring to the table?* Demographically, they are not numerous. Politically, they are atomized much like the nineteenth-century French peasantry that Karl Marx once likened to "potatoes in a sack." Candidates for elected office in the United States are not known for "playing the secular card." This is because it makes little sense to pander to a tiny constituency whose core beliefs about the universe are completely at odds with those held by everyone else in the country.[3]

Secularists – we say this as delicately as possible – are not an electoral prize. It is questionable whether religious progressives actually need (or want) their partnership. But the opposite also holds true. Nonbelievers, as we observed in our discussion of same-sex eroticism, have every right to ask whether those on the religious Left are their natural allies. Going a bit further – we are in a state of emergency after all – we pose the following unspeakable query: is liberalism the *only* legitimate political philosophy for secularists to espouse? Are there no components of either conservative or radical worldviews that share common ground with secular ideals? Our goal is not to prescribe a political plan of action for nonbelievers. We merely suggest that it makes little sense to cling to old and simple articles of faith when so many new and complex possibilities have emerged.

Although the contemporary religious landscape is indeed new and complex, religious attitudes toward secularism are nowhere near as varied. Succumbing to a fate that afflicts all minority groups that happen to be elites, secularists are not tremendously popular. Even Harvey Cox – whose appreciation for the process of secularization is unsurpassed among theologians – could muster few kind words for the movement known as secularism (the distinction between secularization and secularism will be discussed momentarily). The latter in Cox's estimation was "the name for an ideology, a new closed world-view, which functions very much like a new religion." Secularism, he cautioned in 1965, must "be watched carefully." More recently, Martin Marty exclaimed, "Oppose secularism but thank god for the secular." A less benign variant of these sentiments appears today in a "secular tyranny myth" that has proliferated globally. In its American incarnation, the United States is portrayed as suffering under the rule of a secular Apartheid regime. The majority of the nation's God-fearing citizens have been subjected to the domination of a privileged faction. Perched in the judiciary, the media, and universities, these nonbelievers impose on the populace a draconian separation of Church and State. The original framers of the Constitution – pious citizens every last one of them – never had such a radical division in mind.[4]

It is beyond the scope of this study to respond in detail to the American version of the myth promulgated by – but not only by – the Religious Right. Suffice it to say that like all such caricatures it attributes far too much historical significance, power, and organizational cunning to secularists. Throughout this work, and in deference to our less humanist conception of things, we have pointed to consequences that result independent of human will. Much in the way that the Bible produces readings that none of its contributors ever dreamed of, history produces outcomes that are beyond the intentionality of agents. Secularists had little to do with erecting the putatively antireligious foundations of the Constitution that have served them so well. The Establishment Clause – a passage so perfectly vague, so amenable to conflicting interpretations, that one wonders if the Founding Fathers lifted those two verses from an unknown biblical manuscript stashed away in some Masonic lodge – was not born of secular ideals. "The religion clauses," writes one scholar, "were not intended as an instrument of secularization, or as a weapon that the non-religious or anti-religious could use to suppress the effusions of the religious."[5]

Proponents of tyranny myths err in that they blame secularization on secularism. Secularization is a broad sociological process centuries – some would say millennia – in the making. By nearly all accounts, it is not the product of human planning and forethought – no one person or group willed it into existence. Yet, its chief result is experienced by all, namely, the diminishing role that religion plays in the various departments of life. Secularism, in contrast, loosely refers to a diverse array of nontheistic social movements achieving visibility around the early nineteenth century and spiking in popularity toward the mid-twentieth century. The separation of powers may indeed be an early example of secularization's advance. It has little to do, however, with the crafty designs of flesh-and-blood secularists (whose presence in colonial America was not exceedingly large). Separation, moreover, is an idea that has been repeatedly defended by *nonsecularists*. When Alexis de Tocqueville warned about "the dangers that may accrue from a union of church and state," he was not expressing atheist dogma. Rather, he espoused an idea repeatedly championed by religious groups to this day.[6]

In more recent years, well-spoken religious thinkers – precisely the sort of intellectuals who are missing in action in the secular camp – have decried the marginalization of religion in the public sphere. In *The Culture of Disbelief*, Stephen Carter spoke of what he viewed as a misreading of the Establishment Clause. It was not meant as a "guarantor of public secularism" (which is what Carter claims it has become), but "a guardian of religious liberty." Secularism, argued Richard John Neuhaus in *The Naked Public Square*, has had "a perverse and debilitating effect on our public life." Yet if measured by their ability to prevent society-wide religious intolerance and violence, prevailing readings of the Establishment Clause have performed quite capably. A country whose history of racial tolerance is nothing less than deplorable has demonstrated a degree of interreligious tranquility worthy of the world's envy. Many contemporary religious intellectuals fail to realize (or admit) what a boon *to religion* the Separation of Powers and its prevailing judicial interpretations have been. Keeping the public square "naked" is a small price to pay for preventing religions from achieving, yet again, their absolute worst. The irony, the dilemma, is that an undemocratic ideal, an ideal not necessarily rooted in the consensual will of the majority, best serves the interests of that majority.[7]

SECULAR WORKS: NEW PROJECTS FOR SECULAR
INTELLECTUALS

In light of the preceding remarks, the following recommendation may startle the reader: the time has arrived to think and move beyond separation of Church and State. American secularism's immense, nearly exclusive investment in this one issue has not only stunted its growth, but also resulted in a handy stereotype to accompany the aforementioned myth. To conjure up an image of a secularist is to picture a legal scholar or ACLU activist fulminating about why the likeness of Frosty the Snowman should not be gracing the courthouse steps in December. Careful attention to judicial interpretations of the Establishment Clause is undeniably necessary. Yet, this alone is not sufficient for the intellectual, or dare we say, "spiritual," well-being of nonbelievers. The zeal to perform ideological maintenance work on the Wall of Separation has turned American secularism into a movement of nuisance suits. Religious conservatives of the most politicized and media-hawking type have become their conversational partners. With interlocutors such as these, virtues such as self-criticism and analytical nuance tend to get lost in the acrimonious exchange. In hopes of returning some of the luster to a worldview that once spoke the unspeakable with considerable dash, we suggest a few alternative projects.[8]

First, a response to the bruising critique of secularism that has emerged from within the academy is urgently needed. In recent decades, postcolonialist and postmodernist thinkers have cornered, shaken down, and placed in a headlock the formerly indomitable trio of enlightenment, modernity, and secularization/secularism (they also sometimes confuse the process and the social movement). That these critics espouse positions that bear more than a passing resemblance to those held by hardcore religious conservatives has been observed. Wilfred McClay speaks of the "fascinating convergence of what might very loosely be called 'fundamentalist' and 'postmodern' perspectives, each very hostile to secularism, in the emergence of 'postliberal' Christian theologies." Emboldened by the absence of any riposte, the indictment from these quarters has swelled to include a litany of interrelated accusations. Secularism is a legitimating ideology for Occidental imperialism. Secularism has ruthlessly desecrated traditional ways of life. Secularism insists on its own neutrality but actually serves the interests of majoritarian religious groups. Secularism is a shill for advanced capitalism. Secularism retains a "theoretical and practical affinity with political despotism." For many, the political principles of secularism are viewed as something that only work in those Christian polities where they were born. Thus, the grafting of its ideas on non-Christian social bodies is wont to yield catastrophic social mutations.[9]

Although the typical university faculty is disproportionately populated by irreligious and areligious types, few scholars seem interested in responding to these charges. We are not quite there yet, but a day may come when college-educated persons will come to think of secularism as not only reprehensible in the moral sense (as its religious detractors have argued with such finesse), but as a political alternative to be likened to Totalitarianism. Or maybe it will be construed as an ideological curio from the olden days, something on the order of the Futurist movement. In accordance with the self-critical spirit of secularism, the merits of the aforementioned accusations should be acknowledged. The massive and inexcusable human rights' failures of polities such as Algeria, Tunisia, North Korea, and the ex-Soviet Union, among others, should be thought about carefully. Indeed, an autopsy of failed secular regimes, particularly those in the Middle East, will be especially useful in conceptualizing the inhumane possibilities that lurk within worldviews that purport to be deeply concerned about humanity.[10]

But not everything, we repeat, is politics. If we have made this claim throughout this book, then this is because we write at a time in which the discourse of politics pervades everything. A trip to the local aquarium, for example, includes an obligatory harangue on "bad big government," endangered ecosystems, and the irresponsible actions of corporate fishing interests. All are serious and real issues, but can't one merely enjoy the Vaudeville charms of a seal flapping its flippers without the accompaniment of social commentary? In the academy, as in the aquarium, we have gone political. Today's scholar must be prepared to not only connect his or her research to contemporary political concerns, but also to forthrightly articulate his or her own political vision. Whether this has produced better scholarship than that served up in the age that clung to an illusory ideal of objectivity and nonpartisanship is open to debate. We simply note that there are *less* political (although not necessarily apolitical) ways of approaching scholarly subject matter. The projects we suggest in this section are not geared to ideological combat or social change. In terms of public policy decisions, they offer little or no "cash value." They are merely queries and projects that we believe may be of intellectual interest.

Although much has been written – perhaps too much – about secularization, studies of secularists and what we could call "secular culture" are uncommon. A comprehensive history of secularism has yet to appear. Even the term "secular" remains ambiguous. The theologian Gabriel Vahanian writes: "No other word has been more maligned than the word 'secular'. Its connotations encompass so diverse a debauchery of meaning as to throw anyone endowed with the least love of words into a dizzying puzzle of bewilderment." Imbricated designations such as "humanist," "atheist," "agnostic," "freethinker," are also underdefined, as are the interrelations and antagonisms among those who refer to themselves with these terms. The ethnic and cultural composition of such groups has never been studied. Our hunch, by the way, is that diversity is not presently a great strength of nonbelieving movements.[11]

Secularism's well-known infatuation with science and technology has obscured any exploration of its considerable reflexes in the arts. This occurs in spite of the fact that there are legions of novelists, painters, playwrights, poets, dancers, filmmakers, architects, and so on, whose work is animated by a conscious rejection of religious standards of form, truth, and beauty. These figures have been discussed individually qua artists. But no attempt has been made to draw out the connections and recurring themes across their work. The study of "secular aesthetics" would take stock of that tremendous body of work produced in often contentious dialogue with religion. Such inquiries could take us anywhere from the fiction of Philip Roth and Salman Rushdie, to a cinematic appraisal of Fellini's infamous Vatican fashion show in *Roma*, to the architecture of Le Corbusier, to analyses of Chinese and Soviet poster art. If finding novel ways of thinking about the secular is a priority, then perhaps the realm of the arts offers more promise than that of politics or science.

Might we also call attention to the "secular adjective"? Little in the way of theoretical speculation has been devoted to the fact that so many individuals refer to themselves as "secular Jews." The phrase "secular Muslim" is increasingly heard and it is our surmise that there is a growing population in both Islamic countries and the diaspora that might be comfortable with this designation. ("Secular Christian," in contrast, surfaces far less frequently and this too raises interesting questions.) Those who retain the adjective apparently do not want to affect a categorical and dogmatic break with religion. They are therefore quite different from the cartoonesque despisers of religion who star in the passion plays of secular tyranny myths. They are also unlike those true-believing antireligious activists who have always gravitated to positions of prominence in secular movements. Adjectived secularists might profitably be seen as the mirror image of the secularly religious in that they have no particular animus or institutionalized dislike for others. Generally shunned from secularist movements, the time has perhaps arrived to recognize their presence and possibilities. In a similar vein, it must be asked if the secular orientation toward religion must *always* be antagonistic. More curiosity, less hatred. In highly secularized nations that might be a less infantile stance.[12]

Many of the projects mentioned previously need to be undertaken by professional scholars. This is where our program for the rejuvenation of secular intellectual culture encounters obstacles. Irreligious and areligious persons who study matters pertaining to the sacred are few and far between. Further, there exist almost no fora in which the expressly nontheistic study of religion takes place. In theory, the university provides such a space. But as we have observed again and again, the religious studies department is, typically, an ecumenical space. It is an arena in which believing and once-believing critics representing different religious traditions can converse with one another. This is not to deny that many truly enlightening discussions about religion may take place there. Need we repeat again, with even jerkier semaphore strokes, that *WE-RES-PECT BIB-LIC-AL-SCHOL-ARS . . . A-LOT?* Yet, insofar as few new secularists and almost no heritage secularists participate in these conversations, a certain edge seems to be lacking. Our call – note this – is not for a purge that will result in a discipline comprised solely of debunking atheists. We merely maintain that the presence of alternative, nontheistic approaches in biblical (and religious) studies will provide much needed intellectual diversity.

There is no easy or immediate solution to this absence of balance. Not helping matters is the widespread belief, shared by many professors of religious studies and university administrators, that this lack of equilibrium is not a problem. Yet, if the dominance of ecumenical, as opposed to critical, orientations toward the study of religion is indeed a cause for concern, then universities must play a leading role in rectifying this situation. For one, they should reconsider the practice of outsourcing so much of their religious studies instruction to local clergy or seminaries. They might also ask themselves about the propriety of donations and endowed chairs in religious studies. Almost without exception, these behests are provided by religious foundations or individuals. As openminded as such benefactors may sometimes be, they generally have little patience for the type of blasphemous conclusions that secular hermeneuts are so adept at reaching. University administrations – which have neither more nor less integrity than the average multinational corporation – tend to find this arrangement satisfactory. The happy dividend of having the Jew teach the Tanak, the Christian teach the Bible, and the Muslim teach the Holy Qur'ān is a dramatic reduction of those unfortunate campus conflagrations that overly critical lecturers tend to ignite. No believers brandishing percussion instruments and occupying the Provost's office, no burdensome trustees and elected officials demanding "curricular review," no Cardinals or antidefamation leagues calling for a boycott – that's what's so great about not having secularists teach in a religious studies department!

To their credit, believing critics sometimes manage to stumble over the tripwire of pious insecurities and set off the occasional campus meltdown. This is commendable. But we repeat that the academic study of the Bible, and religion in general, desperately needs an infusion of learned critics who are willing to draw blood. This is one way of putting an end to perennial discussions about why these disciplines are viewed as "second-rate" or "weak sisters" among the humanities. Ideally, a particularly forward-looking institution might commit itself to creating a department in which the explicitly nonconfessional study of religion is pursued. Such an endeavor would not necessarily be exclusionary. All researchers would be welcome to participate as long as they pronounce something approximating a secular *shahada*, or profession of faith: to love critique more than God.

DONE?: THE INESCAPABILITY OF RELIGION

The time has arrived to close the show down, as the jazz musicians like to say. Prior to doing so, a few parting words need to be said about the document that has served as the basis for our reflections on the plight of secularism. Like all sacred scriptures, the Hebrew Bible has endured a turbulent modernity. Now it can be rationally assessed. Now it can be interpreted any which way. Now it can be criticized, ignored, or subjected to the ignominy of secular hermeneutics. In an era of science and reason, pious Jews and Christians must wonder if Moses (and Joshua) really parted bodies of water, if the sun stood still at Gibeon, or if Ezekiel was actually transported by his hair from Babylon to Jerusalem. Secularization has subjugated faith to rationality. It has demanded that religious belief account for itself with some semblance of coherence. It has posited the existence of exteral criteria by which to measure this coherence. The pressures created by this request are, in part, responsible for reactions as varied as the global rise of fundamentalist movements on the one hand, and the proliferation of the secularly religious on the other.

But for all its disruption, enlightenment modernity never vanquished religion. The old did *not* die and the new *was*, in fact, born. It is this uneasy coexistence between premodern and modern worldviews that has produced tensions, compromises, and hybrids stranger than any beast conjured up in the Book of Daniel. The modern, or if you will, postmodern, subject is an intriguingly convoluted product of this encounter. A hundred or so years after Dostoyevsky, after Durkheim, after Weber, and after Freud, the interplay of belief and unbelief still deserves to be called a grand civilizational problematic, if not the grandest of them all. This is a dialectic that continues to forge the vast majority of individual and collective identities.

The Bible has been humbled, no doubt. But here in its third millennium of operations, it continues to exert world-altering effects. Sometimes it does so when modern interpreters confuse *a* meaning they have found in the text with *the* God-breathed meaning of the text. From there, they may try to inflict this reading on as many others as possible. They will, ostensibly, encounter resistance, and the protests of nonbelievers are usually the least of their worries. Nor let us ever underestimate what we might call – euphemistically – the Bible's untapped "potential." Skulking about in the unlighted alleys of Scripture are meaning possibilities that have yet to be activated, amplified, and altered by a given community of interpreters. This forthcoming encounter between sacred texts and its expositors may bring about consequences that were previously unthinkable.

In truth, the Bible's recent – and we believe, temporary – furlough from cultural supremacy has done little to lessen its relevance for our lives. The Good Book no longer needs to be the exclusive or central text of the Occident to exert its impact. After thousands of years of imaginative exegesis, after countless trysts with regimes of power, its diverse messages and contradictory readings have become lodged in the muscle memory of civilization. It influences us via channels that are obscure and difficult to discern. Conceptions of morality, sexual ethics, beauty, and so on, derived by biblical interpreters are not so much knowingly thought about and rationally assessed as they are enacted on a daily basis in a reflex-like manner. The seemingly Godless economic sector of the West still largely adheres to a religiously inflected calendar that mandates days of rest and days of labor. The nonbeliever who is about to engage in an evening of Bacchanalia – God bless her, we wish her well! – will experience feelings of guilt or euphoria that have much to do with trespassing on biblical ideas of female chastity. And even among secularists how many can actually accept the apparent and unbearable truth that when we die we are really dead? Finished. Done.

This is what makes the recurring secular hope of achieving a total and decisive break with religion as realistic as trying to eradicate the air. Better to try and understand how religion works – if only to grasp the manner in which it forges even the most secular self, if only to resist and subvert it, just a bit.

Notes

INTRODUCTION: SECULARISTS AND THE NOT GODLESS WORLD

1. On the abolishment of religion and the necessity of human emancipation, see Karl Marx, "The Jewish Question," in *The Marx-Engels Reader*, 2nd ed. Ed. Robert Tucker. New York: W. W. Norton, 1978, pp. 26–52. Sigmund Freud, *The Future of an Illusion*. Trans. James Strachey. New York: W. W. Norton, 1961, p. 55. Émile Durkheim, *The Elementary Forms of Religious Life*. Trans. Karen Fields. New York: The Free Press, 1995, p. 429. In a more recent article, a sociologist of knowledge declared, "once and for all, let us declare an end to social-scientific faith in the theory of secularization, recognizing that it was the product of wishful thinking." Rodney Stark, "Secularization, R.I.P.," *Sociology of Religion* 60 (1999) 249–273. See his remarks on the small demographic presence of atheists (p. 266). Also of interest is Jeffrey Hadden's "Desacralizing Secularization Theory," in *Secularization and Fundamentalism Reconsidered: Religion and the Political Order, Volume III*. Eds. Jeffrey Hadden and Anson Shupe. New York: Paragon House, 1989, pp. 3–26. More cautious assessments of the demise of secularization hypothesis can be found in José Casanova's thoughtful *Public Religions in the Modern World*. Chicago: University of Chicago Press, 1994, and N.J. Demerath III, "Secularization," in *Encyclopedia of Sociology: Volume 4*, 2nd ed. Ed. Edgar Borgatta. New York: Macmillan, 2000, pp. 2482–2491. The Gallup Poll's 1999 survey revealed that 96 percent of Americans believed in God. George Gallup, Jr. and D. Michael Lindsay, *Surveying the Religious Landscape: Trends in U.S. Beliefs*. Harrisburg, PA: Morehouse Publishing, 1999, p. 2. A great amount of demographic research on religious belief and unbelief in the United States is available for analysis on the Lilly Endowment's American Religion Data Archive (www.thearda.com). See Jane Lampman, "Charting America's Religious Landscape," *Christian Science Monitor* (October 10, 2002) 12, for a review of data indicating that 81 percent of Americans expressed a religious preference.

2. As defined, for example, in the *Oxford English Dictionary*. On the etymological possibilities of the term "secular," see Casanova, *Public Religions*, pp. 12–13. See T. N. Madan's discussion in *Modern Myths, Locked Minds: Secularism and Fundamentalism in India*. Delhi: Oxford, 1997, pp. 3–16. The quote about the "dream" of the secular minority can be found in T. N. Madan, "Secularism in Its Place," in

Secularism and Its Critics. Ed. Rajeev Bhargava. Delhi: Oxford, 1998, p. 298 (297–315). For a discussion of secularists as members of a "globalised elite culture," see Peter Berger, "Secularism in Retreat," in *Islam and Secularism in the Middle East.* Eds. John Esposito and Azzam Tamimi. New York: New York University Press, 2000, pp. 38–51.

3. A readable account can be found in Daniel Pipes' *The Rushdie Affair: The Novel, The Ayatollah, and the West.* New York: Birch Lane Press, 1990. On a statement made by the twelve foreign ministers of the European Common Market opposing the *fatwa,* see pp. 30–31. Also of interest is Malise Ruthven, *A Satanic Affair: Salman Rushdie and the Rage of Islam.* London: Chatto and Windus, 1990. A collective 1993 volume, *Pour Rushdie: Cent intellectuels arabes et musulmans pour la liberté d'expression.* Paris: La découverte/Carrefour des littératures/Colibri, 1993, is a document of great import. For an informative summary of the basic tenets of the fundamentalist movement in the United States, see Wade Clark Roof, "The New Fundamentalism: Rebirth of Political Religion in America," in *Prophetic Religions and Politics: Religion and the Political Order, Volume One.* Eds. Jeffrey Hadden and Anson Shupe. New York: Paragon House, 1986, pp. 18–34. The increasingly hostile relation of fundamentalists to secularism and modernity is charted in Gabriel Almond, R. Scott Appleby, and Emmanuel Sivan, *Strong Religion: The Rise of Fundamentalisms Around the World.* Chicago: University of Chicago Press, 2003. Also of use in understanding the attitude of fundamentalists to secularists is Carol Flake, *Redemptorama: Culture, Politics, and the New Evangelicalism.* Garden City, NJ: Anchor Press, 1984.

4. Harvey Cox, *The Secular City: Secularization and Urbanization in Theological Perspective.* New York: Macmillian, 1965, p. 2.

5. For an insightful and balanced discussion of the troubles that afflict secularism, as well as an assessment of its possibilities, see Brenda Cossman and Ratna Kapur, *Secularism's Last Sigh? Hindutva and the (Mis)Rule of Law.* Delhi: Oxford University Press, 1999, pp. 81–135. An equally insightful analysis is offered by Wilfred McClay, "Two Concepts of Secularism," in *Religion Returns to the Public Square: Faith and Policy in America.* Eds. Hugh Heclo and Wilfred McClay. Baltimore: The Johns Hopkins University Press, 2003, pp. 31–61. McClay writes about the demise of secularism and its inability to respond to "a growing, intellectually sophisticated . . . conservative religious counterculture," p. 38.

6. Remarks on the relation between secularism, religion, and the university can be found in Cox, *The Secular City,* p. 217ff. Also see George Marsden, *The Soul of the American University: From Protestant Establishment to Established Nonbelief.* New York: Oxford, 1994; George Marsden and Bradley Longfield (Eds.). *The Secularization of the Academy.* New York: Oxford, 1992; David Gill (Ed.). *Should God Get Tenure: Essays on Religion and Higher Education.* Grand Rapids, MI: Eerdmans, 1997. The concerns of Christian scholars are expressed in William Marty, "Christians in the Academy: Overcoming the Silence," *Journal of Interdisciplinary Studies* 10 (1998) 1–16. Also see Christian Smith, "Introduction: Rethinking the Secularization of American Public Life," in *The Secular Revolution: Power, Interests and Conflict in the Secularization of American Public Life.* Ed. Christian Smith. Berkeley: University of California Press, 2003, pp. 2–3, 32–33.

7. M. H. Goshen-Gottstein, "Christianity, Judaism and Modern Bible Study," *Supplements to Vetus Testamentum* 28 (1975) 83 (68–88). Goshen-Gottstein returns to these themes in "Modern Jewish Bible Research: Aspects of Integration," in *Proceedings of the Eighth World Congress of Jewish Studies, Jerusalem August 16–21, 1981*. Jerusalem: World Union of Jewish Studies, 1983, pp. 1–18. David Clines, *The Bible and the Modern World*. Sheffield: Sheffield Academic Press, 1997, p. 17. John Barton writes, "The vast majority of biblical interpreters until very recently have been religious believers." "Historical-Critical Approaches," in *The Cambridge Companion to Biblical Interpretation*. Ed. John Barton. Cambridge: Cambridge University Press, 1998, p. 15 (9–20). The memorable remarks of Morton Smith should be mentioned, "The Present State of Old Testament Studies," JBL 88 (1969) 19–35. The widespread suggestion that a secularizing current has infiltrated biblical scholarship is contested in Jacques Berlinerblau, "'Poor Bird, Not Knowing Which Way to Fly': Biblical Scholarship's Marginality, Secular Humanism, and the Laudable Occident," *Biblical Interpretation* 10 (2002) 267–304.

8. On the difference between atheists who are refugees from a Christian past and those that never believed in God in the first place (a difference that approximates our distinction between New and Heritage Secularists), see Alasdair MacIntyre and Paul Ricoeur, *The Religious Significance of Atheism*. New York: Columbia University Press, 1969, p. 15. Perceptive criticisms of biblical scholarship have been advanced. Yet, in terms of articulating the basic assumptions of nonconfessional biblical scholarship, little work has been done. For examples of such critical work, see Philip Davies, *Whose Bible Is It Anyway?* Sheffield: Sheffield Academic Press, 1995, and Robert Oden, *The Bible Without Theology: The Theological Tradition and Alternatives to It*. San Francisco: Harper & Row, 1987. The absence of secularistic interpretation is briefly discussed by James Barr, *The Scope and Authority of the Bible*. Philadelphia: Westminster Press, 1980, p. 21. In addition to these works, one can point to other studies that lean in a secular or at least sufficiently critical direction. Most are written by secularly religious intellectuals. See, for example, André Paul. *Et l'homme créa la Bible: d'Hérodote à Flavius Josèphe*. Paris: Bayard, 2000. The French house of Bayard has published a Bible translation that has been accused of being unduly secular. *La Bible: Nouvelle traduction*. Paris: Bayard, 2001. Other works of interest include Zvi Adar, *Humanistic Values in the Bible*. New York: Reconstructionist Press, 1967. There is also a "how to resist the Bible" manual by Jim Hill and Rand Cheadle, *The Bible Tells Me So: Uses and Abuses of Holy Scripture*. New York: Anchor Books, 1996. For an early science-loving, religion-debunking assault, see Joseph Lewis, *The Bible Unmasked*. New York: Freethought Publishing, 1926. An attempt at a somewhat secular reading of the Bible was advanced in the work of Louis Wallis, *The Bible Is Human: A Study in Secular History*. New York: Columbia University Press, 1942. One can also consult Erich Fromm, *You Shall Be as Gods: A Radical Interpretation of the Old Testament and Its Tradition*. New York: Holt, Rinehart and Winston, 1966, which features a good example of the species-loving secular humanism mentioned previously. A more recent submission is that of Tal Ilan, "A Secular, Jewish, Feminist Look at the Bible," in *Feminist Interpretation of the Bible and the Hermeneutics of Liberation*. Eds. Silvia Schroer and Sophia Bietenhard. Sheffield: Sheffield Academic Press,

2003, pp. 94–102. Also see Dennis McKinsey, *Encyclopedia of Biblical Errancy.* Buffalo, NY: Prometheus Books, 1995. An early classic of the genre is William Henry Burr, *Self-Contradictions of the Bible.* Buffalo, NY: Prometheus Books, 1987.

9. For a treatment of Durkheim's notion of the "collective representation," see the articles in W. S. F. Pickering (Ed.). *Durkheim and Representations.* London: Routledge, 2000, and Stjepan Meštrović, *Emile Durkheim and the Reformation of Sociology.* Lanham, MD: Rowman & Littlefield, 1993. Also see Jacques Berlinerblau, "Durkheim's Theory of Misrecognition: In Praise of Arrogant Social Theory," in *Teaching Durkheim.* Ed. T. Godlove. New York: Oxford University Press, 2005, pp. 213–233 Also, see Jacques Berlinerblau, "Free Will and Determinism in First Isaiah: Secular Hermeneutics, the Poetics of Contingency, and Émile Durkheim's *Homo Duplex,*" *JAAR* 71 (2003) 767–791. Voltaire, *Candide.* Trans. and Ed. Robert Adams. New York: W. W. Norton, 1966, p. 65.

10. The species-positive ethos surfaces in, for example, James Hitchcock, *What Is Secular Humanism? Why Humanism Became Secular and How It Is Changing Our World.* Ann Arbor, MI: Servant Books, 1982, pp. 7–17. On the notion of secularism and the perfectibility of human kind, see Madan, *Modern Myths,* pp. 5–25; Michel Houellebecq, *The Elementary Particles.* Trans. Frank Wynne. New York: Vintage International, 2000, pp. 263–264.

11. We have referred to views such as those advocated by our secular "Church Fathers" as "misrecognition theory." In fact, we have elsewhere identified an early variant of this view in parts of the Hebrew Bible. Jacques Berlinerblau, "Free Will," and Jacques Berlinerblau, "Toward a Sociology of Heresy, Orthodoxy, and *Doxa,*" *History of Religions* 40 (2001) 327–351, and Jacques Berlinerblau, "Ideology, Pierre Bourdieu's *Doxa,* and the Hebrew Bible," *Semeia* 87 (1999) 193–214. Michel de Montaigne, "On the Power of the Imagination," in *Essays.* Trans. J. M. Cohen. New York: Penguin, 1958, pp. 36–48. For discussions of Marx's tendency to see humans as deluded, see Berlinerblau, "Ideology." Marx's well-known dream remark can be found in Karl Marx, "For a Ruthless Criticism of Everything Existing," in *The Marx-Engels Reader,* 2nd ed. Ed. Robert Tucker. New York: W. W. Norton, 1978, p. 15. Durkheim speaks of the "anthropocentric postulate" in *The Rules of Sociological Method and Selected Texts on Sociology and Its Method.* Ed. Steven Lukes. Trans. W. D. Halls. New York: The Free Press, 1982, p. 46. On Durkheim's thinking about illusions and its relation to Comte, see Berlinerblau, "Durkheim's Theory of Misrecognition." Peter Berger is responsible for the quote that summarizes Weber's understanding of history. *The Sacred Canopy: Elements of a Sociological Theory of Religion.* Garden City, NJ: Doubleday, 1969, p. 200, fn. 6.

12. John Macquarrie, *God and Secularity: New Directions in Theology Today, Volume Three.* Philadelphia: Westminster Press, 1969, pp. 43–44.

13. For a discussion of the problems involved in dating the Rabbinic period (which we place between the first and sixth centuries AD), see Isaiah Gafni, "The Historical Background," in *The Literature of the Sages: First Part: Oral Tora, Halakha, Mishna, Tosefta, Talmud, External Tractates.* Ed. Shmuel Safrai. Fortress Press: Philadelphia, 1987, pp. 1–34. More detailed discussions concerning debates about when canonization occurred are found throughout this book.

1. WHO WROTE THE BIBLE? (ANCIENT RESPONSES)

1. The question of the canon of the Hebrew Bible as it was understood in antiquity is extremely complicated, and we can only make a few brief observations here. The idea of a canonical collection containing twenty-four books is discernable in the Rabbinic discussion of B. *Baba Bathra* 14b–15a (ca. second century CE). Using this list as a benchmark, we enumerate the twenty-four scrolls in the order in which the books are discussed by the Rabbis. Names in parentheses indicate the individuals whom the Rabbis claimed wrote the books: 1) Genesis (Moses); 2) Exodus (Moses); 3) Leviticus (Moses); 4) Numbers (Moses); 5) Deuteronomy (Moses and Joshua); 6) Job (Moses); 7) Joshua (Joshua, Eleazar, and Phineas); 8) Samuel (Samuel, Gad, and Nathan); 9) Judges (Samuel); 10) Ruth (Samuel); 11) Psalms (David et. al.); 12) Jeremiah (Jeremiah); 13) Kings (Jeremiah); 14) Lamentations (Jeremiah); 15) Isaiah (Hezekiah and his colleagues); 16) Proverbs (Hezekiah and his colleagues); 17) Song of Songs (Hezekiah and his colleagues); 18) Ecclesiastes (Hezekiah and his colleagues); 19) Ezekiel (the Men of the Great Assembly); 20) the Twelve Minor Prophets (the Men of the Great Assembly); 21) Daniel (the Men of the Great Assembly); 22) Esther (the Men of the Great Assembly); 23) Ezra (Ezra); and 24) Chronicles (Ezra and Nehemiah). The notion of twenty-four books is also found in the apocryphal 2 Esdras 14:44–48. The claim of twenty-two books is most famously made in Josephus, *Against Apion* I 38–42 in *Josephus: The Life, Against Apion*. Trans. H. St. J. Thackeray. Cambridge, MA: Harvard University Press, 1997. For a useful review of ancient sources pertaining to the canon of the Hebrew Bible, see Lee Martin McDonald, "Primary Sources for the Study of the Old Testament/Hebrew Bible Canon," in *The Canon Debate*. Eds. Lee Martin McDonald and James Sanders. Peabody, MA: Hendrickson, 2002, pp. 580–582. In the same volume, see Steve Mason, "Josephus and His Twenty-Two Book Canon," pp. 110–127. For a discussion of twenty-two versus twenty-four books, see Otto Eissfeldt, *The Old Testament: An Introduction*. Trans. Peter Ackroyd. New York: Harper & Row, 1965, pp. 562–571.

2. In terms of the twenty-four books enumerated in endnote 1, the following are not ascribed in the Hebrew Bible: Genesis, Exodus, Leviticus, Numbers, Deuteronomy, Joshua, Judges, (I and II) Samuel, (I and II) Kings, Job, Ruth, Lamentations, Esther, and (I and II) Chronicles. Thus, there is no clear claim of authorship in at least fourteen of the twenty-four scrolls. Ambiguous cases can be found in texts that flip between first and third person narrations, such as Ezekiel, Ezra-Nehemiah, Daniel, and so on. Within the twelve minor prophets (which were reckoned as one scroll in antiquity), the texts of Jonah and Haggai seem to lack any clear ascription.

3. Hermann Gunkel, *The Legends of Genesis: The Biblical Saga and History*. Trans. W. H. Carruth. New York: Schocken Books, 1964, p. 7. On the anonymity of biblical texts in general, Morton Smith's article is of great use: "Pseudepigraphy in the Israelite Literary Tradition," in *Pseudepigrapha I: Pseudopythagorica-Lettres de Platon, Littérature pseudépigraphique juive*. Ed. Kurt von Fritz. Geneva: Vandoeuvres, 1972, pp. 191–227. God's immodest assessment of His handiwork occurs in, for example, Gen. 1:10.

4. On the issue of superscriptions, see the article of H. M. I. Gevaryahu, "Biblical Colophons: A Source for the 'Biography' of Authors, Texts and Books," *Supplements to Vetus Testamentum* 28 (1975) 42–59, and Bruce Waltke, "Superscripts, Postscripts, or Both" *JBL* 110 (1991) 583–596. Eccl. 1:1; 1:12. The flip between first and third person is discussed in footnote 5. The Book of Ecclesiastes does this elsewhere. Notice how 12:8 and 12:9 employ third person forms.

5. Eccles. 1:1. C. L. Seow discusses the implausibility of this attribution in *Ecclesiastes. The Anchor Bible.* New York: Doubleday, 1997, pp. 36–38, 98–99. Song 1:1. Many Psalms open with lines like *mizmôr lĕdāwid* and *mizmôr lĕ'āsāph* frequently translated as "A Psalm of [i.e., by] David," "A Psalm of Asaph," and so on. To most laypersons, this suggests a Psalm written *by* David, Asaph, etc. Yet, the Hebrew can offer other possibilities. As Peter Craigie observed, the preposition, *lāmed*, could also mean "for David," "to David," "concerning David," or "for the use of David." In fact, comparison with cognate languages such as Ugaritic suggests "concerning David" might be the most suitable translation. Peter Craigie, *Psalms 1–50.* Word Biblical Commentary. Waco, TX: Word Books, 1983, pp. 33–35. Craigie concludes that the preposition *lāmed* "need not, and probably does not, imply authorship . . . it may be safest to recognize that the majority of psalms are anonymous and that no certain statement can be made concerning their authorship" p. 35. James Kugel has come to a similar conclusion, noting that to translate the preposition as indicating authorship is probably the "least likely hypothesis." "David the Prophet," in *Poetry and Prophecy: The Beginnings of a Literary Tradition.* Ed. James Kugel. Ithaca, NY: Cornell University Press, 1990, p. 49 (45–55). Also see Mitchell Dahood, *Psalms I: 1–50.* Garden City, NJ: Anchor Books/Doubleday, 1966, pp. 15–16. Artur Weiser suggests the original purpose of the superscriptions "was not at all to name the author of the psalm." *The Psalms: A Commentary.* Old Testament Library. Trans. Herbert Hartwell. Philadelphia: Westminster Press, 1962, pp. 95–99. For a discussion of the range of the preposition *lāmed* in Ugaritic that gives little credence to the claim that it refers to "by," see Dennis Pardee, "The Preposition in Ugaritic," *Ugarit Forschungen* 8 (1976) 215–322. Arguing that the formula does indeed refer to authorship is Brevard Childs, "Psalm Titles and Midrashic Exegesis," *Journal of Semitic Studies* 16 (1971) 137–150, and Brevard Childs, *Introduction to the Old Testament as Scripture.* Philadelphia: Fortress Press, 1979, pp. 520–522. Most authors concur that regardless of what the superscriptions in the Psalms mean, they are later, usually second Temple period, insertions into the text. For Rabbinic attributions of the Psalms to David, see B. *Pesaḥim* 117a. *Pesaḥim.* Trans. H. Freedman. London: Soncino Press, 1938, pp. 598–599. Although most laypersons believe David wrote the Psalter, this too is not supported by Scriptures. Of the 150 Psalms in Hebrew Bible, we count 50 that are anonymous. There remain 100 Psalms that do mention a name in the superscription. Assuming the names indicate authorship – an assumption with which we do not agree – then the following breakdown can be noted. The name of David appears seventy-three times; Asaph twelve times; Solomon twice; Ethan, Herman, and Moses once each; and the sons of Korah eleven times (although one of these references occurs in Psalm 88, where the aforementioned Heman is spoken of).

6. The passages of relevance in Proverbs are 1:1; 24:23; 25:1; 30:1; and 31:1. In 1 Kings 5:12, it is said that Solomon composed 3,000 proverbs and 1,005 songs to boot. On traditions of Solomonic authorship in general, see R. B. Y. Scott, "Solomon and the Beginnings of Wisdom in Israel," in *Studies in Ancient Israelite Wisdom*. Ed. James Crenshaw. New York: Ktav, 1976, pp. 262–279; Michael Fox writes: "Historically, it is improbable that many – if any – of the proverbs were written by Solomon." Fox goes on to discuss the question of Solomonic authorship. *Proverbs 1–9*. The Anchor Bible. New York: Doubleday, 2000, pp. 56–58. For similar sentiments, see Roland Murphy, *Proverbs*. World Biblical Commentary. Nashville, TN: Thomas Nelson, 1998, pp. xx–xxi. An apocryphal Psalm from Qumran – mindful perhaps of Solomon's alleged accomplishments – credits king David with 3,600 psalms and 450 songs. For the publication of the text (referenced as 11 QPsa DavComp), see J. A. Sanders, *Discoveries in the Judaean Desert of Jordan*, IV: *The Psalms Scroll of Qumrân Cave 11*. Oxford: Clarendon Press, 1965, pp. 91–93.

7. Thus, notice the difference in narrative voice between Ezek. 1:1–2 and Ezek. 1:3. A similar shift occurs from Zech. 1:7 to 1:8 or from 7:1 to 7:4. In Daniel, compare, for example, Dan. 1:1 with 4:1 and 8:1.

8. As one scholar writes about the composition of Torah: "most of the relevant passages say nothing about the process through which . . . [it] came into being, but think of it as 'written' . . . a complete . . . and authoritative document." H. Haag, "k-t-b," in *Theological Dictionary of the Old Testament: Volume 7*. Eds. G. J. Botterweck, H. Ringgren, and H. J. Fabry. Trans. David Green. Grand Rapids, MI: William B. Eerdmans, 1995, p. 379 (371–382).

9. In Ex. 34:1, the stones were now man made. Also see the parallel account in Deut. 5:19 and Deut. 10:1–2.

10. Also see Isaiah 30:8. In fact, King Jehoiakim dislikes the contents of the scroll so much that he slices it up piece by piece and feeds it to the fire. His theatrical act of desecration is in vain. Yahweh dictates the same message to Jeremiah plus, it would seem, a new one concerning Jehoiakim of the knives. Jeremiah then dictates it all to Baruch. Textual creation, inscription, and even reinscription occur without as much as a glitch. Baruch's unproblematic reinscription occurs in Jer. 36:4. Robert Carroll has wondered if the passage can be seen as "an intimation (or claim of legitimation) of the scribal transformation of oral prophecy into inscripturated scrolls." "The Book of J: Intertextuality and Ideological Criticism," in *Troubling Jeremiah*. Eds. A. R. Diamond, K. O'Connor, and L. Stulman. Sheffield: Sheffield Academic Press, 1999, p. 227. Perhaps the query of 36:17 might be taken to indicate some concern about compositional accuracy. The gradual burning by King Jehoiakim and the recopying is described in 36:21–36:32. No issues of lost data or transcription are explored in the text. Elsewhere, Yahweh commands Jeremiah to "write down in a scroll all of the words that I have spoken to you" (30:1), which Jeremiah does (30:4) without any apparent difficulties.

11. The same holds true for Huram's letter to Solomon (2 Chron. 2:10–15) and the denunciation of Rehum and Shimshai written to Artaxerxes (Ez. 4:7–16). Mordecai dictates letters to Ahasuerus' scribes, which are sent to 127 provinces (Est. 8:9). Scripture does not seem unduly concerned with issues of translation here, nor when Darius writes a letter in every language on earth (Dan. 6:26). Joshua's spies

are told to write a description of the land they are reconnoiting, which they do flawlessly (Josh. 18:8–9).

12. B. *Baba Bathra* 14b. *Baba Bathra 1*. Trans. Maurice Simon. London: Soncino Press, 1935, p. 71. See endnote 1 for a full list of the attributions made in this text. On Moses as author of Job, also see the Tractate P. *Sotah* 5:6 III A. *The Talmud of the Land of Israel: A Preliminary Translation and Explanation. Volume 27: Sotah*. Trans. Jacob Neusner. Chicago: University of Chicago Press, 1984, p. 161. On the Book of Joshua's authorship, see B. *Baba Bathra* 14b. On Jeremiah, Kings, and Lamentations, see B. *Baba Bathra* 15a; on Daniel's authorship, see *Midrash Rabbah*, Genesis 85:2. *Midrash Rabbah: Genesis, Volume Two*. Trans. H. Freedman. London: Soncino Press, 1983, p. 789. On Esther being written under the inspiration of the Holy Spirit, see B. *Megillah* 7a. *Megillah*. Trans. Maurice Simon. London: Soncino Press, 1938, pp. 34–35.

13. B. *Baba Bathra* 14b–15a.

14. B. *Baba Bathra* 14b–15a. There are exceptions to monoauthorist thought as when the Rabbis ascribe texts to Hezekiah and his colleagues, or the Men of the Great Assembly. For these ascriptions, see endnote 1. An intriguing challenge to the theory of Mosaic authorship and monoauthorism in general is recorded in a work of Epiphanius of Salamis entitled "Ptolemy's Letter to Flora." Ptolemy, apparently, was corrupting Flora's mind by telling her that "not all of that Law in the first five books of Moses has been made by one legislator." The heretic insisted that one section was written by God, one by Moses, and one by "the elders of the people." Still, the latter claim comprises the exception to the rule. "Ptolemy's Letter to Flora," in *The Panarion of Epiphanius of Salamis: Book 1 (Sects 1–46)*. Trans. Frank Williams. Leiden: E. J. Brill, 1987, p. 199.

15. The term "Torah" appears 220 times in the Hebrew Bible. G. Liedke and C. Petersen, "tôrâ, instruction," in *Theological Lexicon of the Old Testament. Volume 3*. Eds. Ernst Jenni and Claus Westermann. Trans. Mark Biddle. Peabody, MA: Hendrickson, 1997, p. 1415. The "Book of Moses" can be found in Neh. 13:1, where it seems to be associated with Torah mentioned in 13:3. The same association is made in 2 Chron. 25:4. The construct phrase "Torah of Moses" is mentioned in Josh. 8:32, 1 K 2:3; 2 K 23:25; Mal. 3:22; Dan. 9:11, 13. "Book of the Torah" is found in Deut. 28:61; Deut. 29:20; Deut. 31:26; Josh. 1:8; Josh. 8:34; 2 K 22:8, 11. "Book of the Torah of Moses" can be found in Josh. 8:31; Josh. 23:6; 2 K 14:6; Neh. 8:1. For "Book of the Torah of Elohim," see Josh. 24:26; Neh. 8:18; and see also, Neh. 10:30. "Torah of Yahweh" can be seen in Isaiah 5:24; Isaiah 30:9; Amos 2:4; Psalms 1:2; Psalms 119:1. And see Neh. 9:3, where both divine appellatives are used, and 2 Chron. 34:14 draws the association between Moses and the Book of the Torah of Yahweh. For a discussion of theories of Mosaic authorship, see J. Alberto Soggin, *Introduction to the Old Testament: From Its Origins to the Closing of the Alexandrian Canon*, rev. ed. Trans. John Bowden. Philadelphia: Westminster Press, 1980, pp. 79–83. Alexander Rofé remarks that by the time of Ezra-Nehemiah "the Pentateuch – or at least its legal sections – were already attributed to Mosaic authorship." Although it seems to us that, at best, Neh. 8:1 and 13:1, and the other examples cited, point to an association of Moses with the legal sections. *Introduction to the Composition of the Pentateuch*. Sheffield: Sheffield Academic

Press, 1999, pp. 11–12. On Jewish perspectives concerning the divine origin of the Five Books and Moses's role in copying it down, see the very thorough discussion of Louis Jacobs, *Principles of the Jewish Faith*. Northvale, NJ: Jason Aronson, 1988, pp. 215–301.

16. R. J. Thompson, *Moses and the Law in a Century of Criticism Since Graf. Supplements to Vetus Testamentum* 19 (1970) 4. For similar points about the difficulties inherent in these equations, see J. Alberto Soggin, *Introduction to the Old Testament*, p. 79. Also see Julio Trebolle Barrera, *The Jewish Bible and the Christian Bible: An Introduction to the History of the Bible*. Trans. Wilfred Watson. Leiden: Brill, 1998, p. 158. On the varied meanings of Torah across biblical documents and compositional periods, see S. R. Driver, "Law (In Old Testament)," in *A Dictionary of the Bible*. Ed. James Hastings. Peabody, MA: Hendrickson, 1898/1988, pp. 64–73. The term in Genesis 26:5 is traditionally translated as "teachings." In the "Appendix to 3 Enoch" (48d4), "Torah" would seem to encompass the entire Bible. Torah is said to refer to "The Torah, the Prophets and the Writings." *The Old Testament Pseudepigraphia, Volume 1*. Ed. James Charlesworth. Trans. P. Alexander. Garden City, NJ: Doubleday, 1983, p. 314.

17. Joseph Blenkinsopp, *The Pentateuch: An Introduction to the First Five Books of the Bible*. New York: Doubleday, 1992, p. 1. For another interesting discussion, see S. David Sperling, *The Original Torah: The Political Intent of the Bible's Writers*. New York: New York University Press, 1998, pp. 11–25.

18. For Philo's references to Moses as author, see *On the Creation*, I, 4–8 in *Philo, Volume I*, Trans. F. H. Colson and G. H. Whitaker. Cambridge, MA: Harvard University Press, 1991, pp. 7–11. Even the last eight verses of Deuteronomy (in which Moses's death is discussed) are ascribed by Philo to the Lawgiver. A claim that contradicts the Rabbinic position discussed previously. According to Philo, "the divine spirit fell upon him [Moses] and he prophesied with discernment while still alive the story of his own death." This claim is found in *Moses II*, 291. Also see *Moses II*, 45–52. For Moses as author of "sacred books," see *Moses I*, 4. All these *Moses* texts are found in *Philo VI*. Trans. F. H. Colson. Cambridge, MA: Harvard University Press, 1935. A similar assumption animates Philo's *Genesis I*, I. 1 in *Philo Supplement I: Questions and Answers on Genesis*. Trans. H. Marcus. Cambridge, MA: Harvard University Press, 1971; Josephus, *Against Apion* I, 37–42 in *Josephus: The Life: Against Apion* Trans. H. St. J. Thackeray. Cambridge, MA: Harvard University Press, 1997. The monoauthorist equation between Moses, Torah, and the first Five Books is worthy of a few monographs. For an introduction to many of the passages involved see Phillip Callaway, "The Ancient Meaning of the Law of Moses," in *History and Interpretation: Essays in Honour of John J. Hayes*. Eds. M. Patrick Graham, William P. Brown, and Jeffrey K. Kuan. Sheffield: Sheffield Academic Press, 1993, pp. 160–172. Also see Lester Grabbe, "The Law of Moses in the Ezra Tradition: More Virtual Than Real?" in *Persia and Torah: The Theory of the Imperial Authorization of the Pentateuch*. Ed. James Watts. Atlanta: Society of Biblical Literature, 2001, pp. 91–113. Also of interest is Johann Cook, "The Law of Moses in Septuagint Proverbs," *VT* 49 (1999) 448–461. The New Testament, for its part, refers to "the law of Moses" or "the book of Moses." It is not clear if these terms refer to all or part of the first five books as translated into

Greek. So when Jesus asks his Saduccean interlocutors in Mark 12:26, "Have you not read in the Book of Moses, in the story of the burning bush?", it is difficult to tell whether he is specifically citing a particular passage (Exodus 3:2–6) or the entire five books. For other references to the law of Moses, see John 1:17; John 7:19; Acts 13:39; and Acts 15:5. Also see the apocryphal 1 Esdras 5:49.

19. Thompson, *Moses and the Law*, notes that it is peculiar that the Rabbis would distinguish Num. 22–24 if they believed the Book of Moses is one and the same as the Pentateuch, pp. 1–2. The translation from Sotah can be found in *The Talmud of the Land of Israel*, V 6 III A. B. *Menaḥoth* (30a) also assigns the final eight verses of the Deuteronomy to Joshua. *Menaḥoth.* Trans. Eli Cashdan. London: Soncino Press, 1960. Also see *Aboth* I.1 –3. 1935. *Aboth.* Trans. J. Israelstam. London: Soncino Press, 1935, p. 1.

20. John Chrysostom, "Homily 2:4," in *Saint John Chrysostom, Homilies on Genesis 1–17.* Trans. Robert Hill. Washington, DC: The Catholic University of America Press, 1986. For some of the considerations involved in dating the patristic era, see W. J. Burghardt, "Fathers of the Church," in *New Catholic Encyclopedia, Volume V: Ead to Foy.* Ed. John Whalen. New York: McGraw-Hill, 1967, pp. 853–855.

21. On the Torah coming from heaven and thus God, see B. *Sanhedrin* 99a. *Sanhedrin II.* Trans. H. Freedman. London: Soncino Press, 1935, p. 671. On God communicating the Torah to Moses on Sinai, see *Midrash Rabbah Numbers* 13:15, 16. *Midrash Rabbah Numbers, Volume Two.* Trans. Judah Slotki. London: Soncino Press, p. 534. Josephus opines "we have learned the noblest of our doctrines and the holiest of our laws from the messengers/angels sent by God," *Antiquities* 15:136, in *Jewish Antiquities.* Trans. Ralph Marcus. Cambridge, MA: Harvard University Press, 1998, p. 323. On the translation "angels," see W. D. Davies, "A Note on Josephus, *Antiquities* 15:136," *Harvard Theological Review* 47 (1954) 135–140. And also see Francis Walton, "The Messenger of God in Hecataeus of Abdera," *Harvard Theological Review* 48 (1955) 255–257. In the New Testament, this view of angels can be found in Acts 7:38; Acts 7:53; Gal. 3:19; and Heb. 2:2. This Jewish belief in angels as transmitters can also be found in *Jubilees* 1:27–1:29 and 2:1, and see the discussion in J. Louis Martyn, *Galatians.* The Anchor Bible. New York: Doubleday, 1997, pp. 356–357. On the Ezra counter-tradition, see the excellent article of C. Houtman, "Ezra and the Law: Observations on the Supposed Relation between Ezra and the Pentateuch," in *Oudtestamentische Studiën* 21 (1981) 91–115. Of interest for Rabbinic views concerning Moses's role in the transmission process is Steven Fraade, "Moses and the Commandments: Can Hermeneutics, History, and Rhetoric be Disentangled?" in *The Idea of Biblical Interpretation: Esaays in Honor of James L. Kugel.* Eds. Hindy Najman and Judith Newman. Leiden: Brill, 2004, pp. 399–422. On the Holy Spirit as author of the text, see our discussion in Chapter Three, endnote 1. "Pseudo Philo" 25:13 poses the question of whether God or Moses wrote the text, in *The Old Testament Pseudepigrapha, Volume 2.* Ed. James Charlesworth. Trans. D. J. Harrington. Garden City, NJ: Doubleday, 1985, p. 336. The *"Testament of Jacob"* 7:4 seems to view Moses as writer of the Old Testament and the law. In *The Old Testament Pseudepigraphia, Volume 1.* Ed. James Charlesworth. Trans. W. F. Stinespring. Garden City, NJ: Doubleday, 1983, p. 917, Sigmund Mowinckel echoes a common complaint as

he calls the popular rendering of 2 Timothy 3:16 "an erroneous translation." He preferred: "Every scripture inspired by God is useful for doctrine." *The Old Testament as Word of God.* Trans. Reidar Bjornard. Nashville, TN: Abingdon Press, 1959, p. 23. The translation from Timothy used in the text comes from the *New Revised Standard Version.*

2. "WHO WROTE THE BIBLE?": MODERN RESPONSES

1. Exod. 33:20. The death of Joshua is reported in Josh. 24:26 and Judges 1:1. On the father-in-law of Moses, compare the two variant spellings used in Ex. 4:18 with Num. 10:29.

2. Genesis 2:4b starts the second creation story. In classic documentary hypothesis, it is attributed to J, whereas that of Genesis 1:1–2:4a is ascribed to P. J is believed to have predated P. The most well-known analysis is that of E. A. Speiser, *Genesis.* The Anchor Bible. Garden City, NJ: Doubleday, pp. 3–20. The stories of wives as sisters can be found in Gen. 12:10–20; Gen. 20; and Gen. 26:6–11. On covenants, compare Genesis 15 with Genesis 17:1–14. For Cain's words, see *Targum Neofiti 1: Genesis.* Trans. Martin McNamara. Collegeville, MN: The Liturgical Press, 1992, pp. 65–66. For the lengthier exchange between Cain and Abel, see *Targum Pseudo-Jonathan Genesis.* Trans. Michael Maher. Collegeville, MN: The Liturgical Press, 1992, pp. 32–33. We would expect the line to commence with the Hebrew letter *nûn* in Psalm 145:14, but the text skips from the letter *mêm* to *sāmek.* See the discussion of Alexander Rofé, *Introduction to the Composition of the Pentateuch.* Sheffield: Sheffield Academic Press, 1999, pp. 17–25, for more examples of duplications, contradictions, and inconsistencies in the Pentateuch.

3. For a review of arguments concerning the non-Hebrew provenance of Job, whether Aramaic or otherwise, see Marvin Pope, *Job.* The Anchor Bible. Garden City, NJ: Doubleday, 1965, pp. xlii–xlv. The most daring exposition of this hypothesis can be found in N. H. Tur-Sinai, *The Book of Job: A New Commentary.* Jerusalem: Kiryath Sepher, 1962.

4. Job 42:7–10.

5. For the argument that the modern period of biblical scholarship begins in the renaissance, not the nineteenth century as we have claimed, see James Kugel, "The Bible in the University," in *The Hebrew Bible and Its Interpreters.* Eds. William Propp, Baruch Halpern, and David Noel Freedman. Winona Lake, IN: Eisenbrauns, 1990, pp. 143–165.

6. The quote on the era of Wellhausen comes from Rolf Rendtorff, "The Paradigm Is Changing: Hopes – and Fears," *Biblical Interpretation* 1 (1993) 36 (34–53). Rendtorff continues, however, "I believe that traditional documentary hypothesis has come to an end" (p. 44). Richard Elliot Friedman, in contrast, observes that it still constitutes a standard assumption of most scholarly work in the field. "Some Recent Non-Arguments Concerning Documentary Hypothesis," in *Texts, Temples, and Traditions: A Tribute to Menahem Haran.* Eds. Michael Fox, Victor Hurowitz, Avi Hurvitz, Michael Klein, Baruch Schwartz, and Nili Shupak. Winona Lake, IN: Eisenbrauns, 1996, pp. 87–101. Whatever the case, it is undeniable that documentary hypothesis has endured a few rough decades of late. As

early as 1954, Herbert Hahn could point to the "sterile" nature of exegetical operation that carved out biblical texts into seemingly infinite sources. *The Old Testament in Modern Research*. Philadelphia: Fortress, 1966, p. 22. More recently, documentary hypothesis has weathered an assault by what Robert Carroll described as
an unholy alliance of conservative theologians and postmodernists, "Poststruc-
turalist Approaches: New Historicism and Postmodernism," in *The Cambridge
Companion to Biblical Interpretation*. Ed. John Barton. Cambridge: Cambridge
University Press, 1998, pp. 50–66. Also see Joseph Blenkinsopp's "The Documentary
Hypothesis in Trouble," *Bible Review* 1 (1985) 22–32, and Richard Elliot Friedman's
"The Recession of Biblical Source Criticism," in *The Future of Biblical Studies: The
Hebrew Scriptures*. Eds. Richard Elliot Friedman and H. G. M. Williamson. Atlanta:
Scholars Press, 1987, pp. 81–102.

7. Julius Wellhausen, *Prolegomena to the History of Israel*. Atlanta: Scholars Press,
   1994, p. 6. Particularly important as precursors for Wellhausen were the fragment
   hypothesis and the supplement hypothesis. For an early discussion, see Charles
   Augustus Briggs, *The Higher Criticism of the Hexateuch*. New York: Charles Scribner's Sons, 1893, pp. 46–68. More recent treatments of these precursors can be
   found in Ernest Nicholson, *The Pentateuch in the Twentieth Century: The Legacy
   of Julius Wellhausen*. Oxford: Clarendon Press, 1998, p. 7. On the origin of the
   supplement hypothesis, see R. J. Thompson, *Moses and the Law in a Century
   of Criticism Since Graf*. Leiden: E. J. Brill, 1970. *Supplements to Vetus Testamentum* 19, 27–30. Also see Georg Fohrer, *Introduction to the Old Testament*. Trans.
   David Green. Nashville, TN: Abingdon, 1978, pp. 108–109; John Van Seters, *The
   Pentateuch: A Social-Science Commentary*. Sheffield: Sheffield Academic Press,
   1999, pp. 28–29; and Douglas Knight, *Rediscovering the Traditions of Israel*, rev.
   ed. SBL Dissertation Series 9. Missoula, MT: Scholars Press, 1975, p. 65. As for the
   ructions and the historical development of documentary hypothesis, interested
   readers can consult admirably clear, concise, and accessible works such as R. E. F.
   Friedman's *Who Wrote the Bible?* San Francisco: Harper Collins, 1987, or Joseph
   Blenkinsopp's *The Pentateuch: An Introduction to the First Five Books of the Bible*.
   New York: Doubleday, 1992. Also of interest is the broader study of Emil Krael-
   ing, *The Old Testament Since the Reformation*. New York: Schocken Books, 1969.
   For detailed studies of Wellhausen, see the collected articles in *Semeia* 25, entitled
   Julius Wellhausen and His Prolegomena to the History of Israel. Ed. Douglas Knight.
   Chico, CA: Scholars Press, 1983. For a discussion of many of the issues discussed
   in this footnote and an illuminating contextualization of Wellhausen's thought,
   see William Irwin, "The Significance of Julius Wellhausen," *Journal of Bible and
   Religion* 12 (1944) 160–173. Irwin makes the "charter" remark on page 164.

8. The generic version described here is a descendant of Wellhausen's original
   hypothesis, not the hypothesis itself. On this, see Irwin, "The Significance," p. 164,
   and Herbert Hahn, *The Old Testament*, p. 20 (emphasis mine). Martin Noth took
   a similar view regarding J and E (in contrast to his conjectured Dtr source):
   "The Pentateuch ... does not have an 'author'. ... Even the original writers of the
   so-called sources of the Pentateuch, from which the whole was finally compiled,
   cannot be regarded as 'authors'. ... To be sure, they gave their works a definite final
   formulation, but they did not give them the basic form." *A History of Pentateuchal
   Traditions*. Trans. Bernhard Anderson. Englewood Cliffs, NJ: Prentice Hall, 1972,

p. 2. And see E. W. Nicholson's remarks on the staggering complexity of the process: "The Pentateuch in Recent Research: A Time for Caution," *Supplements to Vetus Testamentum* 43 (1991) 21 (11–21). Rolf Rendtorff charts the shift in biblical scholarship from a view of the sources as composed by many authors to one in which a source is associated with a given authorial personality: "The 'Yahwist' as Theologian? The Dilemma of Pentateuchal Criticism," *JSOT* 32 (1977) 2–9. For discussions of new sigla such as B, L, and K, see, for example, Otto Eissfeldt, *The Old Testament: An Introduction.* Trans. Peter Ackroyd. Oxford: Basil Blackwell, 1965, and Robert Pfeiffer, *Introduction to the Old Testament.* New York: Harper & Row, 1948, as well as the discussion of Blenkinsopp, *The Pentateuch,* pp. 12–15.

9. Nicholson, *The Pentateuch,* p. 7; Otto Eissfeldt, *The Old Testament,* p. 177. Soggin writes: "The Pentateuch was not composed in a single draft; it is the product of a redactional process which proves to be extremely complex. J. Alberto Soggin, *Introduction to the Old Testament: From Its Origins to the Closing of the Alexandrian Canon,* rev. ed. Trans. John Bowden. Philadelphia: Westminster Press, 1980, p. 83.

10. We need not concern ourselves with the countless debates about tradition history – its affinity or lack thereof with Wellhausen's documentary hypothesis, the question of who its founder actually was, and so on. Interested readers may consult the studies mentioned here, especially Douglas Knight's *Rediscovering the Traditions.* Knight suggests that Wellhausen underestimated "the extent to which the tradition could develop at the precompositional stage" and "devaluated the worth of these earlier forms for the exegete" (p. 66). More recently, Rolf Rendtorff forcefully argued that one of the leading lights of the approach, Hermann Gunkel, "inaugurated a methodological approach that moved into a direction quite different from that established by Wellhausen." "The Paradigm is Changing," pp. 38–39. On Gunkel, also see Walter Rast, *Tradition History and the Old Testament.* Philadelphia: Fortress Press, 1972, p. 3; Blenkinsopp, *The Pentateuch,* pp. 14–15. And see Nicholson, *The Pentateuch,* p. 30. Also of interest to understanding this school is the volume edited by Knud Jeppesen and Benedikt Otzen, *The Productions of Time: Tradition History in Old Testament Scholarship.* Sheffield: Almond Press, 1984. David Noel Freedman's remarks in "Pentateuch," in *The Interpreter's Dictionary of the Bible: Volume 3.* Ed. George Arthur Buttrick. New York: Abingdon Press, 1962, pp. 725–726 (711–727), are also of interest. On all the things that the term "tradition history" may signify, see Knight, *Rediscovering the Traditions,* pp. 22–29. Of the various definitions given by Knight, number 4 comes closest to what we have in mind: "The whole history of a literary piece – from its earliest beginnings as independent units of oral tradition, through its development, growth and composition at the oral and written levels, on to its redaction and finalization in its present form" p. 23. R. N. Whybray, following Rendtorff, sees documentary hypothesis and the tradition history method as "*alternatives* which cannot be combined," *The Making of the Pentateuch: A Methodological Study.* Sheffield: JSOT Press, 1987, p. 42, although our approach permits for their selective combination (see Chapter Three).

11. Hermann Gunkel, *The Legends of Genesis: The Biblical Saga and History.* Trans. W. H. Carruth. New York: Schocken Books, 1964, p. 88, 4, 130. As Rast put it, "he [Gunkel] comprehended a stage in the history of the Old Testament literature

during which literary formation was often influenced by means of oral communication" *Tradition History*, p. 3. Martin Noth, *A History*, p. 21. See Rendtorff for a discussion of Noth's belief in collectors as being individual authors, "Martin Noth and Tradition Criticism," in *The History of Israel's Traditions: The Heritage of Martin Noth*. Eds. Steven McKenzie and M. Patrick Graham. Sheffield: Sheffield Academic Press, 1994, p. 95. Ivan Engnell, *A Rigid Scrutiny: Critical Essays on the Old Testament*. Trans., Ed. John Willis. Nashville, TN: Vanderbilt University Press, 1969, p. 6; also see Engnell, "Methodological Aspects of Old Testament Study," *Supplements to Vetus Testamentum* 7 (1960) 13–30. Engnell, it should be noted, was searingly critical of documentary hypothesis, referring to it as "an anachronistic bookish mode of view" and "an *interpretatio europaeica moderna*." Engnell, "Methodological Aspects," p. 21; *A Rigid Scrutiny*, p. 53. On issues pertaining to oral tradition and historicity, and problems of the approach in general, see Robert Culley's interesting studies: "An Approach to the Problem of Oral Tradition," *VT* 13 (1963) 113–125; *Studies in the Structure of Hebrew Narrative*. Philadelphia: Fortress Press, 1976; "Oral Tradition and Historicity," in *Studies on the Ancient Palestinian World: Presented to Professor F. V. Winnett on the Occasion of His Retirement, 1 July 1971*. Eds. J. W. Wevers and D. B. Redford. Toronto: University of Toronto Press, 1972, pp. 102–116; and "Psalm, 102: A Complaint with a Difference," *Semeia* 62 (1993) 19–35. For an early appraisal, see J. Van der Ploeg, "La rôle de la tradition orale dans la transmission du texte de l'ancien testament," *RB* 54 (1947) 5–41. Gunkel pointedly referred to "collectors rather than authors" (*The Legends*, pp. 124, 125). J and E were thus not authors but "schools of narrators" (p. 130). Gunkel also advises us not to bother looking for individual authors, *Water for a Thirsty Land: Israelite Literature and Religion*. Ed. K. C. Hanson. Minneapolis: Fortress, 2001, p. 31. Also see Nicholson, *The Pentateuch*, p. 41, and Alexander Rofé, *Introduction*, p. 89.

12. Engnell (*Rigid Scrutiny*, p. 9) argues in favor of the stability of oral literature and would thus reject our emphasis (and Gunkel's) on the high degree of flux involved in oral transmission. On this latter issue, see Culley, "Psalm 102," p. 21. Also see Samuel Sandmel, "The Haggada Within Scripture," *JBL* 80 (1961) 108 (105–122); A. S. Kapelrud, "The Traditio-Historical Study of Prophets," in *The Productions of Time* (1984) 57 (53–66). On the "theological implications" of tradition history, see Douglas Knight, "Tradition History," in *The Anchor Bible Dictionary, Volume 6: Si–Z*. Ed. David Noel Freedman. New York: Doubleday, 1992, p. 637 (633–638).

13. Our remarks on i.b.e. will be restricted to Michael Fishbane's monumental *Biblical Interpretation in Ancient Israel*. Oxford: Clarendon Press, 1985, in particular, his first section entitled "Scribal Comments and Corrections." This is not to downplay the importance of other studies of this genre, nor the rest of Fishbane's study, but rather to signal the special relevance of this particular line of analysis to our theory of composition by aggregate (discussed in Chapter Three).

14. Michael Fishbane, *Biblical Interpretation*, pp. 27, 23, 6. Fishbane's use of the *traditum/traditio* dichotomy was taken from Knight's, *Rediscovering the Traditions*, pp. 5–20. Fishbane notes, however, that he is not speaking of oral, but literary texts, p. 7. James Kugel has pointed to the difficulties these imprecise terms create, be it in Latin or English, for Fishbane's hypothesis. "The Bible's Earliest Interpreters," Review of Michael Fishbane's *Biblical Interpretation in Ancient Israel*.

Prooftexts 7 (1987) 273–274 (269–283). On the repeated interpretation and copying of texts, see James Kugel, *The Bible as It Was*. Cambridge: The Belknap Press,
2000, p. 1.

15. Fishbane continues "and so interrupted the a-ab parallelism...with the spec-
ifying comment." *Biblical Interpretation*, p. 55. Kugel, in "The Bible's Earliest
Interpreters," p. 278, finds Fishbane's argument about Psalm 68:9 unconvinc-
ing. In fact, this has never been an especially popular interpretation of the verse.
Mitchell Dahood interprets what Fishbane would later see as a gloss as an "epi-
thet of Yahweh," namely, "the One of Sinai." Mitchell Dahood, *Psalms II: 51–100*.
The Anchor Bible. Garden City, NJ: Doubleday, 1968, p. 139. Also see Dahood,
"Hebrew-Ugaritic Lexicography II," *Biblica* 45 (1964) 405, and Theophile Meek,
"Translating the Hebrew Bible," *JBL* 79 (1960) 332. Contra Ernst Vogt, "'Die Him-
mel troffen'" (Ps. 68:9)?," *Biblica* 46 (1965) 207–209; I. L. Seeligmann, "A Psalm
from Pre-Regal Times," *VT* 14 (1964) 80, fn 1, also sees "a faulty gloss." For the
translation "yon Sinai," see A. A. Anderson, *The Book of Psalms: Volume I, Intro-
duction and Psalms 1–72*. New Century Bible. Greenwood: Attic Press, 1972, p. 487.
A completely different translation of *zeh sînay* as "Lord of Sinai" is suggested by
Frank Moore Cross, *Canaanite Myth and Hebrew Epic: Essays in the History of the
Religion of Israel*. Cambridge, MA: Harvard University Press, 1973, pp. 100–101.

16. Fishbane, *Biblical Interpretation*, p. 38. For criticisms of Fishbane, see the following reviews of *Biblical Interpretation*: Lyle Eslinger, "Inner-Biblical Exegesis
and Inner-Biblical Allusion: The Question of Category," *VT* 42 (1992) 47–58
[and the response of Benjamin Sommer, "Exegesis, Allusion and Intertextuality
in the Hebrew Bible: A Response to Lyle Eslinger," *VT* 46 (1996) 479–489], and
H. G. M. Williamson, "History," in *It Is Written: Scripture Citing Scripture, Essays
in Honor of Barnabas Lindars, SSF*. Eds. D. A. Carson and H. G. M. Williamson.
Cambridge: Cambridge University Press, 1988, pp. 27–28 (25–38). On the tendency of Fishbane to see biblical writing as an organic precursor of postbiblical
Rabbinic interpretation, see Kugel, "The Bible's," p. 276; Also, James Sanders,
"Review of Michael Fishbane's *Biblical Interpretation in Ancient Israel*," *CBQ* 49
(1987) 302–305, 303; And finally, Brevard Childs, "Review of Michael Fishbane's
Biblical Interpretation in Ancient Israel," *JBL* 106 (1987) 511–513. For brief remarks
on the relation between i.b.e and documentary hypothesis, see Wolfgang Roth,
"Biblical Interpretation in Ancient Israel," *JQR* 69 (1989) 391 (387–391). For a discussion of the very similar concept of "secondary readings," see Alexander Rofé,
"The Historical Significance of Secondary Readings," in *The Quest for Context
and Meaning: Studies in Biblical Intertextuality in Honor of James A. Sanders*. Eds.
Craig Evans and Shemaryahu Talmon. Leiden: Brill, 1997, pp. 393–402. He writes:
"changes introduced by the scribes into the manuscripts i.e. secondary readings,
sometimes have considerable significance" p. 393. A more skeptical assessment
about glosses and scribal additions in general can be found in Emanuel Tov,
"Glosses, Interpolations, and Other Types of Scribal Additions in the Text of the
Hebrew Bible," in *Language, Theology, and the Bible: Essays in Honour of James
Barr*. Eds. Samuel Balentine and John Barton. Oxford: Clarendon Press, 1994,
pp. 40–66.

17. Bernard Levinson, *Deuteronomy and the Hermeneutics of Legal Innovation*. New
York: Oxford University Press, 1997, pp. 6, 16–17. A clear restatement of the

assumptions of the school of inner-biblical exegesis can be found in Esther Menn, "Inner-Biblical Exegesis in the Tanak," in *A History of Biblical Interpretation: Volume 1, The Ancient Period*. Eds. Alan Hauser and Duane Watson. Grand Rapids, MI: William B. Eerdmans, 2003, pp. 55–79.

18. Samuel Sandmel, "The Haggadah Within Scripture," *JBL* 80 (1961) 105–122, and see pages 110, 120, and 122 for the previous quotes. Also see Frederick Winnett, "Re-examining the Foundations," *JBL* 84 (1965) 12 (1–19). On the tendency of ancient writers to combine or merge different documents that recounted different versions of the same event see Rofé, *Introduction*, pp. 112, 117. The sources were not blended according to Sandmel, rather they were simple recastings of ancient tales. See the assessment of Brevard Childs, "Review of *Biblical Interpretation in Ancient Israel* by Michael Fishbane," *JBL* 106 (1987) 512–513. And see the critique made by Whybray, *The Making*, p. 222. In Sandmel's conception the roots of Haggadic writing would extend further back in Jewish/Israelite history than most would have imagined. In this manner, his emphasis on continuity between the biblical and Rabbinic periods resembles that of Michael Fishbane. Also see Esther Menn's discussion of the differences between biblical and Rabbinic exegesis, "Inner-Biblical Exegesis," p. 75.

19. John Barton, "What Is a Book? Modern Exegesis and the Literary Conventions of Ancient Israel," in *Intertextuality in Ugarit and Israel* (= *Oudtestamentische Studiën* 40). Ed. Johannes de Moor. Leiden: Brill, 1998, pp. 6, 12 (1–14). On the anthological nature of Scripture, see Michael Fishbane's "The Hebrew Bible and Exegetical Tradition," in *Intertextuality in Ugarit and Israel* (= *Oudtestamentische Studiën* 40). Ed. Johannes de Moor. Leiden: Brill, p. 18 n(15–30).

20. Monoauthorism would seem to have made a comeback in the form of biblical literary criticism. For a full discussion, see Jacques Berlinerblau, "The Bible as Literature?" *Hebrew Studies* 45 (2004) 9–26. On the tendency of higher critics to aim for "the intention of the writer," see Ellen van Wolde, "Intertextuality: Ruth in Dialogue with Tamar," in *A Feminist Companion to Reading the Bible*. Eds. Athalya Brenner and Carol Fontaine. Sheffield: Sheffield Academic Press, 1997, p. 430; Regina Schwartz, "Introduction: On Biblical Criticism," in *The Book and the Text: The Bible and Literary Theory*. Ed. Regina Schwartz. Cambridge: Basil Blackwell, 1990, p. 13 (1–15); Jon Levenson, "The Hebrew Bible, the Old Testament, and Historical Criticism," in *The Future of Biblical Studies: The Hebrew Scriptures*. Eds. Richard Elliot Friedman and H. G. M. Williamson. Atlanta: Scholars Press, 1987, pp. 50–51 (19–60). Here we use the term "historical criticism" as roughly equivalent to what we are calling modern biblical scholarship. See Norman Gottwald's remarks on the attempt to reconcile religious and historical approaches in Old Testament scholarship, *The Hebrew Bible: A Socio-Literary Introduction*. Philadelphia: Fortress Press, 1987, pp. 16–20. These tensions are discussed cleverly in John Collins, "Biblical Theology and the History of Israelite Religion," in *Back to the Sources: Biblical and Near Eastern Studies in Honour of Dermot Ryan*. Eds. Kevin Cathcart and John Healey. Dublin: Glendale, 1989, pp. 16–32.

21. The quote from Franz Delitzsch is cited in Rudolf Smend, "Julius Wellhausen and His *Prolegomena to the History of Israel*," *Semeia* 25 (1982) 3 (1–20).

22. John Barton, "Wellhausen's *Prolegomena to the History of Israel*: Influences and Effects," in *Text and Experience: Towards a Cultural Exegesis of the Bible*. Ed. Daniel Smith-Christopher. Sheffield: Sheffield Academic Press, 1995, p. 319.

3. A SECULAR ANSWER TO "WHO WROTE THE BIBLE?"

1. Statements attributing the Old and New Testaments to inspiration by the Holy Spirit can be readily found in the patristic literature. J. T. Forestell writes: "Christian antiquity, in its prayer, preaching, and theological writing, universally recognized that the writings of the OT and NT were the work of the Holy Spirit and were all equally the word of God." "Bible, II (Inspiration)," in *New Catholic Encyclopedia, Volume II. Baa to Cam.* Washington, DC: Catholic University of America, 1967, p. 382. A similar point is made by M. F. Wiles, "Origen as Biblical Scholar," in *The Cambridge History of the Bible, Volume 1: From the Beginnings to Jerome.* Eds. Peter Ackroyd and C. F. Evans. Cambridge: Cambridge University Press, 1970, p. 461 (454–488). A few examples would be Origen, *Genesis Homily* 2:2; *Exodus Homily* 4:2 in *Origen: Homilies on Genesis and Exodus.* Trans. Ronald Heine. Washington, DC: The Catholic University of America Press, 1982. On the Holy Spirit's influence on the Psalms, see Theodoret of Cyprus, "Commentary on Psalm 73" and "Commentary on Psalm 104" in *Theodoret of Cyrus: Commentary on the Psalms, Psalms 73–150.* Trans. Robert Hill. Washington, DC: The Catholic University of America Press, 2001. In Augustine's sermons on the Psalter, the Holy Spirit is often seen as the author. Michael Fiedrowicz in the introduction to a new translation writes: "The words of a psalm are often attributed immediately to the Holy Spirit as to their proper speaker, without human agency." *The Works of Saint Augustine: A Translation for the 21st Century Expositions of the Psalms 1–32.* Ed. John Rotelle. Hyde Park, NY: New City Press, 2000, p. 24. One of the apostolic Church Fathers, Clement of Rome, writes: "You have studied the Holy Scriptures, which are true and inspired by the Holy Spirit." Clement of Rome, "The Letter of St. Clement to the Corinthians," 45 in *The Apostolic Fathers,* Trans. Francis Glimm. New York: Christian Heritage, 1948. Also see Bruce Vawter, "The Bible in the Roman Catholic Church," in *Scripture in the Jewish and Christian Traditions: Authority, Interpretation, Relevance.* Ed. Frederick Greenspahn. Nashville, TN: Abingdon, 1982, pp. 112–133. The Holy Spirit also appears in Rabbinic discussions of biblical authorship as noted in Chapter One. The association between the Holy Spirit and Scripture can be found in many Protestant teachings such as the Westminster Confession, see John Gerstner, "A Protestant View of Biblical Authority," in *Scripture in the Jewish and Christian Traditions: Authority: Interpretation, Relevance.* Ed. Frederick Greenspahn. Nashville, TN: Abingdon, 1982, pp. 42–63. For attributions to God, Moses, angels, and so on, see Chapter One.

2. Just to make things appropriately complex, note that any two juxtaposed texts may each individually have been the victims of earlier acts of superimposition. The Rabbinic sages seem to entertain some sort of notion of juxtaposition. Rabbi Meir once noted: "There are sections [in Scripture] which are close to one another and yet as distant as is the East from the West in subject matter." *Midrash Sifre,*

Numbers, 131 in 1926. *Midrash Sifre on Numbers: Selections from Early Rabbinic Scriptural Interpretations*. Trans. Paul Levertoff. London: A. Golub, 1926, p. 134. And see *Midrash Psalms*, 3:2, where Rabbi Eleazar teaches: "The sections of Scripture are not arranged in their proper order...." *The Midrash on Psalms (The First of Two Volumes)*. Trans. William Braude. New Haven, CT: Yale University Press, 1959, p. 49.

3. We should recall that according to a school such as tradition history (discussed in Chapter Two), even the "first" author, the one who transferred the oral legend to a scroll, was confronted with oral precursors. Presently, many biblical literary critics advocate what we call "final-redactor monoauthorism." This is the designation we use to refer to those who ascribe an astonishing degree of responsibility for the overall form and contents of biblical texts to one person, allegedly the last person to work over the materials. It is a corollary of this view that one need only scrutinize the final version of the text. By looking exclusively at canonized scripture, these scholars conveniently bypass the long, complex compositional history of the Bible (as well as more than a century of higher and lower critical research). "But is it not the task of the critic," asks Gabriel Josipovici, "to try and come to grips with the final form as we have it, and to give the final editor or redactor the benefit of the doubt, rather than to delve behind his work to what was there before?" *The Book of God: A Response to the Bible*. New Haven, CT: Yale University Press, 1988, p. 14. Also see Edward Greenstein, "An Equivocal Reading of the Sale of Joseph," in *Literary Interpretations of Biblical Narratives. Volume II*. Ed. Kenneth Gros Louis. Nashville, TN: Abingdon, 1982, p. 117 (114–125), and Northrop Frye, *The Great Code: The Bible and Literature*. New York: Harcourt Brace Jovanovich, 1982, p. xvii. Final-redactor monoauthorism is especially pronounced in the writings of Robert Alter; see, for example, *The Art of Biblical Narrative*. New York: Basic Books, 1981, and all the works cited in our critique of this approach, "The Bible as Literature?" *Hebrew Studies* 45 (2004) 9–26. Needless to say, the final-redactor approach pays far too little attention to the materials inherited by an editor and the effect that this *traditum* will have on the last person to work over a text. On the notion of authorship being difficult to apply to biblical texts, see Gerald Bruns, *Hermeneutics: Ancient and Modern*. New Haven, CT: Yale University Press, 1992, pp. 64–82.

4. For an interesting discussion of the notion of male authorship, see Athalya Brenner, "Introduction," in *On Gendering Texts: Female and Male Voices in the Hebrew Bible*. Eds. Athalya Brenner and Fokkelien Van Dijk-Hemmes. Leiden: E. J. Brill, 1993, pp. 1–13. On scribes and gender also consult David Baker, "Scribes as Transmitters of Tradition," in *Faith, Tradition, and History: Old Testament Historiagraphy in its Near Eastern Context*. Eds. A. R. Millard, James Hoffmeier, and David Baker. Winona Lake, IN: Eisenbrauns, 1994, pp. 69–77 (65–77). Philip Davies. *In Search of 'Ancient Israel.'* Sheffield: Sheffield Academic Press, 1992, pp. 19, 106–109, 116–120, although in this book Davies disagrees sharply with the type of diachronic models advocated previously. The phrase "plutocratic prerequisites" is used by Max Weber in his famous essay "Science as a Vocation," in *From Max Weber: Essays in Sociology*. New York: Oxford University Press, 1958, p. 129 (129–156).

5. Dexterous and highly motivated types probably performed a few of these activities at once.

6. Jeffrey Tigay. *The Evolution of the Gilgamesh Epic*. Philadelphia: University of Pennsylvania Press, 1982, p. 1. Also see the remarks of S. N. Kramer on the way in which Semitic Babylonians modified the Sumerian prototype. "The Death of Gilgamesh," *BASOR* 94 (1944) 2–12. For an excellent discussion of traditional biblical and ancient Near Eastern methods of textual meddling, see Jeffrey Tigay, "The Evolution of the Pentateuchal Narratives in Light of the Evolution of the *Gilgamesh Epic*," in *Empirical Models for Biblical Criticism*. Ed. Jeffrey Tigay. Philadelphia: University of Pennsylvania Press, 1985, pp. 21–52. In the same study, Tigay scrutinized the compositional history of texts ranging from the *Epic of Gilgamesh* to the Masoretic text of the Hebrew Bible, to the Samaritan Pentateuch, to the Septuagint, and to selected Qumran manuscripts. In each case, it seem clear that (what we call) transhistorical polyauthorism was practiced by ancient Near Eastern scribes. "Conflation as a Redactional Technique," in *Empirical Models*, pp. 53–95. David Carr remarks that scribes in the prebiblical and biblical period "were much more inclined than we are to build on earlier texts, incorporating, combining, and expanding them into a new and complex whole." *Reading the Fractures of Genesis: Historical and Literary Approaches*. Louisville, KY: Westminster John Knox Press, 1996, p. 16. On the consequences of editing, also see Brian Peckham, "Writing and Editing," in *Fortunate the Eyes That See: Essays in Honor of David Noel Freedman in Celebration of His Seventieth Birthday*. Eds. Astrid Beck, Andrew Bartelt, Paul Raabe, and Chris Franke. Grand Rapids, MI: William B. Eerdmans, 1995, p. 382 (364–383). Contra the conlusions of J. P. Weinberg, "Authorship and Author in the Ancient Near East and in the Hebrew Bible," *Hebrew Studies* 44 (2003) 157–169.

7. The biblical scholar Michael Fox makes this point well (albeit using monoauthorist nomenclature) in his discussion of a strangely secular text: "Esther was not written as part of the Bible. Not only could the author not have known that there would be a Bible, but the lack of a reference to God may show that he did not intend his book to be regarded as sacred scripture." Michael Fox, "The Religion of the Book of Esther," *Judaism* 39 (1990) 137 (135–147).

8. Richard Elliot Friedman, "Sacred History and Theology: The Redaction of Torah," in *The Creation of Sacred Literature: Composition and Redaction of the Biblical Text*. Ed. Richard Elliot Friedman. Berkeley: University of California Press, 1981, p. 25 (25–34); Stephen Geller, "Through Windows and Mirrors into the Bible. History, Literature and Language in the Study of the Text," in *A Sense of Text: The Art of Language in the Study of Biblical Literature*. Ed. Stephen Geller. Winona Lake, IN: Eisenbrauns, 1983, p. 23 (3–40). Hahn's remark occurs in a discussion of Gunkel's writings, Herbert Hahn, *The Old Testament in Modern Research*. Philadelphia: Fortress Press, 1966, p. 126.

9. Michael Fishbane, "Jewish Biblical Exegesis: Presuppositions and Principles," in *Scripture in the Jewish and Christian Traditions: Authority, Interpretation, Relevance*. Ed. Frederick Greenspahn. Nashville, TN: Abingdon, 1982, p. 101 (92–110); Nahum Sarna, "The Authority and Interpretation of Scripture in Jewish Tradition," in *Studies in Biblical Interpretation*. Philadelphia: The Jewish Publication

Society, 2000, p. 67 (67–79); Northrop Frye, *The Great Code: The Bible and Literature*. New York: Harcourt Brace Jovanovich, 1982, p. 220.

10. William Blake, "The Everlasting Gospel," in *The Complete Poetry and Prose of William Blake*. Ed. David Erdman. Berkeley: University of California Press, 1982, p. 524; William Shakespeare. *The Merchant of Venice*. New York: Signet, 1998, I. 3. 95 and III. 2. 77–79.

11. On the Torah's "seventy faces" see *Midrash Rabbah Numbers*, XIII 15. A somewhat different translation can be found in *Midrash Rabbah: Numbers, Volume Two*. Trans. J. Slotki. London: Soncino Press, 1983, p. 534. There the translation is "there are seventy modes of expounding the Torah." Nahum Sarna translates: "There are seventy facets to the Torah." "The Authority," p. 68.

12. Israel Knohl, *The Divine Symphony: The Bible's Many Voices*. Philadelphia: JPS, 2003, p. 5.

13. In speaking of editing, Brian Peckham remarks, "the edited version turns out to be a completely different literary work with another structure and another interpretation of history." "Writing and Editing," p. 365. We had believed the phrase "meaning never meant" was of our own invention. More recently, however, we discovered that Professor John Barton had spoken of texts that have "meanings that no one ever meant," so the credit belongs to him. *Reading the Old Testament: Method in Biblical Study*. Philadelphia: Westminister Press, 1984, p. 78.

14. On this attribution of sources, or similar schemes, see Richard Elliot Friedman, *Who Wrote the Bible?* San Francisco: HarperSanFrancisco, 1989, pp. 247–248; Martin Noth, *A History of Pentateuchal Traditions*. Trans. Bernhard Anderson. Englewood Cliffs, NJ: Prentice Hall, 1972, pp. 35, 28–29; S. R. Driver. *An Introduction to the Literature of the Old Testament*. New York: Meridian Books, 1963, p. 15. In a 1981 study of redaction, Friedman used the term "narrative synthesis." He wanted to show how the work of an editor juxtaposing his sources generated what we have called meaning possibilities. Friedman oscillates between seeing the final text as the result of contingencies and seeing the presence of a theological consciousness that intentionally created the final product. "Sacred History," pp. 25–34. A similar interest in the sum being greater than the parts can be seen in Simeon Chavel, "Compositry and Creativity in 2 Samuel 21:1–14," *JBL* 122 (2003) 23–52. Roland Barthes' remark, "We do not read the text in its 'truth' but in its 'production'" would seem apt. "The Struggle with the Angel: Textual Analysis of Genesis 32:23–33," in *Structural Analysis and Biblical Exegesis: Interpretational Essays*. Trans. Alfred Johnson, Jr. Pittsburgh: The Pickwick Press, 1974, p. 24 (21–33).

15. On the tendency of Midrashic commentators to juxtapose remote sources see James Kugel, "Two Introductions to Midrash," in *Midrash and Literature*. Eds. Geoffrey Hartman and Sanford Budick. New Haven, CT: Yale University Press, 1986, p. 93. (77–103).

16. Frye, *The Great Code*, p. 204.

17. On the addition of chapter divisions and numbered verses, see G. F. Moore, "The Vulgate Chapters and Numbered Verses in the Hebrew Bible." *JBL* 12 (1893) 73–78. More recently, see Jordan Penkower, "Verse Divisions in the Hebrew Bible," *VT* 50 (2000) 379–393.

4. WHY IS THERE SO MUCH BIBLICAL INTERPRETATION?

1. The interpretation of every single word has been performed, of course, on the Masoretic, Septuagint, and Vulgatic incarnations (to name but a few) of the Bible. To a far lesser extent, Muslims have exegeted the Hebrew Bible/Old Testament. For an interesting study of this topic, see Hava Lazarus-Yafeh, *Intertwined Worlds: Medieval Islam and Bible Criticism*. Princeton, NJ: Princeton University Press, 1992. We assume more Old Testament interpretation has occurred than New Testament interpretation. Christians interpret both testaments in equal measure. Jews, of course, only exegete the latter (i.e., Hebrew Bible). Further, prior to the canonization of the New Testament, analysis of the Old had been taking place for centuries. R. P. C. Hanson writes: "By far the greater part of Christian exegesis for a hundred and fifty years after the resurrection is of course exegesis of the Old Testament," "Biblical Exegesis in the Early Church," in *The Cambridge History of the Bible, Volume 1: From the Beginnings to Jerome*. Eds. P. R. Ackroyd and C. F. Evans. Cambridge: Cambridge University Press, 1970, p. 414 (412–453). In light of these considerations, the Hebrew Bible would seem to have endured more interpretation than the New Testament. For *The Wrath of Telipinu*, see the Gary Beckman translation in *The Context of Scripture. Volume 1. Canonical Compositions from the Biblical World*. Eds. William Hallo and K. Lawson Younger. Leiden: Brill, 1997, pp. 151–153.

2. On some of those who rejected the authority of the Old Testament, see William Horbury, "Old Testament Interpretation on the Writings of the Church Fathers," in *Mikra: Text, Translation, Reading and Interpretation of the Hebrew Bible in Ancient Judaism and Early Christianity*. Ed. Martin Jan Mulder. Assen/Maastricht: Van Gorcum, 1988, pp. 758–760 (727–787).

3. Paul Raabe, *Obadiah: A New Translation with Introduction and Commentary*. New York: Doubleday, 1996, pp. 32–33. For the discussion of a similar intertextual phenomenon in another prophetic book, see Adele Berlin, *Zephaniah: A New Translation with Introduction and Commentary*. New York: Doubleday, 1994, p. 13. John Day points out that while the prophets quote each other repeatedly, they "almost never admit explicitly that they are quoting," "Prophecy," in *It Is Written: Scripture Citing Scripture: Essays in Honor of Barnabas Lindars, SSF*. Eds. D. A. Carson and H. G. M. Williamson. Cambridge: Cambridge University Press, 1988, p. 49 (39–55). We also cite the early and important article of David Clines, "Nehemiah 10 as an Example of Early Jewish Biblical Exegesis," *JSOT* 21 (1981) 111–117; G. Vermes, "Bible and Midrash: Early Old Testament Exegesis," in *The Cambridge History of the Bible, Volume 1: From the Beginnings to Jerome*. Eds. P. R. Ackroyd and C. F. Evans. Cambridge: Cambridge University Press, 1970, p. 201 (199–231); Regina Schwartz, "Introduction: On Biblical Criticism," in *The Book and the Text: The Bible and Literary Theory*. Ed. Regina Schwartz. Cambridge: Basil Blackwell, 1990, p. 4 (1–15).

4. For a more recent discussion of the date of the closing of the Hebrew canon, see Roger Beckwith, "Formation of the Hebrew Bible," in *Mikra: Text, Translation, Reading and Interpretation of the Hebrew Bible in Ancient Judaism and Early Christianity*. Ed. Martin Jan Mulder. Assen/Maastricht: Van Gorcum, 1988, pp. 39–87. Also see James Sanders, "Canon" in *The Anchor Bible Dictionary, Volume 1: A–C*.

Ed. David Noel Freedman. New York: Doubleday, 1992, pp. 837–852, and Jack
Lewis, "Jamnia Revisited," in *The Canon Debate*. Eds. Lee Martin McDonald and
James Sanders. Peabody, MA: Hendrickson, 2002, pp. 146–162.

5. See Roland Bainton, "The Bible in the Reformation," in *The Cambridge History
of the Bible: The West from the Reformation to the Present Day, Volume Three*, Ed.
S. L. Greendslade. Cambridge: At the University Press, 1963, pp. 1–37.

6. On the name of Deuteronomy, see Moshe Weinfeld, *Deuteronomy 1–11*.
The Anchor Bible. New York: Doubleday, 1991, pp. 1–2; Alfred Bertholet,
Deuteronomium. Freiburg: J. C. B. Mohr, 1899, pp. 9–17; S. R. Driver, *A Critical and Exegetical Commentary on Deuteronomy*. ICC. Edinburgh: T. and T. Clark,
1902, pp. ii–xix. "We are struck by the fact," wrote Gerhard Von Rad, "that a large
part of the laws or maxims of the sacral code is known already from the Book of
the Covenant (Ex. 21–23)," *Deuteronomy: A Commentary*. Trans. Dorothea Barton. Philadelphia: Westminster Press, 1966, p. 13. For a comparison of the passages
from Exodus and Deuteronomy, see John Van Seters, "'Comparing Scripture with
Scripture': Some Observations of the Sinai Pericope of Exodus 19–24" in *Canon,
Theology, and Old Testament Interpretation: Essays in Honor of Brevard S. Childs*.
Eds. Gene Tucker, David Petersen, and Robert Wilson. Philadelphia: Fortress Press,
1988, pp. 111–130. Here we assume, as most do, that the reference to the "Book of
the Covenant" in Exodus 24:7 refers to the preceding collection of laws found in
Ex. 20:22–23:19. On this see John Durham, *Exodus*. World Biblical Commentary.
Waco, TX: Word Books, 1987, p. 315. A similar observation is made in S. R. Driver,
The Book of Exodus: In the Revised Version with Introduction and Notes. Cambridge:
At the University Press, 1953, p. 253. Cassuto, however, challenges the assumption
that Moses was reading the same text. U. Cassuto, *A Commentary on the Book of
Exodus*. Jerusalem: The Magnes Press, 1951, pp. 217–218.

7. These events occur in 2 K 22–23. Since the early nineteenth century, the "discovered" book has always been associated with Deuteronomy or some major part of it.
See Mordechai Cogan and Hayim Tadmor, II *Kings: A New Translation with Introduction and Commentary*. Anchor Bible. New York: Doubleday, 1988, p. 294. Also
see Driver, *A Critical*, p. xlv. N. Lohfink writes: "This document is probably identical with an early edition of Deut-5–28." "Deuteronomy," in *The Interpreter's
Dictionary of the Bible: Supplementary Volume*. Nashville, TN: Abingdon Press,
1976, p. 231 (229–232). Also see Louis Pirot and Albert Clamer, *La Sainte Bible,
TomeIII, Josué-Juges-Ruth-Rois*. Paris: Letouzey et Ané, 1949, p. 782.

8. On dreams and their interpretation, see Gen. 37:5–10; 40:5–8; 41:1–16; Dan. 2; and
Judges 7:9–15. On dreams in general, see Ernst Ehrlich, *Der Traum im Alten Tes-
tament*. Beihefte zur Zeitschrift für die Alttestamentliche Wissenschaft 73. Berlin:
Alfred Töpelmann, 1953. More recently, Shaul Bar, *A Letter That Has Not Been
Read: Dreams in the Hebrew Bible*. Trans. Lenn Schramm. Cincinnati: Hebrew
Union College Press, 2001. Samson's famous riddle story occurs in Judg. 14; also
see Daniel 5. On riddles in general, see Harry Torczyner, "The Riddle in the Bible,"
HUCA 1 (1924) 125–149, and James Crenshaw, "Riddles," in *The Anchor Bible Dictionary, Volume 5: O-Sh*. Ed. David Noel Freedman. New York: Doubleday, 1992,
pp. 721–723. As for toponyms that are explained, see, for example, Gen. 11:9;
16:14; and 19:22. The famous Shibboleth incident occurs in Judges 12:1–6. Failed

interpretations of various nonchosen peoples can be glanced in Gen. 41:8 and Dan. 2:1–12. Strangely, although the prohibition against sculpted images (Exod. 20:4) may have rendered the Israelites aniconic, it seemingly did not succeed in making them asymbolic. Nothing can stand for God. But in the secular realm one thing can stand for another.

9. Marcel Simon, "The Bible in the Earliest Controversies Between Jews and Christians," in *The Bible in Greek Christian Antiquity*. Ed. Paul Blowers. Notre Dame: University of Notre Dame Press, 1997, p. 53 (49–68); Cyril, *Catechesis* IV:33 in *The Works of Saint Cyril of Jerusalem, Volume 1*. Trans. Leo McCauley and Anthony Stephenson. Washington, DC: The Catholic University of America, 1969, p. 135.

10. R. P. C. Hanson, "The Bible in the Early Church" in *The Cambridge History of the Bible: From the Beginnings to Jerome*. Eds. P. R. Ackroyd and C. F. Evans. Cambridge: Cambridge University Press, 1970, pp. 412 (412–453); *Aboth* 1:1 in *Aboth*. Trans. J. Israelstam. London: Soncino Press, 1935, p. 1. Steven Schwarzschild has observed that in Judaism Talmudic teaching "if anything surpasses in authority the Bible itself." "Judaism, Scriptures, and Ecumenism," in *Scripture and Ecumenism: Protestant, Catholic, Orthodox and Jewish*. Ed. Leonard Swidler. Pittsburgh: Duquesne University Press, p. 123 (111–132). For a comprehensive discussion of Rabbinic literature in this period, see the edited volume, *The Literature of the Sages: First Part: Oral Tora, Halakha, Mishna, Tosfeta, Talmud, External Tractates*. Ed. Shmuel Safrai. Philadelphia: Fortress Press, 1987.

11. Albert Outler, "Scripture, Tradition and Ecumenism," in *Scripture and Ecumenism: Protestant, Catholic, Orthodox and Jewish*. Ed. Leonard Swidler. Pittsburgh: Duquesne University Press, 1965, p. 9 (9–22).

12. Philo, *Questions and Answers on Genesis*, Book I, 10. *Philo Supplement I: Questions and Answers on Genesis*. Trans. Ralph Marcus. Cambridge, MA: Harvard University Press, 1971, p. 7.

13. On Augustine's "fascinated preoccupation" with hidden meanings see Gerald Bonner, "Augustine as Biblical Scholar," in *The Cambridge History of the Bible, Volume 1: From the Beginnings to Jerome*. Eds. P. R. Ackroyd and C. F. Evans. Cambridge: Cambridge University Press, 1970, p. 559, and see p. 547 for quotes pertaining to this view (541–562); James Kugel, *The Bible as it Was*. Cambridge: The Belknap Press, 2000, p. 18. Origen, in his Letter to Gregory Thaumaturgus writes: "While you attend to this divine reading seek aright and with unwavering faith in God the hidden sense which is present in most of the passages of divine scripture." in *Bible Interpretation*. Ed. James Megivern. Wilimgton, NC: Consortium, 1978, p. 18. Origen's reference to "stumbling blocks" can be found in Frances Young, *Biblical Exegesis and the Formation of Christian Culture*, Cambridge: Cambridge University Press, 1997, p. 22. The Qumran sectarians also spoke of hidden meanings in the Torah; see Lawrence Schiffman, *The Halakah at Qumran*. Leiden: E. J. Brill, 1975, pp. 22–32, 75–76. Nahum Sarna has spoken of the Rabbinic principle that Scripture retains a "deliberate equivocality." "The Authority and Interpretation of Scripture in Jewish Tradition," in *Studies in Biblical Interpretation*. Philadelphia: Jewish Publication Society, 2000, p. 76 (67–79).

14. C. K. Barrett, "The Interpretation of the Old Testament in the New," in *The Cambridge History of the Bible, Volume 1: From the Beginnings to Jerome*. Eds. P. R. Ackroyd and C. F. Evans. Cambridge: At the University Press, 1970, p. 388 (377–411); Kugel, *The Bible as it Was*, 21–22. On the Rabbinic perception of the Bible as the revealed word of God, also see Irving Jacobs, *The Midrashic Process: Tradition and Interpretation in Rabbinic Judaism*. Cambridge: Cambridge University Press, 1995, p. 4. Robert Carroll writes: "religious communities invariably read the Bible as if it were timeless and addressed to themselves." "The Reader and the Text," in *Text in Context: Essays by Members of the Society for Old Testament Study*, Ed. A. D. H. Mayes. Oxford: Oxford University Press, 2000, p. 19 (4–34).

15. On Williams, see Norman Sykes, "The Religion of the Protestants," in *The Cambridge History of the Bible: The West from the Reformation to the Present Day, Volume 3*. Ed. S. L. Greenslade. Cambridge: Cambridge University Press, 1963, p. 186 (175–198).

16. Exodus 24:7; 2 Kings 23:3; Ezra 9–10; Neh. 8 (and see our discussion of Ezra in the next chapter where we discuss the dissent from a certain Jonathan and his two supporters mentioned in Ezra 10:15): Loring Batten was surely correct in referring to Neh. 8:8 as an "obscure" and "a loosely constructed passage." *The Books of Ezra and Nehemiah*. ICC. New York: Charles Scribner's Sons, 1913, p. 356. We would translate "They (?) read in/from the scroll, in/from the teaching of Elohim *mĕpōrāš wĕśôm śekel* and they understood the reading." The first question mark after "they" is present to indicate the strangeness of having Ezra, who is supposedly doing the reading, spoken of in third person plural. The problems in translation center around the words *mĕpōrāš wĕśôm śekel*. Charles Torrey rendered the verse this way, "And they read in the book of the law distinctly, and gave the sense, so that the reading was understood." *Ezra Studies*. New York: Ktav, 1970, p. 268. Michael Fishbane translates "they read out explicitly," "and gave the sense." *Biblical Interpretation in Ancient Israel*, Oxford: Clarendon Press, 1985, p. 109.

17. Clifford Geertz, *Islam Observed: Religious Development in Morocco and Indonesia*. Chicago: University of Chicago Press, 1971, p. 39; Zechariah 9:12.

5. INTRODUCING BIBLICAL SCHOLARS AND SECULAR HERMENEUTICS

1. Data and speculation on the religiosity of biblicists can be found in Jacques Berlinerblau's "'Poor Bird, Not Knowing Which Way to Fly': Biblical Scholarship's Marginality, Secular Humanism, and the Laudable Occident," *Biblical Interpretation* 10 (2002) 267–304. Adele Berlin's remarks are also of interest in "A Search for a New Biblical Hermeneutics: Preliminary Observations," in *The Study of the Ancient Near East in the Twenty-First Century: The William Foxwell Albright Centennial Conference*. Eds. Jerrold Cooper and Glenn Schwartz. Winona Lake, IN: Eisenbrauns, 1996, p. 197 (195–207).

2. An interesting study of one such university president can be found in James Wind's *The Bible and the University: The Messianic Vision of William Rainey Harper*. Atlanta: Scholars Press, 1987.

3. Martin Marty, "America's Iconic Book," in *Humanizing America's Iconic Book*. Eds. Gene Tucker and Douglas Knight. Chico, CA: Scholars Press, 1982, p. 22 (1–23).

4. Robert Carroll, *Wolf in the Sheepfold: The Bible as a Problem for Christianity*. London: SPCK, 1991, p. 2.

5. David Clines, *The Bible and the Modern World*. Sheffield: Sheffield Academic Press, 1997, p. 23.

6. In a famous article Edward Ullendorff argued that the Masoretes "superimposed an elaborate network of vowels and accents which have effectively disguised many of the distinctive characteristics which the living language must have exhibited. There is little discernible development in the Masoretic pronunciation of Hebrew, and the vocalism applied to the consonants makes Deborah talk in very much in the same manner as Qoheleth or Daniel or Esther almost a thousand years later. It is clear, therefore, that this language is the result of a good deal of subsequent doctoring, of leveling and compromise, resulting in a hybrid language.... In any real sense of the term, BH in its Masoretic garb was scarcely a language which in that form was ever actually spoken. The subsequent process of leveling and averaging has created a structure which neither Deborah nor Daniel would be likely to have recognized." "Is Biblical Hebrew a Language?" in *Is Biblical Hebrew a Language? Studies in Semitic Languages and Civilizations*. Wiesbaden, Germany: Otto Harrassowitz, 1977, p. 7 (3–17).

7. As Claus Westermann notes: "the verse bristles with difficulties." *Genesis 1–11: A Commentary*. Trans. John Scullion. Minneapolis: Augsburg, 1984, p. 373. Gordon Wenham opines: "almost every word in this statement has been the subject of controversy." *Genesis 1–15*. Word Biblical Commentary. Waco, TX: Word Books, 1987, p. 141. John Skinner, who offered something very close to a secular translation, writes: "A complete exegesis of these words is impossible." *A Critical and Exegetical Commentary on Genesis*. ICC. New York: Charles Scribner's Sons, 1917, p. 144. On the difficulties, also see B. Jacob. *Das Erste Buch Der Tora Genesis: Übersetzt und Erklärt*. New York: Ktav, 1934, p. 173. The problems center on the presence of the *hapax legomena yādôn* and *bĕšagam*. E. A. Speiser translated: "My spirit shall not shield man forever, since he is but flesh." *Genesis*. The Anchor Bible. Garden City, NJ: Doubleday, 1964, p. 44. The translation "shield" was proposed by Speiser on the basis of parallels with Akaddian *dinānu* from the root *d-n-n* in the sense of "substitute." See E. A. Speiser, "*YDWN*, Gen 6:3" *JBL* 75 (1956) 126–129, although the logic that leads him from "substitute" to "protect" is not entirely clear. Also see "*dināanu*" in *The Assyrian Dictionary: Volume 3, D*. Ed. A. Leo Oppenheim. Chicago: The Oriental Institute, 1959, pp. 148–150. For another attempt to use Akkadian roots, see George Ricker Berry, who rendered: "The spirit from me shall not be powerful in mankind for an unlimited period." "The Interpretation of Gen. 6:3," *American Journal of Semitic Languages and Literatures* 26 (1899) 49 (47–49). For a brief discussion of Arabic parallels, see Alfred Guillaume, "A Note on the Meaning of Gen. 6:3," *American Journal of Semitic Languages and Literatures* 56 (1939) 415–416. On *bĕšagam*, see C. A. Ben-Mordecai, "B'shaggam: An Obscure Phrase in Gen. 6:3," *American Journal of Semitic Languages and Literatures* 57 (1940) 306–307, who recommends reversing the order of verses 3 and 4. A good review of turn-of-the-century German scholarship on

this issue can be found in Hermann Gunkel, *Genesis.* Göttinger Handkommentar zum Alten Testament. Göttingen, Germany: Vandenhoeck und Ruprecht, 1910, pp. 55–58.

8. Robert Carroll, "Between Lying and Blasphemy or on Translating a Four-letter Word in the Hebrew Bible: Critical Reflections on Bible Translation," in *Bible Translation on the Threshold of the Twenty-First Century: Authority, Reception, Culture and Religion.* Eds. Athalya Brenner and Jan Willem van Henten. Sheffield: Sheffield Academic Press, 2002, p. 63. (53–64).

9. As the postmodern critic, A. K. M. Adam observes: "The meaning that the author intended in composing a text is the single most widely held criterion by which modern interpretations have been judged legitimate or illegitimate." *What Is Postmodern Biblical Criticism.* Minneapolis: Fortress Press, 1995, p. 20. Also see David Clines, *The Bible and the Modern World*, pp. 12–13. James Kugel has also pointed to the preoccupation among biblicists with getting back to the "real Isaiah." Kugel sets this preoccupation within the context of a discipline that he views as profoundly Protestant in its basic assumptions. "The Bible in the University," in *The Hebrew Bible and Its Interpreters.* Eds. William Propp, Baruch Halpern, and David Noel Freedman. Winona Lake, IN: Eisenbrauns, 1990, p. 161. (143–165); *The Bible and Culture Collective, The Postmodern Bible.* New Haven, CT: Yale University Press, 1995, pp. 41, 130. Harry Nasuti observes that the discipline of Old Testament research has "been even more firmly committed to the author's intentions than the rest of the humanities." *Defining the Sacred Songs: Genre, Tradition and the Post-Critical Interpretation of the Psalms.* Sheffield: Sheffield Academic Press, 1999, p. 129. On the search for the intentions or Tendenz of original authors as motivating a scholar such as Wellhausen, see Douglas Knight, "Wellhausen and the Interpretation of Israel's Literature," *Semeia* 25 (1982) 24, 27 (21–36).

10. Adele Berlin, "Literary Exegesis of Biblical Narrative: Between Poetics and Hermeneutics," in *"Not in Heaven": Coherence and Complexity in Biblical Narrative.* Eds. Jason Rosenblatt and Joseph Sitterson, Jr. Bloomington: Indiana University Press, 1991, p. 124 (120–128). In "A Search," Berlin advances an argument very different from our own. She suggests that modern exegetes are no longer concerned with interpreting the text. The "aversion to interpretation" (p. 196) that Berlin discusses strikes us as a phenomenon that is restricted to certain types of biblical literary critics, in particular, postmodern critics. Most exegetes, however, seem to be interpreting as usual. In outlining her ground rules for interpretation, Berlin advances another point quite different from our own: "assume that the text makes sense in its present form." p. 202. A discussion of the playful nature of Midrashic interpretation can be seen in Adele Berlin's "On the Use of Traditional Jewish Exegesis in The Modern Literary Study of Bible," in *Tehillah le-Moshe: Biblical and Judaic Studies in Honor of Moshe Greenberg.* Eds. Mordechai Cogan, Barry Eichler, and Jeffrey Tigay. Winona Lake, IN: Eisenbrauns, 1997, pp. 173–183.

11. That so few are familiar with the work of Betty Carter points to everything – absolutely everything – that is wrong in the contemporary arts. Her exegesis of "Stardust" can be heard on her 1990 album *Droppin' Things.* Polygram.

12. The terms "modern" or "postmodern," of course, are umbrella categories for a diverse array of scholarly approaches. We use both terms with some hesitance and unease insofar as they homogenize a heterogeneous assortment of scholarship.

13. They continue: "The deconstruction of texts relativizes the authority attributed to them, and makes it evident that much of the power that is felt to lie in texts is really in the power of their sanctioning community." David Clines and J. Cheryl Exum, "The New Literary Criticism," in *The New Literary Criticism and the Hebrew Bible*. Sheffield: Sheffield Academic Press, 1993, pp. 19–20 (11–25). Also see *The Post Modern Bible*, p. 130.

14. Adam, *What Is Postmodern Biblical Criticism*, p. 20. *The Postmodern Bible* observes: "writing has often been thought to threaten truth with distortion and mischief. An orphan, no sooner born than set adrift, cut loose from the author who gives birth to it, writing seems fated endlessly to circulate from reader to reader, the best of whom can never be sure that he or she has fully grasped what the author intended to say." p. 123. Postmodernists tend to draw a useful distinction between texts and writing on the one side and authors on the other. As Roland Barthes put it in his "The Death of the Author," "writing is the destruction of every voice, of every point of origin." in *IMAGE/MUSIC/TEXT*. Trans. Stephen Heath. New York: Hill and Wang, 1977, p. 142 (142–148). On the distinction between texts and authors, also see Athalya Brenner and Fokkelien Van Dijk-Hemmes, "Introduction," in *On Gendering Texts: Female and Male Voices in the Hebrew Bible*. Leiden: E. J. Brill, 1993, p. 6. Also Clines, *The Bible*, pp. 13–15.

15. On this charge, see *The Postmodern Bible*, p. 36.

16. Yvonne Sherwood, *A Biblical Text and its Afterlives: The Survival of Jonah in Western Culture*. Cambridge: Cambridge University Press, 2000. This line of analysis is sometimes called "Rezeptionsgeschichte" or the "history of the interpretation of the Bible." Robert Carroll notes that such an endeavor would require teams of researchers and would be well beyond the abilities of any one scholar. "The Discombobulations of Time and the Diversities of Text: Notes on the Rezeptionsgeschichte of the Bible," in *Text as Pretext: Essays in Honour of Robert Davidson*. Ed. Robert Carroll. Sheffield: Sheffield Academic Press, 1992, pp. 61–85. For examples of such studies, see Jeremy Cohen, *"Be Fertile and Increase, Fill the Earth and Master It": The Ancient and Medieval Career of a Biblical Text*. Ithaca, NY: Cornell University Press, 1989. We should recall, when looking at how those in different ages went about interpretation that the body of biblical texts consulted varies across history, as does the conception of what constitutes Scripture. Early Jewish communities, for example, did not conceive of the Hebrew Bible as a single work like they do today. On this point, see the interesting discussion of Frederick Greenspahn, "Does Judaism Have a Bible," in *Sacred Texts, Secular Times: The Hebrew Bible in the Modern World*. Eds. Leonard Greenspoon and Bryan LeBeau. Omaha, NE: Creighton University Press, 2000, p. 5 (1–12).

17. Emphasis in original. Pierre Bourdieu, "Genesis and Structure of the Religious Field," *Comparative Social Research*, 13 (1991) 14 (1–44).

18. Adele Berlin, "The Role of the Text in the Reading Process," *Semeia* 62 (1973) 143 (143–147). A similar approach can be found in André LaCocque and Paul Ricoeur, *Thinking Biblically: Exegetical and Hermeneutical Studies*. Trans. David

Pellauer. Chicago: University of Chicago Press, 1998, p. xi. In addition, both speak of a hermeneutics that is "attentive to the history of reception . . . respectful of the irredeucible plurivocity of the text," p. xv. For an overview of the many things connoted by the term "reader-response criticism," see Jane Tompkins, "An Introduction to Reader-Response Criticism," in *Reader-Response Criticism: From Formalism to Poststructuralism.* Ed. Jane Tompkins. Baltimore: Johns Hopkins University Press, 1980, pp. ix–xxvi. Also of interest is Terry Eagleton, *Literary Theory: An Introduction,* 2nd ed. Minneapolis: University of Minnesota Press, 1996, pp. 48–78, and Ian Maclean, "Reading and Interpretation," in *Modern Literary Theory: A Comparative Introduction,* 2nd ed. Eds. Ann Jefferson and David Robey. London: B. T. Batsford, 1991, pp. 122–144. See Hugh White, "The Trace of the Author in the Text," *Semeia* 71 (1995) 45–64, for a discussion of the "left wing" and "right wing" of reader-response theory. For the most comprehensive and theoretically sophisticated overview of reader-oriented theories as applied to the Bible, see the chapter "Reader-Response Criticism," in *The Postmodern Bible,* pp. 20–69. Also to be consulted is Edgar McKnight, *Post-Modern Use of the Bible: The Emergence of Reader-Oriented Criticism.* Nashville, TN: Abingdon Press, 1988. For a case study on the "reading conventions" of an audience and their impact on interpretation, see Robert Robinson, "Wife and Sister Through the Ages: Textual Determinacy and the History of Interpretation," *Semeia* 62 (1993) 103–128.

19. Our term, "large finite set" is very close to Michael Fox's notion of textual meaning as "a *set,* specifically a fuzzy set, which has definition and conditions and excludes an infinite number of possibilities, and yet may hold an indefinite number of subsets . . . some of them overlapping or with fuzzy partitions between them." "The Uses of Indeterminacy," *Semeia* 71 (1995) 175 (173–192). We generally concur with Fox, who in his assessment of reader-oriented theories in biblical studies concluded: "Ultimately a text is *authoritative,* setting constraints that include some meanings, allow some, and exclude others." "The Uses," p. 176. John Riches uses the phrase "reservoirs of meaning." "A Response to Walter Sundberg," in *Renewing Biblical Interpretation.* Eds. Craig Bartholomew, Colin Greene, and Karl Möller. Grand Rapids, MI: Zondervan, 2000, p. 86 (82–89). There is some similarity between our position and that of Wolfgang Iser, with his emphasis on "the dialectical structure of reading." "The Reading Process: A Phenomenological Approach," in *Reader-Response Criticism: From Formalism to Post-Structuralism.* Ed. Jane Tompkins. Baltimore: Johns Hopkins University Press, 1980, p. 68 (50–69). On the multiplicity of readings that can be extracted from Scripture, see David Clines. "Varieties of Indeterminacy," *Semeia* 71 (1995) 17–27; Mordecai Gafni, "Walking Together: Can Religious and Secular Jews Forge a Common Spiritual Language?" *Conservative Judaism* 52 (2000) 25 (22–37).

6. ON JEWISH INTERMARRIAGE: THE BIBLE IS OPEN TO INTERPRETATION

1. P. *Megillah,* 4: 10. The text actually refers to an "Aramaean" woman, a euphemism apparently for any non-Jewish woman. Geza Vermes discusses this passage and provides the prooftexts that might establish the association between Aramaean women and gentiles. "Leviticus 18:21 in Ancient Jewish Bible Exegesis," in *Studies*

in Aggadah, Targum, and Jewish Liturgy in Memory of Joseph Heinemann. Eds. Jakob Petuchowski and Ezra Fleischer. Jerusalem: The Magnes Press, 1981, p. 115 (108–125). Also of great interest is the extended discussion of Jacob Milgrom, *Leviticus 17–22.* Anchor Bible. New York: Doubleday, 2000, pp. 1551–1565. Jacob Neusner translates as follows: "R. Ishmael taught: 'This is one who marries an Aramaic woman and produces children from her. He sets up enemies of the Omnipresent.'" *The Talmud of the Land of Israel: A Preliminary Translation and Explanation, Volume 19, Megillah.* Trans. Jacob Neusner. Chicago: University of Chicago Press, 1987, p. 168.

2. *Midrash Rabbah, Song of Songs* I. 3, 3. *Midrash Rabbah, Song of Songs.* Trans. Maurice Simon. London: Soncino, 1983, p. 38.

3. Shaye Cohen argues that intermarriage "was not a serious problem" in Rabbinic times. "From the Bible to the Talmud: The Prohibition of Intermarriage," *Hebrew Annual Review* 7 (1983) 27 (23–39). Equally clear and thorough expositions of this problematic can be found in his "The Matrilineal Principle in Historical Perspective," *Judaism* 34 (1985) 5–13; "The Matrilineal Principle," in *The Beginnings of Jewishness: Boundaries, Varieties, Uncertainties.* Berkeley: University of California Press, 1999, pp. 263–307. A text dealing with the matrilineal principle and demonstrating the aforementioned "back and forth" is P. *Kiddushin* 3:12. See *The Talmud of the Land of Israel: A Preliminary Translation and Explanation, Volume 26: Qiddushin.* Trans. Jacob Neusner. Chicago: University of Chicago Press, 1984, pp. 201–211. The subsequent discussion is especially interesting because it features the momentary dissent of one Jacob of Kepar Naborayya. Also to be read in association with the matrilineal decision is P. *Yebamoth.* 7:5. See *The Talmud of the Land of Israel: A Preliminary Translation and Explanation, Volume 21, Yebamot.* Trans. Jacob Neusner, Chicago: University of Chicago Press, 1987, pp. 242–248. A case of seemingly tolerated intermarriage is mentioned in *Midrash Rabbah Lamentations* I. 16, 47. *Midrash Rabbah Lamentations.* Trans. A. Cohen. London: Soncino Press, 1983, p. 128. The inscrutable decision mentioned previously comes from the fourth-generation *tanna* Rabbi Simon b. Yohai's reading of Deut. 7:3–4 preserved in B. *Kiddushin* 68b and B. *Yebamot* 23a (also see the discussion of different authorities in B. *Kiddushin.* 66b). Phillip Sigal, "Halakhic Perspectives on the Matrilineal-Patrilineal Principles," *Judaism* 34 (1985) 89–96, expresses puzzlement at the logic behind the matrilineal decision as does Cohen, "From the Bible," p. 30. Contra Lawrence Schiffman's explanation of the reasoning that led to an emphasis on matrilineality, as well as his insistence that such a practice was in effect in Ezra's time, "Jewish Identity and Jewish Descent," *Judaism* 34 (1985) 78–84, and Lawrence Schiffman, *Who Was a Jew?: Rabbinic and Halakhic Perspectives on the Jewish-Christian Schism.* Hoboken, NJ: Ktav, 1985, pp. 15–16. Solomon Zeitlin viewed the matrilineal principle as taking hold in "the time of Nehemiah." "The Offspring of Intermarriage," *Jewish Quarterly Review* 51 (1960–1961) 137 (135–140). On Rabbinic voices that seem to endorse patrilineal descent, see Bernard Zlotowitz, "A Perspective on Patrilineal Descent," *Judaism* 34 (1985) 129–135. As for Rabbinic observations on intermarriage, see the wide-ranging discussion in P. *Kiddushin* 4:3, as well as that of the Mishnah and Gemara to B. *Megillah.* 25a. *Megillah.* Trans. Maurice Simon. London: Soncino Press, 1938, pp. 148–150. Other

remarks can be seen in *Sifre Deut. piska* 171. *Sifre: A Tannaitic Commentary on the Book of Deuteronomy.* Trans. Reuven Hammer. New Haven, CT: Yale University Press, 1986, pp. 199–200; *Midrash Rabbah Genesis* 80:7 and 85: 1, *Midrash Rabbah Genesis, Volume*I. Trans. H. Freedman. London: Soncino Press, 1983, pp. 739–740, 787. Also see B. *'Abodah Zarah* 31 b and 36b, where an attempt is made to figure out where the prohibition on intermarriage with all gentiles comes from. *'Abodah Zarah.* Trans. A. Mishcon. London: Soncino Press, 1935, pp. 156, 176–180. Of interest is P. *Sotah* 1.8 II F, where R. Abin wants to know why Samson was not permitted to intermarry when there is no Torah prohibition against marrying Philistines. There, too, the problem is pursued of whether the ban on intermarriage applies to certain nations or all non-Israelites. See *The Talmud of the Land of Israel: A Preliminary Translation and Explanation, Volume 27, Sotah.* Trans. Jacob Neusner. Chicago: University of Chicago Press, 1984, p. 42. For a discussion of how the Rabbinic decrees became codified into Jewish law, see David Bleich, "The Prohibition Against Intermarriage," *Journal of Halacha and Contemporary Society* 1 (1981) 5–27. His speculations on the pre-Sinaitic and Sinaitic basis of the prohibition are dubious in the extreme.

4. Barry Kosmin et al., *Highlights of the CJF 1990 National Jewish Population Survey.* New York: Council of Jewish Federations, 1991, p. 14, chart 14. Also see the article of Paul Spickard and the literature cited there. "Ishmael Returns: The Changing Status of Children of Jewish Intermarriage in the United States," in *Jewish Assimilation, Acculturation and Accommodation: Past Traditions, Current Issues and Future Prospects.* Ed. Menachem Mor. Lanham, MD: University Press of America, 1992, pp. 191–203. More recent data can be found in Egon Mayer et. al., *American Jewish Identity Survey, 2001.* New York: The Center for Cultural Judaism, 2003. The figure of 10,420 Jews was the worst-case estimate of Elihu Bergman, "The American Jewish Population Erosion," *Midstream* 23 (1977) 9–19. The sociological *mitzvah* approach tends to surface among Reconstructionist Jews and, occasionally, Reform Jews. See, for example, Fred Massarik, "Rethinking the Inter-Marriage Crisis," *Moment* 3 (1978) 29–33.

5. Considerations of space will force us to concentrate solely on texts that speak about marriage. We forego a discussion about the tricky Mal. 2:11, where it may be said that Judah has metaphorically married the daughter of a foreign God. Passages about sexual relations between Israelites and non-Israelites, as interesting as they might be, are not scrutinized here. These include Deut. 20:14 and Num. 25. Nor do we directly discuss Lev. 18:21, a verse that does not seem to discuss marriage but was interpreted as doing so by early Jewish commentators. For a comprehensive study, see Vermes, "Leviticus 18:21." Rebekkah's misgivings about these women are reported in Gen. 26:34–35 and 27:46. Issac's blessing can be found in Gen. 28:1–4.

6. These events occur in Ex. 34: 10–16. On the term "inhabitant of the land," see the lengthy discussion of F. Langlamet, "Israël et 'l'habitant du pays,'" *RB* 76 (1969) 338–341 (321–350).

7. Deut. 7:3. This legislation differs from the previous one in that expresses concern for the spiritual welfare of the son *and* daughter of the male being addressed. Here we prefer the translation "marry yourselves" to the common "intermarry,"

which carries a misleading modern connotation. In the Hebrew of the MT, constant shifts between first and third person, as well as singular and plural, are often witnessed. See S. R. Driver, *A Critical and Exegetical Commentary on Deuteronomy*. ICC. New York: Charles Scribner's Sons, 1895, p. 99. For examples of what is sometimes called reversion, see Brian Peckham, "Writing and Editing," in *Fortunate the Eyes That See: Essays in Honor of David Noel Freedman in Celebration of His Seventieth Birthday*. Eds. Astrid Beck, Andrew Bartelt, Paul Raabe, and Chris Franke. Grand Rapids, MI: Eerdmans, 1995, pp. 375–382 (364–383). A fascinating discussion of reversion can be found in Morton Smith, "Pseudepigraphy in the Israelite Literary Tradition," in *Pseudepigrapha I: Pseudopythagorica-Lettres de Platon, Littérature pseudépigraphique juive*. Ed. Kurt von Fritz. Geneva: Vandoeuvres, 1972, pp. 191–227. On textual discrepancies between the MT of this verse and other witnesses, see Moshe Weinfeld, *Deuteronomy 1–11*. The Anchor Bible. New York: Doubleday, 1991, p. 359.

8. Joshua 23:6–13. A comparison of lists of nations in the Bible can be found in Robert Boling. *Joshua*, The Anchor Bible. Garden City, NJ: Doubleday, 1982, pp. 165–167. Also see T. Ishida, "The Structure and Historical Implications of the Lists of Pre-Israelite Nations," *Biblica* 60 (1979) 461–490. This verse varies wildly across different witnesses, a point discussed by Robert Boling, "Some Conflate Readings in Joshua-Judges," *VT* 16 (1966) 296–297 (293–298). Yahweh threatens to stop driving these nations out of the land (23:12) if the Israelites keep marrying them. Thus, if they marry these prohibited peoples, the less inclined Yahweh will be to drive them out. Or as one theologian puts it: "Mixing with the nations brings further opportunities for such mixing." Trent Butler. *Joshua*. Word Biblical Commentary. Waco, TX: Word Books, 1983, p. 256.

9. Christine Hayes, *Gentile Impurities and Jewish Identities: Intermarriage and Conversion from the Bible to the Talmud*. New York: Oxford University Press, 2002, p. 26. A similar point was made by Louis Epstein, *Marriage Laws in the Bible and the Talmud*. Cambridge, MA: Harvard University Press, 1942, p. 146. As for the identity of the offspring of mixed unions, a conclusion cannot be reached regarding what the Bible thinks. This is because the passages adduced previously only discuss the harmful effects of intermarriage on one's children. Not a word is uttered about what happens when that exogamous child him- or herself procreates. Hence the necessity for later commentators to connect the dots.

10. Ezra 10:3, 44. On the nature of the Torah, which Ezra is citing, see the speculations of K. Koch, "Ezra and the Origins of Judaism," *Journal of Semitic Studies* 19 (1974)182–183 (173–199). Joseph Blenkinsopp observes that the references to Torah are "puzzling ... since Pentateuchal law nowhere requires an Israelite to divorce his foreign wife." *Ezra-Nehemiah: A Commentary*. The Old Testament Library. Philadelphia: Westminster Press, 1988, p. 189. On the grammatical and thematic inconsistencies of the book, as well as a theory as to its authorship, see Yonina Dor, "The Composition of the Episode of the Foreign Women in Ezra IX–X" *VT* 52 (2003) 26–47.

11. The demurral may or may not occur in Ezra 10:15. The problem of the rainy season is discussed in 10:12–14. Giovanni Garbini is one of the few scholars willing to

confront the "total historical improbability" of the Book of Ezra. Although he is not the first to do so, it is truly astonishing how many exegetes believe the events narrated in the book are references to actual events. *History and Ideology in Ancient Israel.* Trans. J. Bowden. New York: Crossroad, 1988, p. 155. On the highly innovative nature of Ezra's ideas and terminology, see Jonathan Klawans, *Impurity and Sin in Ancient Judaism.* Oxford: Oxford University Press, 2003, pp. 45–46, where it is suggested that Ezra introduced the idea of "the moral impurity of gentiles." Moshe Weinfeld argues that Ezra precipitated a shift from a religious-national conception of identity to a religious-biological conception. "The Universalistic Tendency and the Separatist Tendency in the Period of the Restoration," *Tarbiz* 33 (1963) 238 (228–242) (Hebrew). Saul Olyan, *Rites and Rank: Hierarchy in Biblical Representations of Cult.* Princeton, NJ: Princeton University Press, 2000, sees Ezra as engaging in "a monumental departure from practices represented in earlier texts." p. 85. Jacob Milgrom has noted that Ezra is the first in the Bible to view intermarriage as "a cultic sin against God." Jacob Milgrom. *Cult and Conscience: The Asham and the Priestly Doctrine of Repentance.* Leiden: E. J. Brill, 1976, p. 72. H. Zlotnick Sivan views the idea of penalizing the wives as opposed to the husbands as another novelty of this text. "The Silent Women of Yehud: Notes on Ezra 9–10," *Journal of Jewish Studies* 51 (2000) 13 (3–18); also see Bob Becking. "Continuity and Community: The Belief System of the Book of Ezra," in *The Crisis of Israelite Religion: Transformation of Religious Tradition in Exilic and Post-Exilic Times.* Eds. Bob Becking and Marjo Korpel. Leiden: Brill, 1999, p. 271 (256–275). Gary Knoppers, in contrast, sees less innovation in Ezra and Nehemiah than most have assumed and more of a reliance on the views of the Deuteronomist. "Sex, Religion, and Politics: The Deuteronomist on Intermarriage," *HAR* 14 (1994) 121–141.

12. The translation problem centers on the question of how to translate the preposition *k* in 9:2. Loring Batten in a classic commentary suggested that the phrase in which the preposition appears, "according to (*k*) their abominations" (in our translation "as their abominations"), is a later gloss, as are the nations mentioned subsequently. *A Critical and Exegetical Commentary on the Books of Ezra and Nehemiah.* New York: Charles Scribner's Sons, 1913, p. 331. Given the peculiar syntax of the verse, this suggestion has great merit. (Also see Wilhelm Rudolph. *Esra und Nehemia.* Handbuch zum Alten Testament. Tübingen, Gurmany: J. C. B. Mohr, 1949, p. 86.) H. G. M. Williamson translates "but have acted according to the abominations of the Canaanites. . . . " *Ezra, Nehemiah.* Word Biblical Commentary. Waco, TX: Word Books, 1985, p. 125. David Clines translates "with their abominations." *Ezra, Nehemiah, Esther.* Grand Rapids, MI: W. B. Eerdmans, 1984, pp. 119–120. Most commentators break up the verse after "their abominations," and then proceed to list the nations. This implies that the complaint is specifically directed against these eight nations. See Kurt Galling, *Die Bücher der Chronik, Esra, Nehemia. Das Alte Testament Deutsch.* Göttingen, Germany: Vandenhoeck und Ruprecht, 1954, p. 210. Or Rudolf Kittel who translates the *lāmed* as "namely," "that is," and proceeds to reel off the names of the peoples. *Die Bücher der Chronik und Esra, Nehemia und Esther.* Handkommentar zum Alten Testament. Göttingen, Germany: Vandenhoeck und Ruprecht, 1902, p. 61. A very similar explanation based on Arabic parallels is suggested by Alfred Bertholet,

Die Bücher Esra und Nehemia. Kurzer Hand-Commentar zum Alten Testament. Tübingen, Germany: J. C. B. Mohr, 1902, p. 39. Bertholet was following the analysis of Charles Torrey, *The Composition and Historical Value of Ezra-Nehemiah*. Giessen, Germany: J. Ricker'sche Buchhandlung, 1896, p. 18; also see Charles Torrey, *Ezra Studies*. Chicago: University of Chicago Press, 1910, p. 270. And P. Andres Fernandez who translates "a saber, los cananeos...." *Comentario a los libros de Esdras y Nehemias*. Madrid: Casimiro, 1950, p. 172. Less frequently, the preposition *k* is translated as a simile, and the term "abominations" is seen as being in the construct state with the following list of nations, which is headed by a *lāmed*. According to Gesenius in his section, "Expression of the genitive by circumlocution" the *lāmed* attached to the dependent noun (in this case, "Canaanite") can mean "belonging to." (*Gesenius' Hebrew Grammar*, 2nd Eng. Edition. Eds. E. Kautzsch and A. E. Cowley. Oxford: Clarendon Press, 1983, p. 419). The JPS, for instance, translates: "The people of Israel...have not separated themselves from the peoples of the land whose abhorrent practices are *like those* of the Canaanites, the Hittites" (emphasis ours), and so on. Still, this translation seems very forced, and the use of the construct with a pronominal suffix "their abominations" followed by a long list of peoples introduced by a *lāmed* is hard to find in the Hebrew Bible. The JPS translation suggests that the abominations practiced by the "peoples of the land" are *like* those of the eight nations. Thus, the complaint is not about intermarriage with the listed nations, but intermarriage with unspecified nations that resemble the eight listed nations. The JPS thus remains faithful to mainstream Judaism by having the text say that *any* peoples whose abominations are like those of the Canaanites are not fit to be married to Judahites. This extends the ban beyond just those named in the Bible. A similar translation can be seen in Lester Grabbe, *Ezra-Nehemiah*. London: Routledge, 1998, p. 137.

13. If this surmise is correct, we have a clear example of how scribal meddling can inadvertently stimulate meaning and meanings for pious exegetes and meaninglessness for secular hermeneuts. On inner-biblical exegesis in this chapter, see Michael Fishbane's discussion of the passage in question as being an exegetical blend of Deut. 7:1–6 and 23:4–9. *Biblical Interpretation in Ancient Israel*. Oxford: Clarendon Press, 1985, p. 116. Also see Milgrom, *Cult and Conscience*, p. 73. On inner-biblical exegesis in intermarriage passages in Nehemiah, see David Clines. "Nehemiah 10 as an Example of Early Jewish Biblical Exegesis," *JSOT* 21 (1981) 111–117.

14. The single external usage appears in Is. 6:13. Somewhat similar passages can be found in Neh. 9:2 and Isaiah 61:9. The contrast between the Torah passages cited previously and Ezra's perspective is intriguing. The laws in Exodus and Deuteronomy spoke to a solitary Israelite male. Ezra addresses the entire community. In the legal materials, intermarriage imperils one's children. In Ezra, the dilution of holy semen would appear to endanger the genealogical integrity of the Judahites, past, present, and future. In one, exogamy leads to apostasy; in the other, it leads to moral transgression and communal defilement. For a comprehensive discussion of the Hebrew term, see H. D. Preuss. "*zāra'; zera'*," in *Theological Dictionary of the Old Testament, Volume VI*. Eds. G. Botterweck and H. Ringgren. Trans. David Green. Grand Rapids, MI: Eerdmans, 1980, pp. 143–162. Preuss suggests that the

term refers solely to members of the returning expatriate community (pp. 159–160). H. Zlotnick Sivan observes that "the precise identity of the women to whom they are married remains elusive." "The Silent Women," p. 5. Eskenazi and Judd suggest that three types of women might be the subject of the law: 1) "Judahites or Israelites who had not been in exile or who differed along particular ethnic and socio-economic lines from the returnees", 2) members of foreign nations, and 3) Judahite or Israelite women not of the exile community whose religious practices differed from those of the returning exiles (pp. 268–270). Tamara Eskenazi and Eleanore Judd, "Marriage to a Stranger in Ezra 9–10," in *Second Temple Studies 2. Temple and Community in the Persian Period.* Eds. Tamara Eskenazi and Kent Richards. Sheffield: Sheffield Academic Press, 1994, pp. 266–285. Daniel Smith-Christopher suggests that Ezra is not speaking about foreigners but adversarial Jewish sects. "The Mixed Marriage Crisis in Ezra 9–10 and Nehemiah 13: A Study of the Sociology of the Post-Exilic Judaean Community," in *Second Temple Studies 2. Temple and Community in the Persian Period.* Eds. Tamara Eskenazi and Kent Richards. Sheffield: Sheffield Academic Press, 1994, p. 257 (243–265). Also see Becking, "Continuity and Community," p. 274.

15. Neh. 10:31 ; 13:23–31. Cohen, "The Matrilineal Principle in Historical Perspective," p. 8–9, doubts that this text shows that Ezra introduced the matrilineal principle into Judaism, although he raises the possibility that the Rabbis may have deduced this idea from the book of Ezra. Contra Sigal, "Halakhic Perspectives," who sees Ezra as having "expanded the prohibition of mixed marriage from the 'seven nations' to all gentiles." p. 89. See endnote 3 for other opinions.

16. Josephus, *Jewish Antiquities IV* 143, in *Jewish Antiquities, Books I–IV.* Trans. H. St. J. Thackeray. New York: G. P. Putnam's Sons, 1980, p. 545. Judah's marriage to a Canaanite woman is reported in Gen. 38:2 and 1 Chron. 2:3. Gary Knoppers has noted that in Chronicles we see the line of Judah intermarry at least six times. "Intermarriage, Social Complexity, and Ethnic Diversity in the Genealogy of Judah," *JBL* 120 (2001) 22 (15–30). Joseph's union with Asenath is mentioned in Gen. 41:45, 50–52; 46:20; Claus Westermann observes: "The narrator of the Joseph story and his listeners found nothing scandalous in Joseph becoming the son-in-law of a priest of the God Re." *Genesis 37–50: A Commentary.* Trans. J. Scullion. Minneapolis: Augsburg, 1986, p. 96. On the Egyptian, and perhaps cultic, provenance of her name, see Gordon Wenham, *Genesis 16–50.* Word Biblical Commentary. Dallas: Word Books, 1994, pp. 396–397. On Simeon, see Gen. 46:10; Ex. 6:15.

17. On Zipporah, see Ex. 2:16–22; 4:24–26; 18:2–4; Num. 12. On many of the issues relating to Zipporah, see H. F. Richter. "Gab es Einen 'Blutbräutigam'? Erwägungen zu Ex. 4, 24–26," in *Studies in the Book of Exodus: Redaction, Reception, Intepretation.* Ed. Marc Vervenne. Leuven, Belgium: Leuven University Press, 1996, pp. 433–441. B. A. Levine doubts that Zipporah is one and the same as the unnamed "Cushite wife." *Numbers: 1–20.* The Anchor Bible. New York: Doubleday, 1993, p. 328. Martin Noth, *Numbers: A Commentary.* Trans. James Martin. Philadelphia: Westminster Press, 1968, p. 94, also disassociates her from Zipporah, as does George Buchanan Gray, *A Critical and Exegetical Commentary on Numbers.* New York: Charles Scribner's Sons, 1920, p. 121. On ancient

traditions that associated Zipporah with the Cushite wife, see James Kugel, *The Bible as It Was.* Cambridge: The Belknap Press, 1997, pp. 299–300. Further, nothing indicates that Moses's sons, Gershom and Eliezer, are anything but respectable figures in the Bible's memory.

18. Judges 14–16; Esther 2:17. Adele Berlin notes that even though she is made queen the text never specifically mentions that she is married to the king. *Esther.* JPS Bible Commentary. Philadelphia: JPS, 2001, p. 29. Others insist that she was both his wife and queen. See Lewis Bayles Paton, *A Critical and Exegetical Commentary on the Book of Esther.* ICC. Edinburgh: T. and T. Clark. Continuum Intl Pub Group, 1908/1976, p. 184. André LaCocque sees Esther as "a subversive piece of literature," reacting "sharply against the Jerusalem establishment, especially after the reforms of Ezra and Nehemiah in the fifth century." *The Feminine Unconventional: Four Subversive Figures in Israel's Tradition.* Minneapolis: Fortress Press, 1990, p. 71. Michael Fox, *Character and Ideology in the Book of Esther.* Columbia: University of South Carolina Press, 1991, also points out that the author of Esther seems untroubled by intermarriage. Under David's reign, Uriah the Hittite married Bathsheeba (2 Sam. 11) until David had him killed. The text shows little concern about this intermarriage but seems positively outraged by David's actions (2 Sam. 12). Solomon is criticized in 1 Kings 11 and Neh. 13:26. Shaye Cohen has written an interesting review of the passages dealing with Solomon's marriage to Pharaoh's daughter. "Solomon and the Daughter of Pharaoh: Intermarriage, Conversion, and the Impurity of Women," *Journal of the Ancient Near Eastern Society* 16–17 (1984–1985) 23–37. David's marriage to Maacah is reported in 2 Sam. 3:3 and 1 Chron. 3:2. As for Chronicles, Gary Knoppers observes that in this and other genealogical accounts concerning Judah's line the intermarriages are mentioned without any critique or rebuke. Further, "groups that seem to be non-Israelites or distant relations of the Israelites in other biblical contexts . . . are incorporated into Judah." "Intermarriage, Social Complexity," pp. 26–27. Sara Japhet, *I and II Chronicles: A Commentary.* Old Testament Library. Louisville, KY: Westminster John Knox Press, 1993, p. 74. For a full list of all the intermarried Israelites in Chronicles and a discussion of the relevance of their appearance, see Sara Japhet, *The Ideology of the Book of Chronicles and its Place in Biblical Thought* (Hebrew). Jerusalem: Bialik Foundation, 1977, pp. 295–298. On passages presuming intermarriage, see 1 Chron. 2:17; 2:34; 4:17; 8:8; 2 Chron. 12:13; 24:26.

19. Ruth 4:13. The "congregation of Yahweh" is mentioned in Deut. 23:4–8. Conversely, and puzzlingly, children born of Edomite and Egyptian parents *can* be admitted into the congregation of Yahweh in the third generation (Deut. 23: 8–9). Saul Olyan writes of the phrase "congregation of Yahweh" that "[t]he exact meaning of entering the assembly of Yhwh in this text is uncertain, though such entry probably means to join the covenant community, embracing cultic obligations and privileges." *Rites and Rank: Hierarchy in Biblical representations of Cult.* Princeton, NJ: Princeton University Press, 2000, p. 79. Also see M. H. Pope, "Congregation, Assembly," in *The Interpreter's Dictionary of the Bible: Volume One.* New York: Abingdon Press, 1962, pp. 669–670. And also see Jeffrey Tigay, *Deuteronomy.* Philadelphia: The Jewish Publication Society, 1996, pp. 209–210. Cohen, "From the Bible," p. 32, does not believe that the phrase refers to intermarriage. As

Athalya Brenner remarks: "The Book of Ruth can and has been read as an optimistic, idyllic story of integration, of polemic against exogamy and xenophobia (see Ezra and Nehemiah)." Brenner's suggestion is certainly plausible, but insofar as we do not know who wrote and rewrote Ezra and Ruth (and when), nor if the texts were aware of one another, it can only remain a conjecture. Athalya Brenner, "Ruth as a Foreign Worker and the Politics of Exogamy," in *Ruth and Esther: A Feminist Companion to the Bible (Second Series)* Ed. Athalya Brenner. Sheffield: Sheffield Academic Press, 1999, p. 162 (158–162). Michael Goulder speaks of this text as "covertly" challenging the law from Deuteronomy and misunderstanding others. "Ruth: A Homily on Deuteronomy 22–25?" in *Of Prophets' Visions and the Wisdom of the Sages: Essays in Honour of R. Norman Whybray on his Seventieth Birthday.* Eds. Heather McKay and David Clines. Sheffield: Sheffield Academic Press, 1993, pp. 307–319.

20. Jeffrey Tigay, trying to harmonize this law with that of Deut. 20:10–18, concludes that it must refer to "non-Canaanite women." *Deuteronomy*, p. 194. A similar argument was made by Driver. *Deuteronomy*, p. 244. This verse tacitly endorses intermarriage. Christine Hayes writes: "the women of foreign nations are considered to be ultimately assimilable, while those of the seven Canaanite nations are not." "Intermarriage and Impurity in Ancient Jewish Sources," *HTR* 92 (1999) 8 (3–36). Cana Werman, "*Jubilees 30*: Building a Paradigm for the Ban on Intermarriage," *HTR* 90 (1997) 1 fn. 2 (1–22), writes that that the law of the captive women "takes marriage with a foreign woman for granted." In passing, we also mention Numbers 31:13–18. The text states that every female captured in battle is to be slain, except those who have not had carnal relations with a man. The possible implication of such a verse seems to be that these foreign women can enter the marriage pool available to male Israelites.

21. "To the extent that a community's source of doctrine and practice is its Bible," writes Frederick Greenspahn, "then, one would have to conclude that it is the Talmud or, perhaps better, the halachic corpus as a whole which plays that role in Judaism." "Does Judaism Have a Bible," in *Sacred Texts, Secular Times: The Hebrew Bible in the Modern World* eds. Leonard Greenspoon and Bryan LeBeau Omaha: Creighton University Press, 2000, p. 5 (1–12). Also see Jonathan Magonet, "How Do Jews Interpret the Bible Today? The Sixteenth Montefiore Lecture (17 February 94), University of Southampton." *JSOT* (1995) p. 4 (3–27). The figure regarding the 1,500 Rabbinic commentators is taken from the article of David Goldenberg, "The Curse of Ham: A Case of Rabbinic Racism?" in *Struggles in the Promised Land: Toward a History of Black-Jewish Relations in the United States.* Eds. Jack Salzman and Cornel West. New York: Oxford, 1997, p. 31 (21–51). See endnote 3 for texts that render differing views about intermarriage and the children of the intermarried. *Jubilees* 30:7–8. This text relies explicitly on Ezra's notion of holy seed/semen. James Kugel traces the usage of "holy seed" terminology in *Jubilees* and other works of the era in "The Holiness of Israel and the Land in Second Temple Times," in *Texts, Temples, and Traditions: A Tribute to Menahem Haran.* Eds. Michael Fox, Victor Hurowitz, Avi Hurvitz, Michael Klein, Baruch Schwartz, and Nili Shupak. Winona Lake, IN: Eisenbrauns, 1996, pp. 21–32. Unlike the circles that produced *Jubilees*, the Rabbis, as Christine Hayes

has demonstrated, did not view gentiles as inherently impure. By acknowledging their human commonality, the sages, unlike earlier Jewish sects, were willing to acknowledge possibilities of conversion. On the relative leniency of Rabbinic views on intermarriage, see Hayes, *Gentile Impurities*, p. 162, and the earlier discussion of Epstein, *Marriage Laws*, pp. 183–219. Compare *Jubilees* with *Judith* 14:10 where Achior the Ammonite converts to Judaism unproblematically after his circumcision. No sense of genetic barriers between Jews and gentiles can be found in this text. On the difference between *Jubilees* on the one side and the Pentateuch and *Judith* on the other, see Solomon Zeitlin, "The Book of 'Jubilees' and the Pentateuch," *Jewish Quarterly Review* 48 (1957) 218–235. Shaye Cohen, "From the Bible to the Talmud," pp. 27–28. *The Testament of Levi* (14:6) compares taking a gentile woman to the sins of Sodom and Gomorrah. *Testament of Levi* in *The Old Testament Pseudepigrapha, Volume One*. Eds., Trans. James Charlesworth and H. C. Kee. Garden City, NJ: Doubleday, 1983, p. 793.

22. Schiffman. *Who was a Jew?* p. 81, fn. 23. Cohen, "The Matrilineal Principle in Historical Perspective," p. 7. Also see Cohen's "Conversion to Judaism in Historical Perspective: From Biblical Israel to Postbiblical Judaism," *Conservative Judaism* 36 (1983) 34, 38 (31–45). Sigal, "Halakhic Perspectives," speaks of a "pragmatic fluidity" in the Hebrew Bible regarding a child's identity as opposed to a "hard and fast patrilineal or matrilineal principle" p. 89. Saul Olyan writes: "On the whole, texts of the monarchic and exilic eras give the impression that the intermarriage of an Israelite man and an alien woman was not understood to be much different from the marriage of two Israelites, since the consequences for the children were basically the same: Israelite status." *Rites and Rank*, p. 87. Contra those writers who see a biblical basis for the matrilineal principle. Mayer Gruber, "Matrilineal Determination of Jewishness: Biblical and Near Eastern Roots," in *Pomegranates and Golden Bells: Studies in Biblical, Jewish, and Near Eastern Ritual, Law, and Literature in Honor of Jacob Milgrom*. Eds. David Wright, David Noel Freedman, and Avi Hurvitz. Winona Lake, IN: Eisenbrauns, 1995, pp. 437–443. Gruber locates its origins in the late Bronze Age. Others opt for the adoption of the matrilineal principle in the period Ezra-Nehemiah. See Phillip Hiat and Bernard Zlotowitz, "Biblical and Rabbinic Sources on Patrilineal Descent," *Journal of Reform Judaism* 30 (1983) 43–48. Hayes also discusses the Rabbis' realization that the ban on intermarriage with all gentiles is not of biblical provenance. *Gentile Impurities*, pp. 147–149, 154. As for the matrilineal principle, it too rests on a flimsy foundation. For the scriptural verses at our disposal usually depict the opposite practice as normative. As Cohen observes, "In biblical times the offspring of intermarriage was judged patrilineally. . . . It never occurred to anyone in pre-exilic times to argue that such marriages were null and void, that the foreign women must 'convert' to Judaism, or that the offspring of the marriage were not Israelite if the women did not convert." "The Matrilineal Principle," p. 7.

23. *Aboth* 1. Admittedly, even if ancient Israelite scribes placed a user's manual called "*Sacred Rules and Regulations for Interpreters*" in front of the Book of Genesis, a great deal of varied interpretation would still have taken place. Yet, in terms of the volume and heterogeneity of readings, we believe Scripture will rival any text ever

produced. The reasons for this are many and complex, but throughout this work, we cite three key factors. First, the collective, transhistorical composition and editing of the Hebrew Bible resulted in an anthology abounding in interpretive possibilities (and impossibilities). Second, the text insinuates that it knew God, while making no stipulations as to how its insights about Yahweh should be interpreted. Third, ancient interpreters not only believed the Bible's claim to possess divine proximity, but also obligingly exploited the interpretive freedom it tacitly granted. S. David Sperling, *The Original Torah: The Political Intent of the Bible's Writers*. New York: New York University Press, 1998, p. 14.

24. The distinction between "innovation" and "interpretation" was suggested in James Kugel's article on a different subject. "Reuben's Sin with Bilhah in the *Testament of Reuben*," in *Pomegranates and Golden Bells: Studies in Biblical, Jewish, and Near Eastern Ritual, Law, and Literature in Honor of Jacob Milgrom*. Eds. David Wright, David Noel Freedman, and Avi Hurvitz. Winona Lake, IN: Eisenbrauns, 1995, pp. 525 (525–554).

25. *Midrash Rabbah Ecclesiastes* VIII 10 notes that Asenath was bought into the fold by the righteous Joseph. *Midrash Rabbah Ecclesiastes*. Trans. A. Cohen. London: Soncino Press, 1983, p. 223; *Midrash Rabbah Ruth* II 23. *Midrash Rabbah Ruth*. Trans. L. Rabinowitz. London: Soncino, 1983, p. 40. For Jethro and Zipporah, see *Midrash Rabbah Exodus* I 32. *Midrash Rabbah Exodus*. Trans. S. M. Lehrman. London: Soncino, 1983, p. 40. As for Zipporah's virtue and cleanliness, see B. *Mo'ed Ḳaṭan* 16b, *Mo'ed Ḳaṭan*. Trans. Dayan Lazarus. London: Soncino Press, 1938, p. 103. Also see *Sifre to Numbers* 99. On the tendency of Midrashists to claim that foreign women were not foreign, see Shaye Cohen. "The Matrilineal Principle," in *The Beginnings of Jewishness: Boundaries, Varieties, Uncertainties*. Berkeley: University of California Press, 1999, p. 269 (241–307). On the lack of any scriptural recognition of conversion see Cohen, "Conversion to Judaism," and Jacob Milgrom, "Religious Conversion and the Revolt Model for the Formation of Israel," *JBL* 101 (1982) 169–176.

26. The Rabbinic materials pertaining to Esther are nicely summarized in Leila Leah Bronner. "Esther Revisited: An Aggadic Approach," in *A Feminist Companion to Esther, Judith and Susanna*. Ed. Athalya Brenner. Sheffield: Sheffield Academic Press, 1995, pp. 176–197. Also see Leila Leah Bronner, "A Thematic Approach to Ruth in Rabbinic Literature," in *A Feminist Companion to Ruth*. Ed. Athalya Brenner. Sheffield: Sheffield Academic Press, 1993, pp. 146–169. David's "lawful" intermarriage is discussed in B. *Sanhedrin*. 107a. *Sanhedrin, II*. Trans. H. Freedman. London: Soncino Press, 1935, p. 732. On whether Solomon converted and married his Egyptian bride, see B. *Yebamoth*. 76a–76b. *Yebamoth, II*. Trans. Israel Slotki. London: Soncino Press, 1936, pp. 515–516. On God's intention to destroy Jerusalem in anger at the intermarriage, see *Midrash Rabbah Leviticus* XII 5. *Midrash Rabbah Leviticus*. Trans. Judah Slotki. London: Soncino, 1983, pp. 158–161. On the variety of Rabbinic views pertaining to Solomon, see Cohen, "Solomon."

27. Bleich, "The Prohibition," p. 7. Jack Wertheimer, "Surrendering to Intermarriage," *Commentary* 111 (2001) 25 (25–32).

28. Blu Greenberg, "Lovers and Other Strangers: A *Tikkun* Roundtable on Intermarriage" *Tikkun* 12 (1997) 37 (35–41); Irving Levitz, "Jewish Identity, Assimilation

and Intermarriage," in *Crisis and Continuity: The Jewish Family in the 21st Century.* Eds. Norman Linzer, Irving Levitz, and David Schnall. Hoboken, NJ: Ktav, 1995, p. 87 (73–93).

29. Alan Wolfe, *The Transformation of American Religion: How We Actually Live Our Faith.* New York: The Free Press, 2003, p. 69.

7. SAME-SEX EROTICISM AND JERRY FALWELL

1. Falwell's own account of the PTL debacle and the accusations against Jim Bakker can be read in Jerry Falwell, *Strength for the Journey: An Autobiography.* New York: Simon and Schuster, 1987, pp. 400–441. Also see Jack Kelley and Peter Johnson, "Falwell, Bakker War Gets Ugly," *USA Today* (May 28, 1987) 1 a. For a review of his remarks concerning September 11, 2001, see Laurie Goodstein, "Falwell's Finger-Pointing Inappropriate, Bush Says," *The New York Times* (September 15, 2001) A15. On Tinky Winky, see Anonymous, "Tinky Winky Update: America Laughs, Falwell Fulminates," *Church and State* 52 (1999) 19; Phil Kloer, "On Television Falwell Comes Late to Teletubby Psychobabble," *The Atlanta Journal-Constitution* (Feb. 11, 1999) D14; Lawrie Mifflin, "Falwell Takes on the Teletubbies," *New York Times* (Feb. 15, 1999) C11. Falwell is quoted here as saying that Tinky Winky is "modeling the gay life style." Also see Charles Lane, "Tubby Ache," *The New Republic* 220(10) (1999) 4–5. On the meeting with Mel White, see Anonymous, "Falwell Tames His Rhetoric," *Christianity Today* 43(14) (1999) 29. On Falwell's overtures to the gay community, see Kia Shant'e Breaux, "Falwell Offers Kind Words to Gay Visitors," *The Atlanta Journal Constitution* (Oct. 25, 1999) A.3; Edward Gilbreath, "The Jerry We Never Knew," *Christianity Today* 44 (2000) 113–114; Lynn Rosellini, "An Unlikely Friendship, A Historic Meeting," *U.S. News and World Report* 127(17) (1999) 68; Kia Shant'e Breaux, "Falwell, Gay Christians Unite in Worship Service," *Houston Chronicle* (Oct. 25, 1999) 1; Teresa Watanabe, "Talks with Falwell Leave Gays Full of Hope," *Los Angeles Times* (October 24, 1999) 8. For a few of Falwell's stabs at the liberal media, see Garry Abrams, "Jerry Falwell Starts a Drive Against Sassy," *The Los Angeles Times* (Sept. 15, 1988) 1; Laura Sessions Stepp, "Falwell's 'Temptation' Boycott," *The Washington Post* (Aug. 6, 1988) C1; Robert Scheer, "The Ellen Controversy Revisited," *The Los Angeles Times* (May 6, 1997) 7.

2. These explanations for the Christian Right's antigay offensive are proposed by commentators in Julia Lieblich, "Christian Right Renews Campaign Against Gays," *Times-Picayune* (Dec. 25, 1994) A18, and Rob Boston, "The Religious Right's Gay Agenda," *Church and State* 52 (1999) 205–210. The first quote about homosexuality and the Christian world can be found in Michael Vasey's *Strangers and Friends: A New Exploration of Homosexuality and the Bible.* London: Hodder and Stoughton, 1995, p. 6. The second in P. Deryn Guest's "Battling for the Bible: Academy, Church and the Gay Agenda," *Theology and Sexuality* 15 (2001) 90 (66–93). Michael Perry notes that what is unusual in this conflict is that not only do Christians of different denominations argue, but Christians within the same denomination also do so. "Christians and Political Self-Restraint: The Controversy Over Same-Sex Marriage," in *A Nation Under God? Essays on the Future of Religion in American Public Life.* Eds. R. Bruce Douglass and Joshua Mitchell.

Lanham, MD: Rowman and Littlefield, 2000, pp. 177–202. For useful surveys of various Jewish and Christian positions on homosexuality, see the essays in the edited volume of Saul Olyan and Martha Nussbaum, *Sexual Orientation and Human Rights in American Religious Discourse*. New York: Oxford, 1998. Also see Kathy Rudy, *Sex and the Church: Gender, Homosexuality, and the Transformation of Christian Ethics*. Boston: Beacon Press, 1997. For the basic creedal positions, see J. Gordon Melton, *The Churches Speak on Homosexuality: Official Statements from Religious Bodies and Ecumenical Institutions*. Detroit: Gale Research, 1991. The argument that the ancients possessed no concept comparable to our notion of homosexuality is made by almost all scholarly commentators. The most stimulating and theoretically informed treatment can be found in Daniel Boyarin, "Are There Any Jews in 'The History of Sexuality?'" *Journal of the History of Sexuality* 5 (1995) 333–355. Daniel Helminiak argues that Scripture does not know of homosexuality but homogeniality. "The Bible on Homosexuality: Ethically Neutral," in *Same Sex: Debating the Ethics, Science, and Culture of Homosexuality* Ed. John Corvino. Lanham: Rowman and Littlefield, 1997, pp. 81–92. Last, we note that in this chapter we are concentrating mainly on how Christian biblicists have approached this issue. This does not mean that Jewish exegetes have not made valuable contributions, although their input is relatively small when compared with the massive amount of scholarship produced by Christians.

3. Tom Horner, *Jonathan Loved David: Homosexuality in Biblical Times*. Philadelphia: Westminster Press, 1978, p. 24; Robert Gagnon, *The Bible and Homosexual Practice: Texts and Hermeneutics*. Nashville, TN: Abingdon, 2001, pp. 37, 12.

4. Saul Olyan, "'And With a Male You Shall Not Lie the Lying Down of a Woman': On the Meaning and Significance of Leviticus 18:22 and 20:13," *Journal of the History of Sexuality* 5 (1994) 184 (179–206). Our first English translation comes from the Jewish Publication Society. The Revised Standard Version reads: "You shall not lie with a male as with a woman; it is an abomination."

5. Olyan, "'And With a Male'" raises a variety of intriguing questions about the passages in question. His interpretation of the verse as referring to anal sex strikes us as interesting but ultimately unconvincing. Olyan, however, rightly argues that the Hebrew of these passages is far more problematic than most commentators have imagined. The crux, for him, is "the opaque idiom" *miškĕbê 'iššâ*. p. 183. He translates this as "the lying down of a woman" – a very plausible translation, although we would refrain from adding the definite article (which does not appear in the Hebrew text). Because the idiom appears nowhere else outside Leviticus, Olyan searches for parallels and scrutinizes "a similar and apparently related idiom" *miškab zākār*. p. 184. This expression is found in Num. 31:17, 18, and 35 and Judg. 21:11 and 12 and is translated by Olyan as "the lying down of a male." p. 184. It also occurs in 1 QSa 1.10 published in D. Barthélemy and J. T. Milik, *Discoveries in the Judaean Desert 1: Qumran Cave 1*. Oxford: Clarendon Press, 1955, p. 109. The problem is that in all these allegedly parallel verses that feature *miškab zākār* (including the Qumran materials), we find the verb *y-d-ʿ*, "to know." The translation of Num. 31:17 would be "every young woman that did not know [the] lying down of a male (*miškab zākār*) you will let live." Or, maybe, "every young

woman that did not know [the] bed of a man, you will let live." In fact, "bed, couch, bedding" is the most widely attested translation of *miškab* (*The Dictionary of Classical Hebrew. Sheffield: Volume V: Nun-Mem.* Ed. David J. A. Clines. Sheffield: Sheffield Academic Press, 2001, p. 526), and it is plausible to think that "knowing a man's bed" could have been a euphemism for sex. In any case, Lev. 18 and 20 do not speak of *knowing* lying downs of a woman and for these reasons drawing parallels with the form that appears there (*miškĕbê 'iššâ*), and the form (*miškab zākār*) is somewhat problematic. Olyan, in contrast, sees "an analogue" between the expression found in Num. 31 and that found in Lev. 18. The former refers to "the lying down of a male" the latter to "the lying down of a woman." Following this analogy, Olyan assumes knowing the lying down of a male refers to vaginal penetration and thus it follows that lying down of a woman refers to anal penetration. The suggestion is intriguing, but far more evidence would be needed. Further, his insistence that 18:22 refers to the insertive partner seems too detailed in light of what the text actually says. See the critique of Olyan's argument by Jerome Walsh, "Leviticus 18:22 and 20:13: Who Is Doing What to Whom?" *JBL* 120 (2001) 201–209. Baruch Levine translates the phrase in question as "'after the manner of lying with a woman' by the introduction of the male member." Baruch Levine, *Leviticus.* JPS Torah Commentary. Philadelphia: JPS, 1989, p. 123.

6. Leviticus 20:13

7. For various opinions on the suggestion that anal sex in particular is being prohibited, see Olyan, "And With a Male"; Walsh, "Leviticus 18:22"; Boyarin, "Are There Any Jews," p. 344; Thomas Thurston, "Leviticus 18:22 and the Prohibition of Homosexual Acts," in *Homophobia and the Judaeo-Christian Tradition.* Eds. Michael Stemmeler and J. Michael Clark. Dallas: Monument Press, 1990, p. 16 (7–23); Robert Goss, *Queering Christ: Beyond Jesus Acted Up.* Cleveland: Pilgrim Press, 2002, p. 190. On the inability of these verses to tell us what specific acts are prohibited, see Derrick Bailey, *Homosexuality and the Western Christian Tradition.* Hamden, CT: Archon Books, 1975, p. 59. For issues pertaining to the importance of the status of the active and passive partners, see Daniel Boyarin, "Are There Any Jews." Walsh believes the laws are addressed to "a free adult Israelite… [who] takes the passive sexual role of being penetrated by the other." "Leviticus 18:22," p. 208. On the question of the relation between penetration and status in the Rabbinic period, see Michael Satlow, "'They Abused Him Like a Woman': Homoeroticism, Gender Blurring, and the Rabbis in Late Antiquity," *Journal of the History of Sexuality* 5 (1994) 1–25. Jacob Milgrom, who does not see the question of status as present in the Levitical legislation notes: "This absolute ban on homosexuality contrasts strikingly with the Hellenistic and Roman world, where homosexuality was sanctioned with those of inferior status, such as slaves, foreigners, and youths." *Leviticus 17–22.* Anchor Bible. New York: Doubleday, 2000, pp. 1749, 1566. Milgrom continues to remark that a strict reading of Scripture would show that such a law was binding in Israel, but not other countries, and proceeds to expand on the implications of this for contemporary social policy. p. 1750. Again, regarding the activities involved and the status of the Israelite being addressed, we believe there is not enough data to draw such conclusions. Nissinen argues that

lesbianism is not mentioned in these texts because such relations did not challenge male domination. Martti Nissinen, *Homoeroticism in the Biblical World: A Historical Perspective*. Trans. Kirsi Stjerna. Minneapolis: Fortress Press, 1998, p. 43. M. H. Pope sees this lack of concern regarding female homosexuality as "due in large measure to belief in the sanctity of semen." "Homosexuality," in *The Interpreter's Dictionary of the Bible: Supplementary Volume*. Nashville, TN: Abingdon, 1976, pp. 415–417. Tikva Frymer-Kensky attributes the absence of reference to lesbian interaction as owing to the fact that "it did not result in true physical 'union' (by male entry)" "Sex and Sexuality," in *The Anchor Bible Dictionary: Volume 5, O-Sh*. Ed. David Noel Freedman. New York: Doubleday, 1992, pp. 1145–1146 (1144–1146).

8. For Carroll's remark, see Chapter Five, footnote 8.

9. The two besieged hosts are Lot in Genesis 19:8, and an unnamed man from Ephraim in Judges 19:24 The Reverend Dr. Derrick Sherwin Bailey's study, *Homosexuality and the Western Christian Tradition*, is seen as milestone in this debate. See, for example, Jonathan Sinclair Carey, "D. S. Bailey and 'the Name Forbidden Among Christians,'" in *Homosexuality and Religion and Philosophy*. Eds. Wayne Dynes and Stephen Donaldson. New York: Garland, 1992, pp. 94–115, and D. J. Atkinson, *Homosexuals in the Christian Fellowship*. Grand Rapids, MI: Eerdmans, 1979, p. 78 (78–99). On the verb *y-d-'* and its nuances, see Victor Hamilton, *The Book of Genesis: Chapters 18–50*. Grand Rapids, MI: Eerdmans, 1995, pp. 33–35. Bailey's opinion notwithstanding, the intentions of the men would appear to be of a prurient nature. Bailey's original argument that the form might be translated in a nonsexual sense can be found in *Homosexuality*, pp. 1–8, and the quote on Sodom and Gomorrah is found on p. 1. This reading is challenged in Nissinen, *Homoeroticism*, p. 46. In Judges 19:24, the Ephraimite host offers to cast out his virgin daughter and the concubine of his guest.

10. Bailey demonstrates that nowhere in the Old Testament is the sin of homosexuality explicitly identified with Sodom. He traces the antihomosexual reading of Genesis 19 to the second century BCE, Palestine. *Homosexuality*, pp. 9, 26. Also see Victor Paul Furnish, "The Bible and Homosexuality: Reading the Texts in Context," in *Homosexuality in the Church: Both Sides of the Debate*. Ed. Jeffrey Siker. Louisville, KY: Westminster John Knox Press, 1994, p. 19 (18–35). As for the theory that the traditional interpretation of the sodomy laws developed in Hellenistic Jewish times, we could cite the following. Philo, for example, offers this appraisal of the Sodomites: "Not only in their mad lust for women did they violate the marriages of their neighbors, but also men mounted males without respect for the sex nature which the active partner shares with the passive." *On Abraham* XXVI: 135–136; *Philo: Volume VI*. Trans. F. H. Colson. Cambridge, MA: Harvard University Press, 1994, p. 71. Josephus makes the following enhancement: "on seeing these young men of remarkably fair appearance whom Lot had taken under his roof, [the Sodomites] were bent only on violence and outrage to their youthful beauty." Josephus, *Jewish Antiquities* I XI 3. 1926. *Josephus, IV, Jewish Antiquities, Books I– IV*. Trans. H. St. J. Thackeray. London: William Heinemann Ltd, 1930, p. 99. On Philo, see Roy Bowen Ward, "Why Unnatural? The Tradition Behind Romans 1:26–27," *HTR* 90 (1997) 263–284. For a discussion of texts pertaining

to homosexuality in the intertestamental period, see Lewis John Eron, "Early Jewish and Christian Attitudes Toward Male Homosexuality as Expressed in the Testament of Naphtali," in *Homophobia and the Judaeo–Christian Tradition*. Eds. Michael Stemmeler and J. Michael Clark. Dallas: Monument Press, 1990, pp. 25–49. For examples of those who do not equate a report of homosexual rape with dislike of homosexuality, see Richard Hays, "Awaiting the Redemption of Our Bodies: The Witness of Scripture Concerning Homosexuality," in *Homosexuality and the Church: Both Sides of the Debate*. Ed. Jeffrey Siker. Louisville, KY: Westminster John Knox Press, 1994, p. 5 (3–17); Furnish, "The Bible," p. 19; Martin Samuel Cohen, "The Biblical Prohibition on Homosexual Intercourse," *Journal of Homosexuality* 19 (1990) 4 (3–20); Also Letha Scanzoni and Virginia Ramey Mollenkott, *Is the Homosexual My Neighbor?: Another Christian View*. San Francisco: Harper & Row, 1978, pp. 57–58. Also see Goss, *Queering Christ*, pp. 194, 197. Contra, those who do see a specific prohibition on homosexuality in the tale, for example, Atkinson, *Homosexuals*, 1979, p. 81. Nissinen writes of Gen. 19: "Homoeroticism appears in the story of Sodom only as one aspect of hostile sexual aggression towards strangers. Other than that, the Yahwist's attitude toward same-sex interaction remains unknown." *Homoeroticism*, pp. 49, 50.

11. Genesis 9:22. B. *Sanhderin. 70a, Sanhedrin*, II. Trans. H. Freedman. London: Soncino Press, 1935, p. 477, although a different interpretation of the verse appears in B. *Sanhedrin* 54a. The latter seems to incorporate an equally unclear verse about "your father's nakedness" found in Lev. 18:7. E. A. Speiser writes: "the term itself relates to exposure . . . and does not necessarily imply sexual offenses." *Genesis*. Anchor Bible: Garden City, NJ: Doubleday, 1964, p. 61, although other commentators are less certain. Gerhard von Rad remarks: "Possibly the narrator suppressed something even more repulsive than mere looking." *Genesis: A Commentary*. Trans. John Marks. Philadelphia: Westminster Press, 1972, p. 137. Nahum Sarna, *Genesis*. JPS Torah Commentary. Philadelphia: Jewish Publication Society, 1989, observes: "the Torah has suppressed the sordid details of some repugnant act." p. 66.

12. For a discussion of the term "homosociability," see Nissinen. *Homoeroticism*, p. 17. J. A. Thompson. "The Significance of the Verb *Love* in the David-Jonathan Narratives in 1 Samuel," *VT* 24 (1974) 334–338, argues that the Hebrew term for love has a political significance. Peter Ackroyd, "The Verb Love-'ĀHĒB in the David Jonathan Narratives – A Footnote," *VT* (1975) 25: 213–214, endorses the suggestion and furthers the attempt to read political overtones into these verses. Mainstream commentaries generally refrain from raising the possibility of sexual love between David and Jonathan, and follow the suggestion of either friendship or political alliance. Horner, *Jonathan Loved David*, p. 28. As for Saul's remarks, Horner writes: "The implication of a homosexual relationship is clearly a part of Saul's outburst." p. 32. The dramatic, teary, kissing scene between Jonathan and David occurs in 1 Sam. 20:41. The problems in translating Saul's rant against Jonathan center around the Hebrew phrase *ben-na'ăwat hamardût*. As S. R. Driver pointed out: "The text must be at fault." *Notes on the Hebrew Text and the Topography of the Books of Samuel*, 2nd ed. Winona Lake, IN: Alpha, 1984, p. 171. The inclination among translators is to follow LXX and restore the Hebrew

to *na'ărat* ("girl") in the construct, thus yielding "son of a rebellious slave girl!" See, for example, Henry Preserved Smith, *A Critical and Exegetical Commentary on the Books of Samuel*. ICC. New York: Charles Scribner's Sons, 1899, p. 193, and Ralph Klein, *1 Samuel*. Word Biblical Commentary. Waco, TX: Word Books, 1983, p. 202. Others argue for the MT reading of the niphal form of the root '-*w-h* ("to be bent, twisted, perverted) and translate "You son of a degenerate, rebellious women." See, for example, Hans Hertzberg, *I and II Samuel: A Commentary*. The Library. Trans. J. S. Bowden. Philadelphia: Westminster Press, 1964, p. 170. Also see P. Kyle McCarter, Jr., *I Samuel*. The Anchor Bible. Garden City, NJ: Doubleday, 1980, p. 339.

13. David's adulterous and murderous activities are chronicled in 2 Sam. 11. His curious stay with the despised Philistines is described in 1 Sam. 27–30. Impotence is insinuated in 1 Kings 1:1–4. For a discussion of the antimonarchic tone sometimes found in the Hebrew Bible and its implications for thinking about the social position of the biblical authors, see Jacques Berlinerblau, *Official Religion and Popular Religion in Pre-Exilic Ancient Israel*. The Rabbi Louis Feinberg Memorial Lecture in Judaic Studies. University of Cincinnati, Department of Judaic Studies, 2000.

14. John McNeill, *The Church and the Homosexual*, 4th ed. Boston: Beacon Press, 1993, p. 53. On the centrality of this passage to Christian views on homosexuality, also see Gagnon, *The Bible*, p. 229, and Nissinen, *Homoeroticism*, p. 103. The translation we are using is furnished by Joseph Fitzmyer, *Romans*. The Anchor Bible. New York: Doubleday, 1993, p. 269. Fitzmyer writes: "Homosexual behavior is the sign of human rebellion against God, an outward manifestation of the inward and spiritual rebellion." p. 276. On what is meant in this text by "unnatural," see the interesting discussion of Roy Bowen Ward, "Why Unnatural? The Tradition Behind Romans 1:26–27," *HTR* 90 (1997) 263–284, and Robin Scroggs, *The New Testament and Homosexuality: Contextual Background for Contemporary Debate*. Philadelphia: Fortress Press, 1983, p. 115. James Miller, "The Practices of Romans 1:26: Homosexual or Heterosexual?" *Novum Testamentum* 37 (1995) 1–11, argues that the reference in 1:26 to women, although accepted by most as indicative of same-sex relations between women, actually refers to some type of heterosexual sex viewed as deviant. David Fredrickson proposes that Paul's remarks are "not an attack on homosexuality as a violation of divine law but a description of the human condition informed by the philosophic rejection of passionate love." "Natural and Unnatural Use in Romans 1:24–27: Paul and the Philosophic Critique of Eros," in *Homosexuality, Science, and the 'Plain Sense' of Scripture*. Ed. David Balch. Grand Rapids, MI: Eerdmans, 2000, p. 208 (197–221). A contestation of "revisionist views" of this passage can be found in Thomas Schmidt, "Romans 1:26–27 and Biblical Sexuality," in *Same Sex: Debating the Ethics, Science, and Culture of Homosexuality*. Ed. John Corvino. Lanham, MD: Rowman and Littlefield, 1997, pp. 93–104.

15. John Boswell, *Christianity, Social Tolerance, and Homosexuality: Gay People in Western Europe from the Beginning of the Christian Era to the Fourteenth Century*. Chicago: University of Chicago Press, 1981, p. 109. "Paul apparently refers," writes John McNeill in *The Church and the Homosexual*, "only to homosexual acts

indulged in by those he considered to be otherwise heterosexually inclined." p. 55. Also see Bailey, *Homosexuality*, p. 38. Nissinen rejects this argument, viewing the emphasis on sexual orientation as an anachronism. Paul's words, he argues, are simply directed to persons who "participate in same-sex erotic acts." *Homoeroticism*, p. 109. As many have observed, it may be deduced that too much sex with the other gender results in a desire to have sex with members of one's own gender, see Dale Martin, "Heterosexism and the Interpretation of Romans 1:18–32," *Biblical Interpretation* 3 (1995) 343 (332–355).

16. On the strangeness of the term, see Robin Scroggs, *The New Testament*, p. 107. The most comprehensive study is that of Dale Martin, "*Arsenokoitês* and *Malakos*: Meanings and Consequences," in *Biblical Ethics and Homosexuality: Listening to Scripture*. Ed. Robert Brawley. Louisville, KY: Westminster John Knox Press, 1996, pp. 117–136.

17. On the history of English translations of this verse, see McNeill, *The Church*, p. 50; Bailey, *Homosexuality*, pp. 38–39; Martin, "*Arsenokoitês* and *Malakos*," pp. 118, 121, 123, for the quotes cited in this paragraph. Boswell, *Christianity*, sees the term as having connoted "male prostitute" to Paul and his contemporaries, p. 107. Also see Furnish, "The Bible," p. 24. Atkinson says it refers to "a male bed-partner for a male in sexual intercourse." *Homosexuals*, p. 91.

18. McNeill, *The Church*, p. 52. He continues: "Neither the *malakoi* nor the *arsenokoitai* were necessarily homosexuals; the former were simply debauched individuals and the latter were probably male prostitutes or those given to anal intercourse, which is not necessarily nor exclusively a homosexual activity," *The Church*, p. 56; Martin, "*Arsenokoitês*, p. 126. The Revised Standard Version renders both the words *malakoi* and *arsenokoitai* with one English word, "homosexuals." Gagnon translates the former as "males who function in the role of passive homosexual partners and who also undertake to erase their distinctively masculine nature." *The Bible*, pp. 310, 307. Bailey, *Homosexuality*, p. 38, says the terms denote "males who engage passively or actively in homosexual acts." Of *malakos*, Boswell writes: "The word is never used in Greek to denigrate gay people as a group or even in reference to homosexual acts generically...." *Christianity*, p. 107. Scroggs, *The New Testament*, p. 108, sees the terms as referring to an "effeminate call-boy" and the one who keeps the latter as a mistress.

19. Robin Scroggs, *The New Testament*, p. 115. Scroggs says Paul is speaking about a dehumanizing pederasty in which the passive boy partner is humiliated (42–43, 126, 127–128). For a challenge to Scrogg's view, see Mark Smith, "Ancient Bisexuality and the Interpretation of Romans 1:26–27," *JAAR* 64(1996) 223–256. Smith writes: "Paul probably proscribed at least all forms of homosexual behavior with which he was familiar." p. 250. And for a critique of Smith, see James Miller, "Response: Pederasty and Romans 1:27: A Response to Mark Smith," *JAAR* 65 (1997) 861–866. A discussion of the confessional nature of Smith's assumptions can be found in Daniel Helminiak, "Response: Ethics, Biblical and Denominational: A Response to Mark Smith," *JAAR* 65 (1997) 855–859. On pederasty, see the remarks of Philo, *Special Laws*, III 37–42 in *Philo VII*. Trans. F. H. Colson. Cambridge, MA: Harvard University Press, 1937, pp. 499–501. Furnish, "The Bible and Homosexuality," p. 23, interprets Jesus' silence as a sign that

homosexuality "was not a matter of special concern within the Church that pre-served and applied his sayings."

20. Falwell, Jerry. (Ed.). *The Fundamentalist Phenomenon: The Resurgence of Con-servative Christianity*. Garden City, NJ: Doubleday, 1981, pp. 8, 203–204. The second remark is cited in Edward Gilbreath, "The Jerry," pp. 113–114. In that same passage, Falwell continues: "But with the violence of the last decade . . . and the attacks against gays, like Billy Jack Gaither and Matthew Shepard – something has to change."

21. Pim Pronk, *Against Nature? Types of Moral Argumentation Regarding Homosex-uality*. Trans. John Vriend. Grand Rapids, MI: Eerdmans, 1993, pp. 324–325. This issue was deftly handled by P. Deryn Guest, "Battling for the Bible," who notes: "when scholarly exegesis runs in harness with a confessional proclamation the alliance can become a powerful disseminator of truth claims." p. 75. For a review of the ways in which Christian writers from across the spectrum confront the question of homosexuality, see David Blamires, "Recent Christian Perspectives on Homosexuality – The Context for the Debate," in *Towards a Theology of Gay Liberation*. Ed. Malcolm Macourt. London: SCM Press, 1977, pp. 9–23.

22. Judith Plaskow, "Sexual Orientation and Human Rights: A Progressive Jewish Perspective," in *Sexual Orientation and Human Rights in American Religious Dis-course*. Eds. Saul Olyan and Martha Nussbaum. New York: Oxford University Press, 1998, p. 29 (29–45). On the merits of restraining the imposition of one's religious belief when discussing this issue, see Perry, "Christians." P. Deryn Guest points to the manner in which biblically based views played a role in recent court disputes about gay civil rights. Guest writes that the religious discourse on homosexuality "spreads far beyond this specific debate and affects translesbigay people within the secular world." p. 69. On the way in which biblical interpreta-tions played a role in Vermont's Civil Unions bill (albeit unofficially), see Susan Ackerman, "When the Bible Enters the Fray," *Bible Review* 16 (2000) 6, 50. Saul Olyan and Martha Nussbaum write: "There are many public contexts in which religious discourse has been brought to bear on this divisive debate." "Introduc-tion," in *Sexual Orientation and Human Rights in American Religious Discourse*. Eds. Saul Olyan and Martha Nussbaum. New York: Oxford University Press, 1998, p. xiv (xiii–xix). Also see Jim Hill and Rand Cheadle, *The Bible Tells Me So: Uses and Abuses of Holy Scripture*. New York: Anchor Books, 1996, pp. 68–76. For a premier as to the "inescapable coupling" of religion and political policy in the United States, see the article of Hugh Heclo, "An Introduction to Religion and Public Policy," in *Religion Returns to the Public Square: Faith and Policy in America*. Eds. Hugh Heclo and Wilfred McClay. Baltimore: The Johns Hopkins University Press, 2003, pp. 3–30.

23. When it comes to the Bible many gay persons evince, in the words of Raymond-Jean Frontain, "spiritual indifference before a seemingly inhospitable authority." "Introduction: Reclaiming the Sacred: The Bible in Gay and Lesbian Culture," *Journal of Homosexuality* 33 (1997) 13 (1–23). For an example of uncompromising critique of the Bible on homosexuality, see Rictor Norton, "The Biblical Roots of Homophobia," in *Towards a Theology of Gay Liberation*. Ed. Malcolm Macourt. London: SCM, 1977, pp. 39–46. And see the response in the same volume of James Martin, "An Old Testament Scholar Replies," pp. 47–56.

24. Thomas Clark, "Secularism and Sexuality: The Case for Gay Equality," *The Humanist* 54 (1994) 23 (23–30). A similar point about the limits of religious toleration in the Indian context is made in Brenda Cossman and Ratna Kapur, *Secularism's Last Sigh? Hinduvta and the (Mis)rule of Law.* New Delhi, India: Oxford University Press, 1999, p. 122.

25. None of this means that social factors alone condition intellectual production. For a discussion of this problematic, see the author's *Heresy in the University: The Black Athena Controversy and the Responsibilities of American Intellectuals.* New Brunswick, NJ: Rutgers, 1999.

26. Christopher Seitz, "Sexuality and Scripture's Plain Sense: The Christian Community and the Law of God," in *Homosexuality, Science, and the "Plain Sense" of Scripture.* Ed. David Balch. Grand Rapids, MI: Eerdmans, 2000, p. 182 (177–196). On the positions of the Fathers, see Boswell, *Christianity, Social Tolerance,* pp. 136–166.

8. THE SECULAR QUR'ĀN?

1. In surveying the rise of modern biblical scholarship, James Kugel says the following about issues of authorship: "Such questions obviously touched on the texts' authority: a divine revelation granted to the true prophet Moses was fine – but what gave authority to anonymous additions, expansions, nay, the work of impostors? The pursuit of the authentically Mosaic, Davidic, etc, thus acquired a certain nervous urgency, and ultimately led, as is well known, to the birth of source criticism." James Kugel, "The Bible in the University," in *The Hebrew Bible and Its Interpreters.* Eds. William Propp, Baruch Halpern, and David Noel Freedman. Winona Lake, IN: Eisenbrauns, 1990, p. 153 (143–165).

2. These arguments are made in Chapter One. The reader will notice different transliterations of the term Qur'ān. Whenever possible we try to employ this usage, although when citing others who transliterate differently, we keep their rendering. All translations from the Qur'ān used in this chapter come from *The Koran: With a Parallel Arabic Text,* Trans. N.J. Dawood. London: Viking, 1990.

3. Stefan Wild, "We Have Sent Down to Thee the Book with the Truth," in *The Qur'ān as Text.* Ed. Stefan Wild. Leiden: E. J. Brill, 1996, p. 140 (137–153). On the Qur'ān as a glorious book, see 12:1; 27:1; 43:2; 44:2; and 56:77. As a "book with the truth" 3:3 and 4:105. As being "wise," see 36:2. References to the Qur'ān's clarity can be found in Daniel Madigan, "Book," in *Encyclopaedia of the Qur'ān. Volume One, A–D.* Ed. Jane Dammen McAuliffe. Leiden: Brill, 2001, pp. 250, 243 (242–251). Madigan expands on the arguments made here in *The Qur'ān's Self-Image: Writing and Authority in Islam's Scripture.* Princeton, NJ: Princeton University Press, 2001. The challenge issued to other would-be Qur'ān bearers can be found in 2:23. For other claims of superiority and responses to critics, see 10:38 and 11:13. On the recitation's flawlessness, see 39:28.

4. 25:32, and see 34:31 and 41:26, where the protestations of critics/unbelievers are aired. For the verses about ambiguity, see 3:7. On this astonishing pericope, see Jane Dammen McAuliffe, "Text and Textuality: Q 3:7 as a Point of Intersection," in *Literary Structures of Religious Meaning in the Qur'ān.* Ed. Issa Boullata. Richmond: Curzon, 2000, pp. 56–76. Shabbir Akhtar, "The Limits of Internal

Hermeneutics: The Status of the Qur'ān as Literary Miracle," in *Holy Scriptures in Judaism, Christianity and Islam: Hermeneutics, Values and Society*. Eds. Hendrik Vroom and Jerald Gort. Amsterdam: Rodopi, 1997, p. 107 (107–112). 17:45–46 attributes misunderstanding of the text to God's design (also see 9:127). In other words, the deity has brought about their inability to understand His own message. This is an argument rather reminiscent of Isaiah 6:9–10. For a discussion of the latter, see Jacques Berlinerblau, "Free Will and Determinism in First Isaiah: Secular Hermeneutics, the Poetics of Contingency, and Emile Durkheim's," *Homo Duplex*" *JAAR* 71 (2003) 767–791. The Qur'ān, anticipating dissent, also prescribes punishments for those who will ignore it: 3:5; 7:50–55. For other examples of the text anticipating and voicing potential objections to itself, see 10:16; 11:13; 17:89; and 30:58–59; also see 84:20–23. A similar sense of impending dissent can be seen in the New Testament, albeit with far less specificity. See, for example, Romans 16:17–18.

5. 10:38; 18:28; 27:6; 32:2; also see 3:3; 5:15; 13:1; 18:1; 40:2; 42:17; 45:2; 46:2. In the New Testament context, 2 Timothy 3:16 comes to mind as a text that is equally explicit about its divine authorship. Although see our remarks on the proper translation of this verse in Chapter One, endnote 21.

6. See Chapter Seven for our discussion of homosexuality. We are veering very close to the notion of *doxa*, ideas about the world so taken for granted that they are never spoken. On this issue, see Jacques Berlinerblau, "Toward a Sociology of Heresy, Orthodoxy, and *Doxa*," *History of Religions* 40 (2001) 327–351, and Jacques Berlinerblau, "Ideology, Pierre Bourdieu's *Doxa*, and the Hebrew Bible," *Semeia* 87 (1999) 193–214.

7. Hava Lazarus-Yafeh, "Self-Criticism in Jewish and Islamic Traditions," in *Judaism and Islam: Boundaries, Communication and Interaction: Essays in Honor of William Brinner*. Eds. Benjamin Hary, John Hayes, and Fred Astren. Leiden: Brill, 2000, p. 312 (303–317). Akhtar, "The Limits," p. 108. In the words of Wild: "The importance of the Qur'ān for Muslims and Islam is tantamount to the importance of the person of Jesus Christ for Christians and Christianity." "We Have Sent," p. 136. "For most devout Muslims," observes Alford Welch, "The Qur'ān is first and foremost the eternal speech of God." "Introduction," in *Introduction to a Thematic Issue of JAAR, Supplements (47:4, December 1979) "Studies in Qur'ān and Tafsir*," *JAAR* 47 (1980) 622 (619–634). This same article explores the dogma of the text as being the speech of God and uncreated.

8. Richard Martin, Mark Woodward, and Dwi Atmaja, *Defenders of Reason in Islam: Mu'tazilism from Medieval School to Modern Symbol*. Oxford: Oneworld, 1997, p. 9. On various rationalist thinkers in Islamic history, one can consult the fifth chapter of Pervez Hoodbhoy's *Islam and Science: Religious Orthodoxy and the Battle for Rationality*. London: Zed Books, 1991, pp. 109–117. Hoodbhoy's work also features a searing critique of scientific inquiry in the Muslim world. On polemics between Jewish, Christian, and Muslim thinkers, see Andrew Rippin, "Interpreting the Bible Through the Qur'ān," in *Approaches to the Qur'ān*. Eds. G. R. Hawting and Abdul-Kader A. Shareef. London: Routledge, 1993, pp. 249–259. R. W. Southern, *Western Views of Islam in the Middle Ages*. Cambridge, MA: Harvard University Press, 1962. For discussions of Muslim views of Jewish Scripture (which are equally

polemical), see Camilla Adang, *Muslim Writers on Judaism and the Hebrew Bible: From Ibn Rabban to Ibn Hazm.* Leiden: E. J. Brill, 1996. Theodore Pulcini, *Exegesis as Polemical Discourse: Ibn Hazm on Jewish and Christian Scriptures.* Atlanta: Scholars Press, 1998. Also see Hava Lazarus-Yafeh, *Intertwined Worlds: Medieval Islam and Bible Criticism.* Princeton, NJ: Princeton University Press, 1992. The comment about 60,000 readings is from Ghazzāli as cited in F. E. Peters, *Judaism, Christianity and Islam: The Classical Texts and Their Interpretation* Princeton, NJ: Princeton University Press, 1990, p. 148.

9. For an interesting and early discussion of what is meant by this phrase, see M. Friedlaender, *Essays on the Writings of Abraham Ibn Ezra.* London: Trübner and Co., 1877, pp. 62, 60–67. Friedlander doubts that it contains the heretical overtones heard by later commentators (such as R. E. F. Friedman in *Who Wrote the Bible?* San Francisco: HarperSanFrancisco, 1997, p. 19). On the constant challenges to Mosaic authorship, see J. Alberto Soggin, *Introduction to the Old Testament: From Its Origins to the Closing of the Alexandrian Canon,* rev. ed. Trans. John Bowden. Philadelphia: Westminster Press, 1980, p. 80.

10. For examples of the aforementioned critical assessments of the text's history, see endnote 17.

11. Needless to say, these activities are not engaged in by all biblical scholars, although a large number spend their time doing precisely this. For a lengthy treatment of the issues discussed in this section, see Jacques Berlinerblau, "'Poor Bird Not Knowing Which Way to Fly': Biblical Scholarship's Marginality, Secular Humanism, and the Laudable Occident." *Biblical Interpretation* 10 (2002) 267–304.

12. Interested readers can consult admirably clear, concise, and accessible works such as Friedman's *Who Wrote the Bible?*; Joseph Blenkinsopp's *The Pentateuch: An Introduction to the First Five Books of the Bible.* New York: Doubleday, 1992, pp. 1–30; or Emil Kraeling's *Old Testament Research Since the Reformation.* New York: Schocken, 1969. Also see James Kugel, "The Bible in the University."

13. For a thorough treatment of William Robertson Smith, see the volume edited by William Johnstone, *William Robertson Smith: Essays in Reassessment.* Sheffield: Sheffield Academic Press, 1995. Also see Warner Bailey, "William Robertson Smith and American Biblical Studies," *Journal of Presbyterian History* 51 (1973) 285–308, and George Anderson, "Two Scottish Semitists," *Supplements to Vetus Testamentum* 28 (1975) ix–xix. On the friendship between Smith and Wellhausen, see in the same volume edited by Johnstone, Rudolf Smend's "William Robertson Smith and Julius Wellhausen," pp. 226–242. Also to be consulted is J. W. Rogerson, *The Bible and Criticism in Victorian Britain: Profiles of F. D. Maurice and William Roberston Smith.* Sheffield: Sheffield Academic Press, 1995. Rogerson makes reference to Smith's "believing criticism." p. 109. For a useful assessment of Wellhausen's approach see Albert de Pury, *La Pentateuque en question,* 2nd ed. Ed. Albert de Pury. Geneva: Labor et Fides, 1989. On Smith and the period in general, see Nigel M. de S. Cameron, *Biblical Higher Criticism and the Defense of Infallibilism in 19th Century Britain.* Lewiston: Edwin Mellen, 1987.

14. Solomon Schechter, "Higher Criticism-Higher Anti-Semitism," in *Seminary Addresses and Other Papers.* The Burning Bush Press, 1959, pp. 35–39. The address was delivered on March 26, 1903. S. David Sperling, *Students of the Covenant: A*

History of Jewish Biblical Scholarship in North America. Atlanta: Scholars Press, 1992, p. 115. For the first two Church decisions, see James Megivern (Ed.). *Bible Interpretation.* Wilmington, NC: McGrath, 1978. An interesting discussion of the most recent document can be found in Peter Williamson, "Catholic Principles for Interpreting Scripture," *Catholic Biblical Quarterly* 65 (2003) 327–349. Of interest is Robert Bruce Robinson, *Roman Catholic Exegesis Since Divino Afflante Spiritu: Hermeneutical Implications.* Atlanta: Scholars Press, 1988. On the increasing acceptance of Wellhausen's work between 1891 and 1925, see Brevard Childs, "Wellhausen in English," *Semeia* 25 (1982) 85 (83–88). An interesting overview of the varied religious responses to higher criticism can be found in Irwin, "The Significance."

15. Richard Riesen, *Criticism and Faith in Late Victorian Scotland: A. B. Davidson, William Robertson Smith and George Adam Smith.* Lanham, MD: University Press of America, 1985, p. 119. Also see Richard Riesen, "Scholarship and Piety: The Sermons of William Robertson Smith," in *William Robertson Smith: Essays in Reassessment.* Sheffield: Sheffield Academic Press, 1995, p. 93 (86–84).

16. Currently, the most infamous case is that of Nasr Abū Zaid, an Egyptian scholar – by our estimation a believing critic – who was forced to leave his native land for Holland. For discussions of the case, see Charles Hirschkind, "Heresy or Hermeneutics: The Case of Nasr Hamid Abu Zayd," *The American Journal of Islamic Social Sciences* 12 (1995) 463–476. Stefan Wild. "Preface," in *The Qur'ān as Text.* Ed. Stefan Wild. Leiden: E. J. Brill, 1996, pp. vii–xi. A broad examination of the problems involved for critical Muslim scholars can be found in Rotraud Wielandt, "Exegesis of the Qur'ān: Early Modern and Contemporary," in *Encyclopaedia of the Qur'ān: Volume Two, E–I.* Ed. Jane Dammen McAuliffe. Leiden: Brill, 2002, pp. 124–142. Vincent Cornell speaks of a "stagnation of Muslim intellectual life and an inhibition of original inquiry that persists to this day." "Where is Scriptural Truth in Islam?" in *Holy Scriptures in Judaism, Christianity and Islam: Hermeneutics, Values and Society.* Eds. Hendrik Vroom and Jerald Gort. Amsterdam: Rodopi, 1997, p. 74 (69–76). Mohammed Arkoun writes: "With the exception of a handful of scholars who have had no lasting influence, all qur'ānic scholars have little regard for any methodological debate and reject, if they are not actually unaware of, questions of an epistemological nature." "Contemporary Critical Practices and the Qur'ān," in *Encyclopaedia of the Qur'ān. Volume One, A–D.* Ed. Jane Dammen McAuliffe. Leiden: Brill, 2001, p. 413 (412–431). A discussion of the 'ulamā can be found in J. O. Hunwick, "'ulamā," in *The Encyclopaedia of Islam: Volume X,* new ed. Eds. P. J. Bearman et al. Leiden: Brill, 2000, pp. 809–810. The definition of this group is taken from the same source.

17. A. T. Welch, "al-Kur'ān," *The Encyclopedia of Islam: Volume V, Khe-Mahi.* Eds. C. E. Bosworth, E. van Donzel, B. Lewis, and Ch. Pellat. Leiden: E. J. Brill, 1986, pp. 426–427 (400–432). John Wansbrough, *Quranic Studies: Sources and Methods of Scriptural Interpretation.* Oxford: Oxford University Press, 1977, p. ix. On the lack of a skeptical approach and the importance of John Wansbrough's work in introducing this orientation to Qur'ānic studies, see Andrew Rippin, "Literary Analysis of Qu'rān, Tafsīr, and Sīra: The Methodologies of John Wansbrough," in *Approaches to Islam in Religious Studies.* Ed. Richard Martin. Tuscon: University

of Arizona Press, 1985 pp. 151–163. The study of Patricia Crone and Michael Cook, *Hagarism: The Making of the Islamic World*. Cambridge: Cambridge University Press, 1977, is also to be mentioned in this breath. Also of interest are the works of the pseudonymous Ibn Warraq, a sort of one-person Islamic reformation project. See, for example, his collection of critical Qur'ānic scholarship. *What the Koran Really Says: Language, Text and Commentary*. Amherst: Prometheus Books, 2002. Of especial interest are the comparisons he draws with biblical scholarship on pp. 85–92. On the other end of the spectrum are the works of scholars who seem so preoccupied with combating Western stereotypes of the Islamic world that they cannot bring themselves to engage in critical studies of Qur'ānic composition. See, for example, Carl Ernst's discussion of "revisionist" and "hypercritical" theories of European scholars, *Rethinking Islam in the Contemporary World*. Chapel Hill: University of North Carolina Press, 2003, p. 97. The secular mantra of "criticize and be damned" strikes us as a better alternative.

18. Daniel Brown, "The Triumph of Scripturalism: The Doctrine of Naskh and its Modern Critics," in *The Shaping of an American Islamic Discourse: A Memorial to Fazlur Rahman*, Eds. Earle Waugh and Frederick Denny. Atlanta: Scholars Press, 1998, p. 60 (49–66). Arkoun, "Contemporary Practices," p. 428. In another essay Arkoun opines: "It is unfortunate that philosophical critique of sacred texts – which has been applied to the Hebrew Bible and the New Testament without thereby engendering negative consequences for the notion of revelation-continues to be rejected by Muslim scholarly opinion." *Rethinking Islam: Common Questions, Uncommon Answers*. Boulder: Westview Press, 1994, p. 35.

19. Shabbir Akhtar, "Critical Qur'ānic Scholarship and Theological Puzzles," in *Holy Scriptures in Judaism, Christianity and Islam: Hermeneutics, Values and Society*. Eds. Hendrik Vroom and Jerald Gort. Amsterdam: Rodopi, 1997, p. 122 (122–127). On the dangers and logical impossibility of Muslims acknowledging a human component in the composition of the text, see Shabbir Akhtar, "An Islamic Model of Revelation," *Islam and Christian-Muslim Relations* 2 (1991) 95–105.

20. Shabbir Akhtar writes: "Many modern Muslims believe that the theologians and exegetes of the early centuries of Islam were authorities empowered to interpret the Qur'ān – once and for all. Who gave them the authority to speak with authority? The answer is, predictably enough, Allah himself. Thus for many Muslims, both the Qur'ān and its interpretation are the perfected gifts of God's grace." "The Limits," p. 107. Milton Viorst, "Puritanism and Stagnation," in *The Place of Tolerance in Islam*. Eds. Joshua Cohen and Ian Lague. Boston: Beacon Press, 2002, pp. 27–30, sees the "conventional interpretation" of Islamic scholars as partly responsible for recent manifestations of militancy. A similar concern for the prevailing interpretive narrowness is seen in another article in the same collection. Sohail Hashmi, in "A Conservative Legacy," advises Muslims "to chart a new exegetical course." p. 36 (31–36). Vincent Cornell argues that "the Muslim fundamentalist suffers from an epistemology that denies the legitimacy of modern hermeneutical methods." "Where Is Scriptural Truth." pp. 74–75. Another more textually oriented critique of the "orthodox literal" reading of the Qur'ān can be found in the writings of the aforementioned Nasr Abū Zaid. "Divine Attributes in the Qur'ān: Some Poetic Aspects," in *Islam and Modernity: Muslim*

Intellectuals Respond. Eds. John Cooper, Ronald Nettler, and Mohamed Mahmoud. London: I. B. Tauris, 1998, p. 193 (190–211). Regarding social structure, the legal scholar Khaled Abou El Fadl pointed to a "disintegration of the traditional institutions of Islamic learning." p. 47. In his analysis, the traditional class of religious specialists has been overrun by a new class of less skilled thinkers. These now speak authoritatively about the text without being bogged down by the accumulated complexity and subtlety of the Islamic exegetical tradition. "The Ugly Modern and the Modern Ugly: Reclaiming the Beautiful in Islam," in *Progressive Muslims: On Justice, Gender and Pluralism.* Ed. Omid Safi. Oxford: Oneworld, 2003, pp. 33–77. More reflections on the intelligentsia can be found in Khaled Abou El Fadl, "Reply," in *The Place of Tolerance in Islam.* Eds. Joshua Cohen and Ian Lague. Boston: Beacon Press, 2002, pp. 93–111. Rotraud Wielandt sees the mutual dependence of the religious establishment and various Muslim governments as making "the suppression of disagreeable innovations in the field of exegetical methodology relatively simple." "Exegesis," p. 140.

21. Here approximating a schema of "heretics" presented in Jacques Berlinerblau, "Toward a Sociology, of Heresy, Orthodoxy, and *Doxa*," *History of Religions* 40 (2001) 327–351.

22. Tariq Ali, "Theological Distractions," in *The Place of Tolerance in Islam.* Eds. Joshua Cohen and Ian Lague. Boston: Beacon Press, 2002, p. 40 (37–41).

23. Omid Safi, "Introduction: *The Times They Are A-Changin'* – A Muslim Quest for Justice, Gender Equality, and Pluralism," in *Progressive Muslims: On Justice, Gender and Pluralism.* Ed. Omid Safi. Oxford: Oneworld, 2003, p. 8 (1–29). There is, however, some reason for optimism. We should recall the speed by which the skeptical orientation came to win converts among Jewish and Christian intellectuals who were once beholden to their own doctrines of scriptural inerrancy.

CONCLUSION: BEYOND CHURCH AND STATE: NEW DIRECTIONS
FOR SECULARISM

1. According to journalistic accounts a few weeks after September 11, 2001, church attendance returned to normal levels. See Katy McLaughlin, "The Religion Bubble – Churches Try to Recapture Their 9/11 Crowds," *The Wall Street Journal* (September 11, 2002) D1. Gerald Zelizer, "Quick Dose of 9–11 Religion Soothes, Doesn't Transform," *USA Today* (January 8, 2002) A13. Anonymous, "Post 9/11 Survey Shows Religion Trend Tipping Other Way," *Free Inquiry* 22 (2002) 29. Amitai Etzioni, "The Silver Lining of 9/11," *Christian Science Monitor* (September 13, 2002) 11.

2. On the situation in Turkey, see John Esposito, "Islam and Secularism in the Twenty-First Century," in *Islam and Secularism in the Middle East.* Eds. John Esposito and Azzam Tamimi. New York: New York University Press, 2000, pp. 1–12. V. S. Naipaul, *Among the Believers: An Islamic Journey.* New York: Vintage, 1982, p. 107.

3. Karl Marx, "The Eighteenth Brumaire of Louis Bonaparte," in *The Marx Engels Reader*, p. 608. (594–617). The political marginalization of secularists was noted

by Daniel Dennett in his "Bright" manifesto, "The Bright Stuff," *New York Times* (July 12, 2003).

4. Harvey Cox, *The Secular City: Secularization and Urbanization in Theological Perspective*. New York: Macmillan, 1965, p. 21. Martin Marty, "Thank God for the Secular," *Christian Century* 121 (2004) 47. As Carol Flake put it: "For the fundamentalist crusader, secular humanism had become the source of all the sins of America, the multiformed beast of modern liberalism: the cold idol of godless science; the brazen serpent of pornography and homosexuality; the unpainted temptress of woman's liberation; the meddling giant of big government." *Redemptorama: Culture, Politics, and the New Evangelicalism*. Garden City, NJ: Anchor Press, 1984, p. 218. The relation of fundamentalists to secularism and modernity is charted in Gabriel Almond, R. Scott Appleby, and Emmanuel Sivan, *Strong Religion: The Rise of Fundamentalisms around the World*. Chicago: University of Chicago Press, 2003, and Wade Clark Roof, "The New Fundamentalism: Rebirth of Political Religion in America," in *Prophetic Religions and Politics: Religion and the Political Order, Volume One*. Eds. Jeffrey Hadden and Anson Shupe. New York: Paragon, 1986, p. 24 (18–34).

5. Michael McConnell, "Taking Religious Freedom Seriously," in *Religious Liberty in the Supreme Court: The Cases that Define the Debate over Church and State*. Ed. Terry Eastland. Washington, DC: Ethics and Public Policy Center, 1993, p. 499 (497–511).

6. Alexis de Tocqueville, *Democracy in America: Volume One*. New York: Vintage, 1990, p. 311. On the prominence of Baptists in the pro-separation movements, see Gordon Stein, "Secularism," in *The Encyclopedia of Unbelief, Volume Two, L–Z*. Buffalo, NY: Prometheus Books, 1985, pp. 612–614. A discussion of the many definitions of secularization can be found in Jeffrey Hadden, "Desacralizing Secularization Theory," in *Secularization and Fundamentalism Reconsidered: Religion and the Political Order. Vol. 3*. Eds. Jeffrey Hadden and Anson Shupe. New York: Paragon House, 1989, pp. 3–26. Also see Karel Dobbelaere, "Secularization," in *Encyclopedia of Religion and Society*. Ed. William Swatos, Jr. Walnut Creek, CA: Altamira, 1998, pp. 452–456. For the argument that the process of secularization in the United States was not so much a process as a "contested revolutionary struggle," see Christian Smith, "Introduction: Rethinking the Secularization of American Public Life," in *The Secular Revolution: Power, Interests and Conflict in the Secularization of American Public Life*. Ed. Christian Smith. Berkeley: University of California Press, 2003, p. 1 (1–96). On the possibility that secularism does not generally contribute to secularization, see Bryan Wilson, "Secularization," in *The Encyclopedia of Religion: Volume 13*. Ed. Mircea Eliade. New York: Macmillan, 1987, p. 159 (159–165). The theory that secularism begins thousands of years ago, in the Bible, deserves to be made the object of a study in and of itself. For some well-known expositions of this theme, see Peter Berger, *The Sacred Canopy: Elements of a Sociological Theory of Religion*. Garden City, NJ: Doubleday, 1969, pp. 113, 119. Cox, *The Secular City*, pp. 17–37. Herbert Schneidau, *Sacred Discontent: The Bible and Western Tradition*. Baton Rouge: Louisiana State University Press, 1976, pp. 24–25. Alasdair MacIntyre and Paul Ricoeur, *The Religious Significance of Atheism*. New York: Columbia University Press, 1969, p. 18.

Willis Glover, *Biblical Origins of Modern Secular Culture: An Essay in the Interpretation of Western History.* Macon, GA: Mercer University Press, 1984. Bas van Iersel, "The Alternation of Secularizing and Sacralizing Tendencies in Scripture," in *The Persistence of Religion.* Eds. Andrew Greeley and Gregory Baum. New York: Herder and Herder, 1973, pp. 82–90. Bernard Cooke, "Secularity and the Scriptures," in *The Spirit and Power of Christian Secularity.* Ed. Albert Schlitzer. Notre Dame: University of Notre Dame Press, 1969, pp. 71–87. And T. N. Madan, *Modern Myths, Locked Minds: Secularism and Fundamentalism in India.* Delhi, India: Oxford University Press, 1997, pp. 5–25. Whereas many trace the advent of secularization to biblical times, Renée Fregosi traces it to the Middle Ages, "From the Secular to the Politco-Religious: Reflections on *The Name of the Rose,*" *Contemporary European Affairs* 2 (1989) 15–27. Studies of secular movements usually concentrate on the development of secularism within one nation. A "global" assessment has yet to be attempted. Of interest in terms of national and regional assessments are Owen Chadwick, *The Secularization of the European Mind in the Nineteenth Century.* Cambridge: Cambridge University Press, 1975, and David Berman, *A History of Atheism in Britain: From Hobbes to Russell.* London: Croom Helm, 1988. For a definition of secularism similar to our own, as well as a concise and insightful discussion of the history of secularism, see Edoardo Tortarolo, *Il laicismo.* Bari: Gius, Laterza & Figli, 1998.

7. Stephen Carter, *The Culture of Disbelief: How American Law and Politics Trivialize Religious Devotion.* New York: Basic Books, 1993, p. 123; Richard John Neuhaus, *The Naked Public Square: Religion and Democracy in America.* Grand Rapids, MI: Eerdmans, 1984, p. 25.

8. See the remarks on separation of Church and State in Charles Taylor, "Modes of Secularism," in *Secularism and Its Critics.* Ed. Rajeev Bhargava. Delhi, India: Oxford University Press, 1998, p. 52 (31–53).

9. Wilfred McClay, "Two Concepts of Secularism," in *Religion Returns to the Public Square: Faith and Policy in America.* Eds. Hugh Heclo and Wilfred McClay. Baltimore: The Johns Hopkins University Press, 2003, p. 39 (31–61). On secularism and despotism see John Keane, "The Limits of Secularism," in *Islam and Secularism in the Middle East.* Eds. John Esposito and Azzam Tamimi. New York: New York University Press, 2000, p. 34 (29–37). One detractor phrases it as follows: "secularity . . . is from the very start a Christian ambition and a Protestant necessity!" S. Parvez Manzoor, "Desacralizing Secularism," in *Islam and Secularism in the Middle East.* Eds. John Esposito and Azzam Tamimi. New York: New York University Press, 2000, p. 90 (81–96). On secularism's Occidental providence and thus its inability to translate to non-Western societies see T. N. Madan, "Secularism in Its Place," in *Secularism and Iits Critics.* Ed. Rajeev Bhargava. Delhi, India: Oxford University Press, 1998, pp. 297–315. In the same volume, an equally penetrating analysis of its Christian origins and external applicability can be found in Charles Taylor, "Modes of Secularism," in *Secularism and Its Critics.* Ed. Rajeev Bhargava. Delhi, India: Oxford University Press, 1998, pp. 31–53. Also see the analysis of Janet Jakobsen and Ann Pellegrini, "Getting Religion," in *One Nation Under God? Religion and American Culture.* Eds. Marjorie Garber and Rebecca Walkowitz. New York: Routledge, 1999, pp. 101–114, and Fregosi, "From the Secular," p. 23,

although Fregosi's assessment of secularism is much more sanguine (p. 26). Similar reflections on Christian origins can be found in Azzam Tamimi, "The Origins of Arab Secularism," in *Islam and Secularism in the Middle East*. Eds. John Esposito and Azzam Tamimi. New York: New York University Press, 2000, pp. 13–28. On secularism as serving to benefit the majority religion in a given society, see the discussion of Brenda Cossman and Ratna Kapur, *Secularism's Last Sigh? Hinduvta and the (Mis)rule of Law*. New Delhi, India: Oxford University Press, pp. 98–101. A variety of criticisms of secularism are nicely summarized in Amartya Sen, "Secularism and Its Discontents," in *Secularism and Its Critics*. Ed. Rajeev Bhargava. New Delhi, India: Oxford University Press, 1998, pp. 454–485. For a defense of secularism against some of these charges and an informative discussion in general, see Rajeev Bhargava, "What Is Secularism For?" in *Secularism and Its Critics*. Ed. Rajeev Bhargava. Delhi, India: Oxford University Press, 1998, pp. 486–550. In terms of philosophical and theological attacks on secularism, see Phillip Blond (Ed.). *Post-Secular Philosophy: Between Philosophy and Theology*. London: Routledge, 1998.

10. For the criticisms of secularism's effects in the modern Middle East, see the essays in Espositio and Tamimi, *Islam and Secularism*, in particular, Rachid Al-Ghannouchi, "Secularism in the Arab Maghreb," in *Islam and Secularism in the Middle East*. Eds. John Esposito and Azzam Tamimi. New York: New York University Press, 2000, pp. 97–123. Also of interest are Charles Smith's less polemical observations, "Secularism," in *Oxford Encyclopedia of the Modern Islamic World, Volume 3*. Ed. John Esposito. New York: Oxford University Press, 1995, pp. 20–30.

11. Gabriel Vahanian, "Theology and the Secular," in *Secular Theology: American Radical Theological Thought*. Ed. Clayton Crockett. London: Routledge, 2001, p. 11 (10–28). A similar concern for the lack of precision in defining the term is expressed in Rustom Bharucha's *In the Name of the Secular: Contemporary Cultural Activism in India*. Delhi, India: Oxford University Press, 1998, p. 2.

12. See the exploration of the relation between secularism and Judaism in Sidney Brichto's "Judaism in a Secular World," in *Two Cheers for Secularism*. Eds. Sidney Brichto and Richard Harris. Northamptonshire: Pilkington, 1998, pp. 23–35. On secular possibilities in Islam, see Tariq Ali, "Theological Distractions," in *The Place of Tolerance in Islam*. Eds. Joshua Cohen and Ian Lague. Boston: Beacon Press, 2002, p. 40. In fact, if one hears "secular Christian," it is usually in the context of Christian death-of-God theologians. See the works cited throughout this chapter.

Index of Biblical Citations

Index of Qur'ānic Citations

Index of Rabbinic, Early Jewish,
and Patristic Citations

Index

A. C. L. U., 135
Aaron, 93
Abel, 31
Abishag the Shunammite, 105
Abraham, 38, 48–49, 89
Abrams, Garry, 181 n1
Achior the Ammonite, 179n21
Ackerman, Susan, 188n22
Ackroyd, Peter, 185n12
Adam, A. K. M., 80, 84, 168n9, 169n14
Adang, Camilla, 191 n8
Adar, Zvi, 145n8
aggregate, (also see "composition by aggregate")
    defined, 45–46
Agur, 21
Ahasuerus, 149n11
Akhtar, Shabbir, 120, 125, 128, 189n4, 190n7, 193n19, 193n20
Akiva, 72
Al-Ghannouchi, Rachid, 197n10
Al-Qaeda, 117, 131
Algeria, 136
Ali, Tariq, 127, 194n22, 197n12
allegory, 64
Almond, Gabriel, 144n3, 195n4
Alter, Robert, 160n3
American Jews and intermarriage, 88, 97–99
Anabaptism, 59
ancient Near East,
    compositional methods, 45–46
Anderson, A. A., 157n15
Anderson, George, 191 n13

angels
    assisting Moses with writing of Torah, 27
Antonio, 47
apocryphal literature, 59
Appleby, R. Scott, 144n3, 195n4
Aramaic, 31
Aramaic Targumim, 31, 77
Artaxerxes, 149n11
Arkoun, Mohammed, 125, 128, 192n16, 193n18
Asaph, 148n5
Asenath, 93, 96, 176n16
Atkinson, D. J., 184n9, 185n10
Atmaja, Dwi, 190n8
Augustine, 64, 72, 159n1, 165n13

B (biblical document), 33
Babylonian Talmud, 105
Bailey, Derrick Sherwin, 104, 183n7, 184n9, 184n10, 187n15, 187n17
Bailey, Warner, 191 n13
Bainton, Roland, 164n5
Baker, David, 160n4
Bakker, Jim, 101, 181 n1
Baptists, 195n6
Bar, Shaul, 164n8
Barr, James, 145n8
Barrere, Julio Trebolle, 151 n16
Barrett, C. K., 65, 166n14
Barthes, Roland, 162n14, 169n14
Barton, John, 38, 145n7, 158n19, 159n22, 162n13
Baruch, 23, 149n10
Bassanio, 47

Made in the USA
Lexington, KY
29 April 2013